MW01641118

The Emergence of Insurgency in El Salvador

Ideology and Political Will

Yvon Grenier
Associate Professor of Political Science
St Francis Xavier University
Antigonish
Nova Scotia

Foreword by Mitchell A. Seligson
Daniel H. Wallace Professor of Political Science
and
Research Professor, University Center for International Studies
University of Pittsburgh

University of Pittsburgh Press

Published in the U.S.A. by the University of Pittsburgh Press
Pittsburgh, PA 15261

Published in Great Britain by Macmillan Press Ltd.

ISBN 0–8229–4094–9

A catalogue record for this book is available from the Library of Congress
0*and the British Library.

This book is printed on paper suitable for recycling and
made from fully managed and sustained forest sources.

10 9 8 7 6 5 4 3 2 1

Printed in Great Britain

For Norine and Francis Michel

'Madmen in authority, who hear voices in the air, are distilling their frenzy from some academic scribbler of a few years back... soon or late, it is ideas, not vested interests, which are dangerous for good or bad.'

John Maynard Keynes, *The General Theory of Employment, Interest and Money*

Content

List of Tables and Figures

Tables

Figure

Foreword

Many scholars are growing increasingly frustrated by studies of revolution that rely upon structural conditions such as land tenure, poverty and inequality. Despite decades of effort, social scientists seem no closer to predicting or explaining revolution. What we need to do is to go back to the drawing board and find additional variables that may yield more satisfying results. Social injustice is nothing new in Latin America. Conversely revolts, and especially full-fledged revolutions, are few and far between. This suggests that political variables must be analysed more seriously, something that students of the 'Great Revolutions' (France, Russia and China) have understood sooner than Latin Americanists. Furthermore it should not mean focusing only on *the state*, as in the old dichotomy 'civil society' versus 'the state'. It also means studying the agents of social and political change, their beliefs and ideologies, the particular structure of incentives in their environment, and so on.

In this path-breaking work, Yvon Grenier, one of the leading younger-generation Canadian political scientists, offers a new interpretation of the civil war in El Salvador, one that also appears promising for the understanding of other countries in the region and beyond. He focuses on the role of ideology, especially as it relates to activists within revolutionary parties, universities and the church. He demonstrates convincingly that, in the case of El Salvador at least, ideas matter and actors matter. As Grenier asserts in his conclusion: 'Central American political actors are power seekers, not solely social class spokespersons. Their political agenda is shaped by a variety of conditioning factors; not just those derived from some compelling socioeconomic "reality".' In short, the point is to 'bring the actor back in'.

This is undoubtedly a controversial book, one that questions the dominant paradigm in the area. I have no doubt that many scholars will take issue with some of the ideas developed in this study. This being said, all serious students of social movements and revolutions should read this important new book.

MITCHELL A. SELIGSON
Daniel H. Wallace Professor of Political Science, and Research Professor at the University Center for International Studies, University of Pittsburgh

List of Abbreviations

ADUES	Asociación de Docentes de la Universidad de El Salvador (Association of Professors of the University of El Salvador)
AGEUS	Asociación General de Estudiantes Universitarios Salvadoreños (General Association of Salvadoran University Students)
ANDES	Asociación Nacional de Educadores Salvadoreños (National Association of Salvadoran Educators)
ANEP	Asociación Nacional de la Empresa Privada (National Association for Private Enterprise)
ARENA	Alianza Republicana Nacionalista (National Republican Alliance)
ASTUES	Asociación de Trabajadores de la Universidad de El Salvador (Association of Workers of the University of El Salvador)
BPR	Bloque Popular Revolucionario (People's Revolutionary Bloc)
CAPUES	Consejo Administrative Provisional de La Universidad de El Salvador (Provisional Administration Council of the University of El Salvador)
CEB	Christian Base Communities
CELAM	Conferencia Episcopal Latinoamericana (Latin American Conference of Bishops)
CONIP	Conferencia Nacional de la Iglesia Popular (National Conference of the Popular Church)
CPD	Comisión Politico-Diplomática (Politico-Diplomatic Commission)
CRM	Coordinación Revolucionaria de las Masas (Revolutionary Coordination of the Masses)
DRU	Directorio Revolucconario Unificado (Unified Revolutionary Directorate)
EPL	Ejército Popular de Liberación (Popular Army of Liberation)

ERP	Ejercito Revolucionario del Pueblo (People's Revolutionary Army)
FAL	Fuerzas Armada de Liberación (Armed Forces of Liberation)
FAPU	Frente de Acción Popular Unificada (United Popular Action Front)
FARN	Fuerzas Armadas de Resistencia Nacional (Armed Forces of National Resistance)
FDR	Frente Democrático Revolucionario (Democratic Revolutionary Front)
FECCAS	Federación Cristiana de Campesinos Salvadoreños (Christian Federation of Salvadoran Peasants)
FENASTRAS	Federación Nacional de Sindicatos de Trabajadores Salvadoreños (National Federation of Unions of Salvadoran Workers)
FEPRO	Federación de las Asociaciones de Profesionales Acadénicos de El Salvador (Federation of Academic Professionals' Associations of El Salvador)
FESINCONTRANS	Federación de Sindicatos de la Industria de la Construcción, Similares, Transporte y de otras Actividades (Federation of Unions of the Construction Industry, Kindred Activities, Transportation and other Activities)
FMLN	Frente Farabundo Martí de Liberación Nacional (Farabundo Marti National Liberation Front)
FPL	Frente Popular de Liberación (Popular Liberation Front)
FRTS	Frente Regional de Trabajadores Salvadoreños (Regional Federation of Salvadoran Workers)

FUDI	Frente Unido Democrático Independiente (United Independent Democratic Front)
FUSADES	Fundación Salvadoreña para el Desarollo Económico y Social (Salvadoran Foundation for Social and Economic Development)
FUSS	Frente Unificado de Sindicatos Salvadoreño (United Federation of Salvadoran Trade Unions)
LP-28	Ligas Populares 28 de Febrero (Popular Leagues–28 February)
ISTA	Instituto Salvadoreño de Transformaceón Agraria (Salvadoran Institute of Agrarian Transformation)
MIPTES	Moviniento Independiente de Profesionales y Técnicos de El Salvador (Independent Movement of Salvadoran Professionals and Technicians)
MNR	Movimiento Nacional Revolucionario (National Revolutionary Movement)
MPSC	Movimiento Popular Social Cristiano (Social Christian Popular Movement)
MCU	Moviniento Concertación Universitaria (Movement of University Dialogue)
ORDEN	Organización Democrática Nacionalista (Nationalist Democratic Organisation)
PAR	Partido de Acción Renovadora (Renewal Action Party)
PCN	Partido de Conciliación Nacional (National Pralogus Party)
PCS	Partido Comunista de El Salvador (Communist Party of El Salvador)
PDC	Partido Demócrata Cristiano (Christian Democratic Party)
PRAM	Partido Revolucionario de Abril y Mayo (Revolutionary Party of April and May)
PRI	Partido Revolucionario Institucional (Institutional Revolutionary Party)
PRTC	Partido Revolucionario de Trabajadores Centroamericanos (Revolutionary Party of Central American Workers)

PRUD	Partido Revolucionario de Unificación Democrática (Revolutionary Party of Democratic Unification)
PSD	Partido Social Demócrata (Social-Democratic Party)
RN	Resistencia Nacional (National Resistance)
UCA	Universidad Centroamericana 'José Simeón Cañas' (Central American University 'José Simeón Cañas')
UDN	Unión Democrática Nacionalista (Nationalist Democratic Union)
UES	Universidad de El Salvador (University of El Salvador)
UNO	Unión Nacional Opositora (National Opposition Union)
UNTS	Unión Nacional de Trabajadores Salvadoreños (National Unity of Salvadoran Workers)
UPD	Unión de Partidos Democráticos (Union of Democratic Parties)
UR-19	Universitarios Revolucionarios 19 de Julio (19th July Revolutionary Students)
UTC	Unión de Trabajadores del Campo (Rural Workers' Union)
UU	Unión Universitaria (University Unity)

Introduction

Plus un événement est lourd de conséquences, moins il est possible de le penser à partir de ses causes. (François Furet, 1995)

By virtually all measures found in the literature on political violence, El Salvador comes across as a country ripe for revolution. Inequality and poverty have been an historical invariant. The diminutive nation was ruled like a personal estate by oligarchs until the early 1930s, when military dictators took over and retained power until October 1979. From that military coup until the peace agreement of January 1992, civilian rulers, whether elected (congresspersons after 1982; president after 1984) or not (members of the civil–military juntas from late 1979 to mid 1982), failed to claim a monopoly on the legitimate use of violence in the national territory.

Along with Colombia, Guatemala and Peru, El Salvador is one of the most violent countries in Latin America. In 1932 the first communist-led uprising in the continent was crushed by the army; this tragic episode is now remembered as *la matanza* (the massacre). Since this massacre inaugurated a period of praetorianism in El Salvador, after only a few months of civilian rule and decades of patrimonial–oligarchic domination, one can conclude that the modern Salvadoran nation state was born in a bloodbath. This sad episode clearly hinted at the extent to which dominant groups were willing to use violence to 'solve' social problems. By the same token, the illegitimate foundation of the new political order granted *a priori* legitimacy to the option of social violence as an expression of popular sovereignty against unjust rulers.[1]

In sum, secular social injustice, a despotic regime and precious little historical inhibition about using guns as a substitute for discussion and negotiation (what the Christian-Democratic leader Fidel Chávez Meña called '*la pistoletiza-*

ción de la realidad nacional') are conceivably more than sufficient to establish a solid probability of revolt in any country.

And yet the present book makes the case that another factor needs to be added to the top of the list: *the role of insurgents*. As obvious as this proposition may seem at first glance, a review of the literature on the roots of revolt in El Salvador reveals that insurgents are rarely considered as a fairly autonomous group of actors. Rather they are presented as *the voice of those who have no voice*. They translate into rhetoric and bullets a deeper 'reality', as understood by academics. As Theda Skocpol once asserted, revolutions are made by 'countries', not by 'revolutionaries'.

The thesis of this book can be summarised as follows: *in contemporary developing countries, insurgencies are initiated by insurgents, not by 'countries.' 'Countries' make them more or less successful, but insurgents provide the impetus*.

Interestingly enough, the insurgents themselves have proven most helpful to my endeavour. Some very interesting material published recently by former insurgents hints at a story that is substantially different from that which emanated from the university presses of North America. For instance Tommie Sue Montgomery's *Revolution in El Salvador* (1982), and the collection of interviews conducted by Marta Harnecker (1993) with leaders of the FPL (the Popular Liberation Front, one of the five factions of the Farabundo Marti Front for National Liberation–FMLN) provide two different portraits of the insurgents.[2] Montgomery pictures them as an eclectic collection of genuine heroes, animated by an overpowering sense of social justice, insurgents roaming amongst the masses like fish in water, or gliding like surfers on a gigantic popular wave. Pictures of them in their own environment suggest a world inhabited by women, children and the elderly. Some are radicals, true, but not all of them. And in any case they are only calling for some commonsensical changes long demanded by the impoverished masses. In fact one can only wonder why they are not more radical than they actually are.

Former insurgents are quite ready to restate their commendable commitment to social justice. However, in contrast with their fervent supporters, they readily confess historical sins of dogmatism, sectarianism, caudillism and mistrust of the people's common sense. To take the aquatic metaphor a step further, they appear more like salmon, leaping into the air and often swimming against the current. Water is their element. But not their conductor.

All this would be of little interest if it wasn't hinting at some major flaws in the way social scientists have interpreted the nature of the insurgency in El Salvador. What explains such different assessments by insurgents in El Salvador and pro-insurgent observers in the US? In my view there are two factors: one is political, the other theoretical.

Politically, most academics working on El Salvador (especially in the US) were also activists. Until the end of the Cold War they were engaged in a battle against Reagan's foreign policy towards Central America. There was a very strong pressure in solidarity milieus and academia to *sell* the FMLN (among other radical insurgencies) to the American public – especially to students and church organisations. Failure to do so was tantamount to helping Reagan and D'Aubuisson.

Here the example of neighbouring Nicaragua, where the insurgents seized power, is appropriate. Countless times I have personally heard pro-Sandinista students and professors describing their favourite regime to a non-specialised audience as some kind of budding Costa Rica, with democracy and elections, popular participation and a mixed-economy, and even Catholic priests in power. One really had to be evil to criticise such a progressive human experiment. Obviously the overwhelming majority of these self-appointed ambassadors would not have paid attention to Nicaragua for a second if it had really been the way they were describing it. The Sandinistas' totalitarian proclivity (*partially* fleshed out in a political formula that included *de facto* military rule, neighbourhood committees, vertically controlled mass organisation, state–party fusion, official ideology and censorship of the media) was never something with which the Sandinistas in Nicaragua had moral problems or second thoughts. As Léo Moulin used to say, totalitarians, unlike less immodest guardians, always say openly what they want to do.[3]

In contrast with gringo *farabundistas* (Farabundist), insurgents are ready to confess their mistakes, probably because they have already paid a price for them. For insurgents, internal war is not merely a concept, a political stand or an attitude. For years it was *a way of life*. They can sit down and tell you the good and the bad, very much like old veterans of war who, while remaining staunchly patriotic and mostly proud of what they did, are not going to fool you or themselves about what really happened on the battlefield or what the war was about. Both the FMLN in El Salvador and the FSLN in Nicaragua have displayed a remarkable capacity to adapt to changing circumstances, and to admit their errors. They see themselves as responsible adults, mastering their destiny; not as innocent children impermeable to criticism.

On the *theoretical* side, Jeff Goodwin and Theda Skocpol aptly point out that 'with some notable exceptions, the literature that emphasizes the role of peasants in revolutions tends to ignore the role of professional revolutionary organizations, groups that tend to be disproportionately middle class in social composition'.[4]

This has been true for some time in the historiography of 'great revolutions' such as the French, the Russian and the Chinese. It has certainly been the case in Central American studies over the past two decades. An important segment of political sociology is still the hostage of nineteenth-century sociology, according to which politics essentially mirrors the social and economic environment. For both Durkheim and Marx, nothing of real magnitude can possibly originate from the 'superstructure' of politics. Real changes come from below and must have deep historical/structural roots.

Of course there is a lot to be said about the linkages between socioeconomic and political variables. A handful of excellent books and articles have been written on the political economy of land tenure, agribusiness, coffee and cotton in El

Salvador. Nevertheless this should not prevent scholars from looking at the crucial contribution of *political will* and *ideology*, if only because grand, socioeconomic causes of revolution have been a permanent fixture of Latin American countries for centuries, whereas full-fledged revolutions have been quite rare.

All 'revolutions' are unique, but they all involve revolutionaries, an old regime, violence and a clash of ideologies. The idea that insurgents and their ideology, or the 'agency,' matter as much as structural factors is far from new. In fact it is hard to find a genuinely new idea about revolution since de Tocqueville. But it has had better days. And in Central American studies, explanations of political change and violence have traditionally been deterministic, economistic and rudimentary.

One way of reintroducing the idea of 'agency' into the discussion on Salvadoran politics is to break down the concept of revolution in order clearly to distinguish different sequences of what we prefer to call the 'internal war'.

The period of emergence was, in my view, specific. Far from being directly connected to those structural factors that supposedly 'caused' the revolution, the emergence of insurgency seems to have been in response to both smaller and larger sets of incentives: *smaller* – the immediate environment, or incentive structure, of the insurgents; *larger* – the dominant and general passions of the time, in Latin America and beyond. The peasants, the poor, the lower strata may have had a key role to play if a truly 'national revolt' was to succeed and if an agenda of radical change was to be successfully implemented. (I have serious doubts about this, but it is not my concern here.) Yet they had very little to do with the political process by which mostly middle-class young people, mostly university actors,[5] shifted their attitudes *vis-à-vis* the government from one of demand for reform to one of confrontation and a call for liberation.

The point here is not to engage in some kind of vendetta against the insurgency and its supporters ('some of my best friends...') El Salvador is now enjoying a painfully realised peace. The FMLN is not only a strong political party but also an essential actor in the democratic reconstruction of the country. It is an invaluable counterweight to the ultraconservative ARENA government, whose antidemocratic bent must be permanently kept in check. Few observers of Salvadoran politics need to be reminded that the overwhelming responsibility for the widespread violation of human rights in the country falls plainly on the lap of the extreme right. Finally, it is easy but not advisable to seize the moral high ground against people who have had the courage to put their lives on the line in the name of values that are mostly admirable.

My point is rather to satisfy a limited academic ambition: to show that *some of the basic premises embraced by most of my colleagues are mistaken*. And though the demonstration is limited to the Salvadoran case, my kicking the tyres will hopefully prove useful for a clearer understanding of other insurgencies in particular and radical political mobilisation (left or right) in general.

Finally, it must be pointed out that this book is conceived as an *essay*, in the sense suggested by the first practitioner of the genre, Montaigne: an initial or tentative attempt to scrutinise an overlooked or contentious dimension of a problem. A much more ambitious work would be needed to challenge systematically what we like to call the 'dominant paradigm' in the discipline. Nevertheless I think that this essay presents sufficient ideas and empirical material to question the validity of some assumptions about the root causes of revolt in El Salvador.

* * *

The Emergence of Insurgency in El Salvador draws on more than ten years of research on politics in El Salvador.[6] Many people enriched this book by contributing their time and insights. Jean Daudelin, Steve Holloway, Jacques Zylberberg Mitch Seligson and Alberto Cuzán were especially helpful with encouragement and judicious comments. Lisa Kowalchuk helped me, through a vigorous electronic exchange, to clarify some of the theoretical questions raised in the first chapter. I would also like to acknowledge with thanks the editor of the IPE series, Timothy Shaw, Macmillan's editor Aruna Vasudevan, as well as Monica McKinnon for helping me with the editing of the manuscript. Finally, I am indebted both to the Social Sciences and Humanities Research Council of Canada and to the University Committee for Research at the St Francis Xavier University for their financial support.

1 Challenging the Dominant Paradigm

> A powerful idea communicates some of its strength to him who challenges it. Being itself a part of the riches of the universal Mind, it makes its way into, grafts itself upon the mind of him whom it is employed to refute, slips in among the ideas already there, with the help of which, gaining a little ground, he completes and corrects it; so that the final utterance is always to some extent the work of both parties to a discussion. It is to ideas which are not, properly speaking, ideas at all, to ideas which, founded upon nothing, can find no support, no kindred spirit among the ideas of the adversary, that he, grappling with something which is not there, can find no word to say in answer. (Marcel Proust, *Within a Budding Grove*)

The cumulative message of two decades of writing on internal wars in Central America is that they were the direct and inexorable result of two phenomena:

- An historical situation of social injustice.
- The oligarchies' resistance to change.

The causal explanation (injustice + reactionary governments = revolution) is obvious enough for an historian to proclaim, in a soon to be re-edited book, that Central American revolutions are inevitable. Over the past two decades this dominant paradigm has become a litmus test of one's suitability to be taken seriously as a student of Central American politics.[1]

The dominant paradigm is usually displayed in a structuralist, 'political economy' fashion. Political development, relatively or potentially autonomous, at least to some extent, never really strays away from the socioeconomic reality. Students of the Central American revolutions also display a strong tendency to look for causes in the countryside, where the roots of revolt are to be found. In the early 1980s it was common to see scholars setting out for El Salvador or Nicaragua to look for evidence of an agrarian revolution. Some were disenchanted, realising that in these two city states the politicians, generals, intellectuals and the US ambassador (none of whom were from the countryside) often left the armed peasants in the dark. However, most of them retained their illusions because their theoretical framework allowed them to sail safely through the storm of contradictions.

Overall, most observers paid precious little attention to the causes of revolt *per se*, for they were so evident. Rather the task at hand was to find new evidence and collect data, in order to fill the boxes of an essentially functionalist model: box one, the people and its vanguard struggling for fundamental change; box two, the oligarchy and the US resisting change.[2] How many books and articles on Guatemala, El Salvador and Nicaragua over the past fifteen years have been entitled 'Revolution and Counterrevolution in...'?

SUMMARISING THE DOMINANT PARADIGM

John A. Booth is one of the few scholars to look at the Central American internal wars from a theoretical perspective, as opposed to an historical or purely partisan perspective.[3] In a successful attempt to summarise what he calls the 'most promising theories' on the 'roots of national revolts' in Central America, Booth highlights a 'complicated combination of developmental changes and internal and external political processes' in the region. Political factors 'also play key roles' in those revolts, since 'aggrieved citizens will not generate overt political conflict'. Recent contributions quoted by the author support 'the importance of the state in the political process of rebellion'.[4]

Booth plainly rejects the 'economically deterministic theories of revolution'. Nevertheless, once the most vulgar economically deterministic approach has been cast off, Booth invariably construes political processes (typically confined to 'popular mobilization ... due to socioeconomic conditions' and 'government response to popular mobilization') as dependent variables, ultimately determined by socioeconomic factors.

In what could be considered as a 'dominant paradigm in a nutshell' passage, Booth argues that:

> according to what may be the most promising theories, recent economic development trends worsened the region's historically extreme maldistribution of wealth and income, intensifying grievances in the '70s with the rapid expansion of Central America's rural and industrial proletariats, declining urban and rural real incomes, and increasing concentration of wealth (especially agricultural land). Such problems led the aggrieved to demand change and sparked growing opposition to incumbent regimes by political parties, labor unions, religious community organizers, and revolutionary groups. Violent repression of opposition demands for reform in Nicaragua, El Salvador, and Guatemala not only failed to suppress mobilization for change but actually helped forge revolutionary coalitions that fought for control of the state.[5]

The chain of causality leading to 'national revolt' can be broken down as follows:

(1) The persistent maldistribution of wealth and income leads the aggrieved to demand change; (2) this invariably meets with repression, which, far from suppressing mobilisation for change, actually (3) radicalises the aggrieved, thus contributing to the formation of revolutionary coalitions. The causal link between these three moments, especially between the second and third, is predicated on two questionable, though usually unchallenged premises. First, the radical politico-military organisations (without which there would be no national revolt) are expressions of, or even descend from, the aggrieved (primarily the poor). Second, and concomitantly,

the radical – or revolutionary – agenda put forward by these organisations, including the use of violence, is in fact a reaction, in the last resort, to:

- The regime's initial rejection of reformist demands.
- Repressive measures against the opposition.
- The outright failure of tirelessly tested alternative strategies.

According to Booth, questions that warrant further study, such as the 'critical process by which popular forces – especially opposition organizations – have formed' and 'the role played by external actors', are tossed in to his concluding remarks, finding little room in an otherwise comprehensive theoretical framework.[6] When the socioeconomic structure ultimately determines political development, it is indeed difficult to find room for 'conjunctural' factors such as resource mobilisation and ideology building.

AN OLD DEBATE: POLITICS VERSUS THE ECONOMY

The dominant paradigm, spelled out with some sophistication by Booth, is indeed plausible and, up to a point, valid. The main assumption (injustice breeds revolt) enjoys an enviable track record in the history of political analysis. The uneven distribution of wealth has been seen as a universal and prime cause of revolt – presented as a war between 'factions' in the *Federalist Papers*, a class struggle in socialist writing, and so on – by too many great thinkers (from Aristotle to Madison, de Tocqueville and, of course, Marx) to be overlooked.

What is more El Salvador does not strike many as the place to undertake a falsification as it is a poor country fraught with injustice and misery. The data on this predicament is nevertheless interesting. El Salvador does have a highly skewed distribution of income, but so have other Latin American countries as well as the US at the end of Jimmy Carter's mandate and Canada at the twilight of Pierre Trudeau's 'Just Society' experiment (Table 1.1). In fact, El Salvador has a *less* unequal distribution than the Latin American average! Income distribution does not tell the whole story of social injustice and exploitation, and at face value it does not appear to be a very useful indicator of the probability of political instability and rebellion.

What appears to be particularly noticeable in El Salvador is not the distribution of income *per se*[7] – which is deplorable but not exceptional – but the overall poverty of the country and, more significantly, the actual poverty of the lower strata. During the 1970s, for instance, 68 per cent of the population was undernourished; only Guatemala and Haiti, as shown in Table 1.2, had an even less enviable record. As regards social

Table 1.1 Income distribution in various countries in the Americas (% share of household income by percentile groups of households)

	Lowest 20%	*Second quintile*	*Third quintile*	*Fourth quintile*	*Highest 20%*	*Highest 10%*
Argentina (1970)	4.4	9.7	14.1	21.5	50.3	35.2
Brazil (1972)	2.2	5.0	9.4	17.0	66.6	50.6
Chile (1968)	4.4	9.0	13.8	21.4	51.4	34.8
Costa Rica (1971)	3.3	8.7	13.3	19.9	54.8	39.5
El Salvador (1976–77)	*5.5*	*10.0*	*14.8*	*22.4*	*47.3*	*29.5*
Mexico (1977)	2.9	7.0	12.0	20.4	57.7	40.6
Panama (1973)	2.0	5.2	11.0	20.0	61.8	44.2
Peru (1972)	1.9	5.1	11.0	21.0	61.0	42.9
Venezuela (1970)	3.0	7.3	12.9	22.8	54.0	35.7
United States (1980)	5.3	11.9	17.9	25.0	39.9	23.3
Canada (1978)	3.9	10.4	17.7	25.5	42.5	—

Sources: James W. Wilkie (ed.), *Statistical Abstract of Latin America*, UCLA Latin American Center Publications, vol. 29, part 1, table 1420; for Canada, David P. Ross, *The Canadian Fact Book on Income Distribution* (Ottawa: Canadian Council on Social Development, 1980), p. 12.

Table 1.2 Indicators of poverty and social welfare in various Latin American countries 1970–80

	Percentage undernourished			*HEC total index**			
	Total	*Rural*	*Urban*	*1950*	*1960*	*1970*	*1980*
Argentina	8	19	5	46.4	39.9	34.0	38.2
Bolivia	—	—	—	79.8	76.1	70.6	67.8
Brazil	49	73	35	73.9	68.5	61.5	56.4
Chile	17	25	12	61.8	57.9	54.1	55.1
Colombia	45	54	38	73.8	69.7	65.6	61.7
Costa Rica	24	34	14	65.8	60.9	57.2	49.9
Cuba	—	—	—	57.5	55.2	54.3	40.3
Dominican Rep.	—	—	—	77.5	70.2	66.7	67.2
Ecuador	—	—	—	76.3	71.2	67.7	60.6
El Salvador	*68*	*76*	*61*	*78.8*	*74.1*	*69.7*	*69.9*
Guatemala	79	82	75	81.2	79.1	77.0	76.1
Haiti	90	4	71	89.7	86.7	86.2	83.9
Honduras	61	75	40	81.0	77.2	71.7	73.1
Mexico	34	45	20	75.5	70.1	63.8	54.9
Nicaragua	64	80	50	76.9	73.3	68.9	66.8
Panama	35	—	—	61.9	60.3	56.6	48.0
Paraguay	—	—	—	71.8	67.9	67.3	63.8
Peru	50	61	35	75.5	67.6	61.2	56.8
Uruguay	—	—	10	42.3	40.6	40.4	34.9
Venezuela	25	36	20	69.9	61.2	55.8	49.2
Latin America	40	62	26	73.8	68.6	63.7	59.7

* HEC = aggregate of data on health, education and communications (average for 12 indicators; 0 = US equality with Latin America).

Source: James W. Wilkie (ed.) *Statistical Abstract of Latin America*, UCLA Latin American Center Publications, vol. 29, part 1, tables 1337, 801.

mobilisation (health, education and communications, or HEC), from 1950 to 1980 El Salvador had slightly less than the Latin American average.

One can find in these two tables more than enough reasons to revolt, but no clear variable that, by itself, can help explain why it happened in El Salvador and not, or not as much, in other countries with similar characteristics.

In addition to socioeconomic explanations, an imposing body of literature on political change, including political violence, underlines the pertinence of political variables in explaining political change and violence.[8] According to John Foran, we are in fact witnessing the emergence of a 'fourth generation' of theories of revolution, characterised by a critique of structuralist explanations *à la* Skocpol (or Barrington Moore, her mentor) and by a new emphasis on culture, ideology and agency.[9] This approach ties in with an even larger school of analysts (from Marx himself – at least in some of his writings – to Clifford Geertz and Michel Foucault) who conceive power as a distinct and autonomous modality of social relations. In fact even the third generation (structuralist) was dominated by state-centred approaches, not by economically deterministic models.[10] Hence, stressing agency and ideology hardly constitutes a new approach among students of revolution, though it never seems to have caught on in Latin American studies.

A focus on agency and ideology has yielded interesting results in recent historiographies of 'great' or 'social' revolutions. For instance recent publications on the French Revolution, in the wake of François Furet's seminal work, emphasise the political process by analysing political culture and highlighting the role of ideologues and ideologies in the eighteenth century. After decades of scholastic domination by Marxist schools, with a narrow class analysis and a penchant for economic determinism, it is now possible to highlight the importance of actors and ideas without falling off academe's bandwagon. Furet recently published a remarkable essay on the adventures of the communist idea in the twentieth century, stressing the central role of ideas, the power of utopia – that is, the human capacity to disregard reality – , the self-determination of actors, and so on.[11] Likewise the resounding success of Daniel Jonah Goldhagen's book on the Holocaust arguably stems in large part from his refreshing quest to restore 'the perpetrators to the center of our understanding of the Holocaust'.[12] Finally, the historian Martin Malia argues that the communist utopia, and the regime built upon such a premise, was the Soviet Union's real 'infrastructure,' with the economy and society being its derived superstructure.[13]

Social scientists typically underestimate or ignore the significant degree of autonomy among ideologues *vis-à-vis* the supposed diktat of their socioeconomic environment. As Jean-François Revel once said, it seems difficult for us to conceive politics, let alone ideas, as a key factor in explaining mega-events such as the total collapse of an economy, a revolution, a major technological mutation or even a famine.[14] They are more easily understood as long-term, structural calamities obeying rules quite heterogeneous to political will. Even after the tragic experiences of extermination camps in Germany, concentration camps and politically manufactured famines in China and the Soviet Union, and mass murder in Cambodia, social scientists persist in denying that one individual or group of individuals can impose themselves as key ingredients of history.[15]

The controversy does not merely pit Marxists against non-Marxists. Authors strongly influenced by Marxist sociology, such as Charles Tilly or Theda Skocpol, have paid careful attention to the political process, by following a tradition pioneered by the author (Karl Marx) of the *18th Brumaire of Napoléon Bonaparte*. In parallel, most exponents of modernisation theory (a 'Marxism with the class struggle left out' – Raymond Aron) never overcame their propensity to crush every facets of the human experience into corresponding stages of economic growth.[16]

To be sure, the dominant paradigm outlined by John Booth does not utterly discard political variables. And in books and articles on El Salvador, one certainly finds discussions of the authoritarian legacy, the failure to implement reforms, the pivotal role of the Church, the emergence of popular sectors, and the adverse role played by the US. Indeed it is common to suggest that in countries such as El Salvador 'everything is political.'

Nevertheless all these political factors are mostly presented, with various degrees of subtlety, as emanations from the overarching socioeconomic structure. Incidentally, to say that everything is political is tantamount to saying that nothing is specifically political, that the whole of 'reality', as it were, is totally engulfed in the ubiquitous enterprise of exploitation. Hence revolt is caused by injustice, even though a political 'critical juncture' might have provided the opportunity for its emergence at one particular moment instead of another. In all fairness, in their valuable contribution to the understanding of Salvadoran politics, Sara Gordon and Enrique Baloyra have gone quite far in that direction. The former perceptively studies the central role of the state, whereas the latter focuses on the importance of ideologies.[17] Both demonstrate that one can certainly move forward (but not far enough!) within the confines of the dominant paradigm.

In studies on Latin American revolutions it is not clear why structuralist, mostly economistic and often mechanistic approaches to political change are still celebrated.[18] It is facile (yet irresistible) to point out that the extreme disparity of income south of the Rio Grande lends itself to the crudest of deterministic explanations. In Latin America the ready-made, one size fits all, bluntest analysis seems to *work*.[19]

Yet this explanation is inadequate. After all internal war is the exception in Latin America, a region where shocking social injustice and the exclusion of the many from the body politic have been a fixture for centuries.[20] For as James DeNardo has suggested, the real intellectual challenge is essentially to 'understand why revolutions happen hardly at all in a world that abounds with misery, deprivation, injustice, and spellbindingly rapid change'.[21]

ECONOMIC DOWNTURN AND DEMOCRATISATION IN LATIN AMERICA DURING THE 1980s

In any general discussion on political development south of the Rio Grande, one has to reckon with the great event of the 1980s: the democratisation of Latin America.[22] The adventure of the so-called 'lost decade' invites scholars to question some of their basic assumptions about the linkages between economy and politics in the region. Indeed, the remarkable – though contradictory and fragile – wave of democratisation in the region, including El Salvador, occurred without substantial alteration to the secular socioeconomic structure of injustice.[23] What is more, the harsh recession of the 1980s, coupled with the growing adoption of neoliberal economic policies, conspired to sharpen the gap between rich and poor. In most Latin American countries one finds more social injustice now than two decades ago.[24]

Far from triggering instability and polarisation, some innovative authors recently suggested that the economic crisis of the 1980s actually favored democratisation, not polarisation. Juan Linz questioned the usual linkage between economic development and democratisation as early as the late 1970s. At that time Spain was offering a telling case of democratisation in the midst of a harsher economic and financial crisis than the one underwent by Latin American countries in the 1980s.[25]

One remembers that, during the 1960s and 1970s, the first proponents of the dependency school proclaimed the absence of alternatives to fascism or socialism in the region. (Without wishing to overstretch the point, one recalls that the Nazis made the same apocalyptic prediction for Europe during the Second World War.) Following some rebuttal from academia, reconstructed *dependentistas* eventually admitted the possibility of 'associate dependent development'; that is, growth coupled with some limited possibility of liberalisation and democratisation.[26] The concept of 'bureaucratic authoritarianism', articulated by Guillermo O'Donnell, rejuvenated the notion that growth, even development, in the Latin American context not only fails to generate democratisation, but requires authoritarianism – in this case a more 'modern', technocratic form of dictatorship.

All in all the theoretical paraphernalia inherited from the two-decade quest for a comprehensive interpretation (both scholarly and political) of the region's socioeconomic ordeal is largely obsolete today.[27]

Going back to the 1980s, the following comments by Terry Karl provide a good encapsulation of the intellectual bottle-neck that is still dominant in the literature:

> most observers assume that crises in growth, employment, foreign exchange earnings, and debt repayments necessarily bode ill for the consolidation of democratic rule, and few would question the long-run value of an increasing resource base for stability. But austerity may have some perverse advantages, at least for initial survivability. In the context of the terrible economic conditions of the '80s, the exhaustion of utopian ideologies and even of rival policy prescriptions has become painfully evident. To the extent that this situation diminishes both the expected benefits and rewards from antisystem activity, it enhances the likelihood of democracies to endure.[28]

This insightful comment was further developed by Karen Remmer, who convincingly made the case that 'the outbreak of severe economic crisis, as distinct from cyclical economic trends, may dampen popular expectations, providing incumbents with unexpected room for maneuver. Available survey data establish no basis for linking the Latin American economic crisis of the '80s with diminished popular support for democratic institutions.'[29] In fact, as she points out in a more recent publication, the dominant economicist theories fail to explain why 'Latin America shifts in the direction of authoritarian rule in the '60s under conditions of relative prosperity and rapid growth and reverts to democracy in the '80s under precisely the opposite set of conditions'.[30]

In sum, politics is influenced by *many* factors, none of which are univocal. Economic crisis might breed polarisation, revolt and repression, but equally or it might breed democratisation. Or it may not breed much at all. Other factors – such as cultural evolution, international events, individual contributions and so on – may outweigh the majestic productive forces as the engine of history.[31] Almost anything can cause revolt and political change. Injustice is doubtless *the* moral justification for revolt in Latin America; however it does not follow that social scientists ought to accept the insurgents' vindication as their obligatory independent variable. As a group, scholars must resist the temptation to bank on the most obvious cause, if only because, unlike the dependent variable (revolt), *the absence of variation* is what makes them so obvious.[32]

POTENTIAL AND LIMITATIONS

A final word on the dominant paradigm. *This book proposes a better understanding of the etiology of revolt in El Salvador through an analysis of the role of ideas and ideologues in the recent political development of that country.* This is not necessarily an antithesis to the dominant model. For one thing, this essay does not pretend to be a comprehensive survey, or a mega-model of analysis. Doubtless, a rigorous cross-national analysis would be necessary to test, and conceivably to falsify, the dominant paradigm synopsised by Booth (1991). Such a task is well beyond the scope of this essay. Although the propositions presented here clearly contradict some assumptions underlying the dominant paradigm, one could equally construe them as complementary avenues, inviting a reformulation within the dominant discourse more than a theoretical *tabula rasa*. After all, the dominant paradigm's limitations appear to be unequivocal even for Booth, who openly deplores the fact in his conclusion. I like to think that he was inviting scholars to explore this avenue.

Part of the problem with the dominant paradigm stems from the misuse of concepts. Thus in the following sections I propose to look at the key notions employed in this book: i.e. *internal war*, *ideology* and the question of *sequences in internal wars*. This clarification will prepare the groundwork for the formulation of alternative hypotheses on the emergence of insurgency in El Salvador.

INSURGENCY AND INTERNAL WAR

Among the different concepts available to describe the kind of political situation studied in this book, internal war, insurgency, and revolt are arguably the most appropriate. All of them conjure up a situation of armed pluralism, where the government is militarily challenged on a continuous basis by a fairly organised group of (mostly) civilian actors. 'Insurgency' describes the military opposition and its course of action, whereas 'revolt' refers more specifically to the action proper. 'Internal war' characterises the situation where a government is militarily challenged on a continuous basis by a fairly organised group of mostly civilian actors.[33] All these terms accord with the angle of analysis adopted in this book, and are preferable to the three concepts generally used in the literature; namely civil war, guerrilla warfare and revolution.

At first glance, civil war and, to a lesser extent, guerrilla warfare are quite acceptable terms. They are vague, but so are most social science concepts. The problem is that in their vagueness they may imply attributes that are far from being fixtures of the situations described.

Civil war initially meant 'war in the city', but is now heavily connoted as war that surges from civil society, war from below, popular war and so on. Yet internal wars are often in opposition to factions that are well entrenched in the ruling class, thus conferring to the conflict a dynamic that is closer to a *coup d'état* than to whatever 'stalagmitic' logic is being subsumed under the term 'civil' war.

'Guerrilla warfare' is no less problematic. It dates back to two historical events: the counterrevolutionary war in France in the wake of the French revolution, that is, when the *Chouans* of North-Western France conducted a *petite guerre* ('small war') against the revolutionary army,[34] and the other famous 'small war', conducted by Spaniards opposing Napoleon's army and the French occupation of Spain in 1808 (guerrilla = Guerr(a) plus the sufix 'illa', which suggests 'small').[35] In both cases 'guerrilla' meant a *defensive mobilisation* featuring peasants and their local leaders (such as the lower clergy), and a strategy of irregular warfare involving small and mobile, offensive combat units.

The term still has this connotation today (the term 'urban guerrilla' is used when the urban component is overwhelming). In sharp contrast with the rebel movements of the first half of the twentieth century in Latin America (Mexico, Bolivia and Guatemala), the guerrilla movements of the post-Castro generation have primarily been led by urban, middle-to-upper-class intellectuals.[36]

What is more, modern Latin American guerrilla warfare can hardly be defined as essentially defensive in nature, unlike most, if not all, peasant mobilisations. The initial impetus and the process by which an offensive political agenda is established bear little resemblance to the equation of interest plus passion that is historically associated with peasant mobilisations. This does not mean that modern Latin American guerrillas warfare has no defensive component; quite the contrary, peasant support of this form of political mobilisation is often a prerequisite for its expansion and consolidation. But the political mobilisation of peasants is predicated on a structure of threat/opportunity, or a 'framing', that forces them to choose between resistance and inordinate loss. This makes their mobilization essentially defensive and local, *not* offensive and national.[37] As Octavio Paz reminds us, Hidalgo and his army of peasants fought their way to the threshold of an abandoned Mexico city, and then turned back.[38]

Incidentally, although peasant insurrections played a fundamental role in the French, Russian and Chinese Revolutions, neo-Marxist and structuralist scholars such as Theda Skocpol and Barrington Moore recognise the subsidiary role of peasants in defining the ideological and political logic of these momentous events. For Skocpol, 'Peasants participated in these Revolutions without being converted to radical visions of a desired new national society, and without becoming a nationally organized class-for-themselves. Instead they struggled for concrete goals – typically involving access to more land, or freedom from claims on their surpluses.'[39] Barrington Moore also contends that:

> By themselves the peasants have never been able to accomplish a revolution. On this point the Marxists are absolutely correct, wide of the mark though they are on other crucial aspects. The peasants have to have leaders from other classes. But leadership alone is not enough. Medieval and late medieval peasant revolts were led by aristocrats or townsmen and still were crushed. This point should serve as a salutary reminder to those modern determinists, by no means all Marxists, who feel that once the peasants have become stirred up, big changes are necessarily on the way.[40]

In the same perspective, James C. Scott notices that the typical dissident behaviour of peasants is 'resistance'; that is, resistance in order to defend themselves. Peasants are not interested in capturing power in the capital city in order to revolutionise the whole polity from above.[41] Peasants have precious little time for or interest in thinking up institutional utopias that could have a universal or even national resonance. Indeed 'dissident intellectuals from the middle or upper classes may occasionally have the luxury of focusing exclusively on the prospects for long-term structural change, but the peasantry or the working class are granted no holiday from the mundane pressures of making a living.'[42]

Finally, the term 'revolution' is arguably the most problematic, for historical as well as theoretical reasons. The concept of revolution has probably been used and abused in Latin America more than in any other region of the world. Right-wing officers, Christian Democrats in search of a third way, fascistic populist leaders, and of course the whole spectrum of left-leaning actors have manipulated it for their own political purposes. To be 'revolutionary' confers an aura of respectability in a region of the world where (1) the wars of independence failed to bloom into true national revolutions, thus leaving an aftertaste of non-fulfillment; (2) the social, economic and political environment generates so much frustration and desire for change; and (3) deference to the nation's legal construct is fainthearted at best.[43] Not surprisingly, in El Salvador as in most Latin American countries, few if any political actors have refrained from calling themselves revolutionary at some point or other over the past twenty years. When a notion is so stretchable and 'enchanted' it becomes a slogan that, even though it is inspiring as an object *of* research, can hardly be used as a sufficiently neutral and circumscribed concept *for* research.

Theoretically the notion of revolution is not as indispensable as it may appear. Radical change is the only true indicator that allows some operationalisation of the concept. That is, one can only know when the putative revolutionaries are in command of state power. Even then, enchanted by the siren song of revolutions – the sex of politics! – scholars tend to exaggerate the depth and magnitude of the change, as John Walton has correctly pointed out.[44] This book refuses to construe the different sequences of an internal war as homogeneous (as will be explained later), and it fails to see the heuristic advantage of hand-picking from, among the various eloquent candidates for the praised label, those who probably constitute the *true* revolutionary. Therefore the concept of revolution may as well be dropped and replaced by the more specific and ideologically neutral notions presented above (internal war, insurgency, and revolt), or if necessary by the more specific concept of radical change (or aspiration to radical change).

THE WORLD OF IDEOLOGIES

Appreciating the self-determination of political actors entails our paying attention to the role of ideologies in political action, because ideology is the organising principle of modern political action. The famous slogan of the French revolution – liberté, égalité, fraternité (ou la mort!) – highlights the essential ingredients that enter into all modern political recipes:

liberalism, socialism and nationalism (fascism being when nationalism turns into vinegar, ravaging all other ingredients beyond recognition).[45]

Very much like the worlds of mythology and religion, the world of ideology is an *orderly world* whose time-span transcends the short, haphazard and *a priori* absurd life of the individual. Powerful in charismatic periods of history such as self-proclaimed revolutions, ideology is nevertheless a poor substitute for religion and mythology in a routinised liberal society, where immortality is confiscated by disenchanting institutions. Being born with the advent of reason as the new 'supreme being', ideology is also a genuine parasite of science, usurping its procedure (explanation, involving cursory verification of some of its assumptions) without the rules of the procedure (comprehensive experimentation and falsification).[46]

Revolutions are always conceived as the absolute triumph of ideology over reality, a last redemptive fiesta where the ideologues become one with the masses and their own heavenly creature. It supposes the illusion of a *temps zéro*, a utopia of new beginning, at once outside the realm of history and pregnant win a new one (during the French Revolution Michelet offered '*le temps n'existait plus, le temps avait péri*')[47] In this line of thought, totalitarian ideology is perhaps more straightforward and transparent than its diluted counterparts because it calls for a *tabula rasa*, followed by what Octavio Paz called a 'mandatory communion,' or a police-manufactured social fusion of the masses.[48] It is both reactionary and progressive, a path to both the lost village and the new Jerusalem. Not surprisingly, 'revolutionary regimes' of the totalitarian variety always strive to preserve the original illusion by *freezing time*, through institutionalisation of revolutionary myths, central planning and expurgation of those 'worms' who recoil from the vanguard-led social fusion.

The relative autonomy of ideologies means that *no ideology is the mere translation of its material environment*. For one, thing ideology is necessarily built, as Carl Schmitt has explained, around the structuring pattern of 'friends and foes'. For the ideologue it is therefore imperative to select and discard information according to political expediency. Ideology is a political strategy. The ideology's criterion of validity is not truthfulness; rather it is to be convincing enough to win political battles.[49]

Even if ideologues are not interested in scoring political points, no discourse can be total, embracing the entire human experience. Pointing out this characteristic is fundamental since ideology tends to be presented as all-encompassing. The more an ideology is constructed for universal application and a wide array of human activity, ordering the world according to one transcendental principle, the more it has to be cut off from the fundamental uncertainty and indeterminacy of the human experience. In Octavio Paz's terms: 'Todo lenguaje, sin excluir al de la libertad, termina por convertirse en una cárcel.'[50] Stretched to its limits, which means being in total awe of its own circular logic, ideology is impermeable to counterargument ('you cannot reason a person out of something he has not been reasoned into' – Swift).[51] Reassuring like a religion, empowering like a unique key to heaven, wrapped in the mantle of science, an ideology needs nothing but a suitable historical moment to intoxicate the many, from hyperactive students and other dissident elements of the ruling class, to hard-working men and women. The extent to which individuals can convince themselves of almost anything is seemingly unlimited.[52]

Intellectuals, who are the main producers and transmitters of ideologies, conjure up the image of Italo Calvino's 'Il Barone Rampante'. Permanently perched at the peak of the tallest trees and looking down on the chaotic world, intellectuals entertain themselves in the illusion of their exclusive grasp of the whole picture of history. Having exclusive access to the laws that underpin the human experience generates an aristocratic contempt for the daily ritual of conflict and accommodation enacted by down-to-earth individuals.[53] One invariably finds, sifting through the initiation to ideology – in a political organisation or in the classroom – the seeds of disdain for ordinary people, their choices and values. And even when the ideologue's aristocratic haughtiness is hidden behind populist slogans (the people, the masses, the proletariat, the nation), these slogans are nothing but abstract fig leaves cherished by the ideologue precisely because they are his own holy creation.

Intellectuals might master an extraordinary quantum of information while being powerfully wrong on the essentials, in contrast to 'average' individuals, who on the whole offset their general ignorance of details by a solid and prudent common sense on fundamental issues concerning their own lives. As the great moralist George Orwell once remarked, ordinary citizens are both too ignorant and too healthy to imagine totalitarian ideologies.[54]

Ideology without Borders

It is a mistake always to analyse ideologies by rummaging through the soil where they bloomed. Ideologies are connected 'vertically', so to speak, to the social base where they are reproduced, but also – perhaps even more importantly – 'horizontally', to a period of history or a generation.[55] The American and the French Revolutions were part of an Atlantic revolution of universal proportions. Hegel was moved to tears when he witnessed Napoleon's tour in Iena: the emperor was more than a general from Corsica or France's new autocrat: he embodied a new European product – reason. (Incidentally the passions unleashed by the revolution, many of which had little to do with reason, captured German minds at least as much as those of the *citoyens français*, and long after they ceased to have much impact in the hexagon.)[56]

Communism, according to Marx, was the intellectual product of the time: an explosive mixture of English political economy, German philosophy and French political radicalism. This bouquet bloomed where the *ideological conditions*, not the *material* ones, were ripe: in France and Germany more than in England and the US.[57] But it was first fleshed out in countries such as Russia and Mongolia, not in France and Germany. In the postwar period the intellectual influence of ideas producers such as Sartre, Wright Mills, Marcuse and even Franz Fanon is more easily confined to historical rather than geographic bounds.

Needless to say, the whole history of Latin American political culture is one of importing and accommodating foreign ideas, starting with the imposition of a pre-Renaissance Mediterranean ethos and followed by the more complex import/export process of the post-independence period.[58] Positivism, romanticism, liberalism and socialism are European transplants, or perhaps more accurately, Western ideas shared by generations of Western-educated individuals. Why does an ideology, or even a philosophical current, emerge or die in one place at a certain point in time?[59] Jean-François Revel claims that 'utopias die the same way they are born: without real causes'.[60] But not all ideologies promote outright utopias. Moreover the socioeconomic as well as the political conditions in a nation or a region certainly contain some of the 'causes' needed in the explanation. Dependency theory and the theology of liberation are neither Latin American inventions nor pure intellectual imports from Belgium or Germany. In a way they are both: that is, the product of the conjugation, mostly in the American continent, of a number or ideas available virtually everywhere during a certain period of time.

The Power of Ideology

Finally, it is possible to identify several conditions that are likely to increase the influence of both ideas and ideologues in a given political situation. Arguably, situations that are likely to convert ideologues into movers and shakers are deep collective traumas such as external or internal war, the collapse of political institutions, a crisis of collective identity, a nationalistic upsurge, a generational clash and so on. In short, this process of conversion occurs during what Max Weber called a charismatic period. This phenomenon has been observed by many great sociologists, most of whom, at one point or another during their careers, have pondered on the nature and role of the intellectual. For instance Lewis Coser argues that:

> In periods marked by relatively stable social structures and routinized politics, the affairs of state prove recalcitrant to intellectuals' attempts to gain political ascendance. But revolutionary periods may afford them the chance to gain state power. In ordinary periods, individual intellectuals may upon occasion be co-opted into seats of power, but only in revolutionary times will groups of intellectuals be in a position to conquer the state. It is then that revolutionary intellectuals wrest power and rule society, even if only for a short but pregnant moment in history. We can witness this process in many of the new nations of the contemporary world.[61]

In the following chapters we shall see the specificity of the conditions in which intellectuals and ideologues emerged as a potent political force in El Salvador. Suffice to say here that, in periods when neither traditions nor the ascendancy of institutions offer guidance to the people, manufacturers of ideas, especially political ideas, can have an inordinate influence upon the course of events. Mario Vargas Llosa once said that literature does not 'reflect' nations; it invents them. The same could certainly be said about ideas – especially bad ones, as Revel would add.[62]

* * *

In sum, revolt or insurgency is a complex and always unique phenomenon – there is no historical law of revolt. Insurgency is made by insurgents, whose political motivations are shaped by such a wide array of factors that it is pointless to reduce insurgency only, or even primarily, to redundant conditions of injustice. Injustice enters into the equation, but so does ideology, and of course the proper conditions favourable to ideology's mobilisational capacity. From the domestic structural conditions of revolt, the case is made here that our attention must be largely shifted to the conditions that allow for the emergence of both the insurgents and the ideas that are instrumental in organising their political action. These conditions are to be found in the relatively autonomous and generational realm of ideologies and in the distinct social environment of ideologues.

IDEOLOGIES AND THE SEQUENCES OF INTERNAL WAR

The enchanted concept of revolution, to which the concept of internal war is preferred in this book, routinely encompasses three different sequences of events:

- The *emergence* of an insurgency.
- The *epicentre* of the revolution, that is when the old regime is being overthrown and replaced by the new revolutionary regime.
- The ensuing period of *implementation of radical changes* by the new government.

The internal war covers the first period, the second period and part of the third period (until the new government reinstalls what Tilly (1978) called the 'unique sovereignty' over the national territory).

Ideology arguably plays an important role in all stages of the process, but the proposition that the key impact of ideologies is during the last stage is the least contentious.[63] Even structuralists such as Theda Skocpol, who provocatively asserted in her famous *State and Social Revolutions* that 'revolutions are not made; they come',[64] subsequently admitted that ideologies 'do independently affect the scope of transformations that revolutionary politicians attempt to institute when they rise to state power amidst ongoing social revolutions'.[65] Some authors contemplate the possibility that ideology does affect the chances of building a strong opposition coalition, as well as the capacity of the regime to maintain itself in power.[66]

In recent years Forrest D. Colburn has probably made the strongest case for rehabilitating 'revolutionary politics' and ideologies as independent variables in the study of 'revolution in the poor countries'.[67] He claims that 'perhaps the two most remarkable characteristics of contemporary revolutions are, first, the extent to which they have shared a common intellectual culture, and, second, just how ambitious that intellectual culture has been, especially given the material poverty of the respective polities'.[68] This ties in with previously cited comments by François Furet, Martin Malia and Jean-François Revel, all of which hinted at the crucial role played by ideas, and by what Furet calls 'political will', in shaping politics during periods of rapid political change.

This being said, this essay focuses on just one of these periods: the first – the emergence of insurgency (in El Salvador this was roughly between 1970 and 1981). It explores the extent to which ideologies and political will are important variables in the emergence of internal war.

Ideologies carry more weight during the first period than during the ensuing ones. Full-fledged national revolt and the implementation of radical changes are complex, multifaceted, multidimensional societal phenomena, involving a variety of actors and constraints. The emergence of an insurgency, on the other hand, is a phenomenon whose social scope is relatively limited, where the main actors form a relatively homogeneous group of people. Social conditions of action (both constraining and enabling) are likely to influence the probability of an insurgency maturing into a full-fledged national revolt and the eventual, capture of state power. But these conditions play a relatively limited role during the emergence of an insurgency *per se*. Conversely ideologies are likely to be predominant in a relatively less constraining environment. And as stated in the previous section, the more an ideology is constructed to embrace universal application and a wide array of human activity, ordering the world according to one transcendental principle, the more it allows itself to be cut off from the fundamental uncertainty and indeterminacy of the human experience. This explains why the insurgents' ideology *was more radical during the period of emergence than at any time thereafter, not less, as the dominant paradigm suggests* (radicalism crops up as a last resort when patience wears out).

The all-encompassing and spellbinding notion of revolution – which, incidentally, was the Virgin of Guadalupe of most Central Americanists during the 1980s[69] – blurs the distinct configurations of each of the three periods, as though they were all 'structurally' the same. An unsuccessful insurgency is not necessarily identical to a successful one in nature and origin.[70] It is a common mistake to assume that all Latin American revolutions are structurally similar, with the proviso that some are (unfortunately) defective and do not develop to their fullest extent. The fact that arms are taken up in a country where indicators of relative deprivation abound is not tantamount to the emergence of a social revolution.[71]

For instance, Central American nations such as El Salvador, Nicaragua, Guatemala and Honduras (democratic Costa Rica again being the exception) embody characteristics that open them to political activism and destabilisation by active minorities. They are city-states, where power and wealth are centralised and concentrated in an authoritarian fashion. The 'civil society', outside the interlocked clans who monopolise power and wealth, is mostly powerless. In such countries, a relatively small but highly organised (that is, these with the proper connections abroad) and motivated group of armed individuals (from coup plotters to guerrillas) can sustain an internal war for a long period of time, even without widespread popular support.[72] Arguably, two or three thousand armed activists could survive for a very long period of time as a serious national counterpower in El Salvador, Guatemala or Nicaragua; it is harder to imagine this scenario in Brazil, Argentina, Chile, Mexico, Venezuela and so on. Ernesto 'Che' Guevara was not all that wrong when he asserted that 'a nucleus of 30 to 50 men' is 'sufficient to initiate an armed fight in any country of the Americas', if the verb 'to initiate' is understood properly and with some change in nuance from one region to another.[73]

NEW PROPOSITIONS ON THE ETIOLOGY OF INTERNAL WAR

The political development of El Salvador over the past three decades has been significantly shaped by factors that are overlooked, underestimated or disputed by exponents of the dominant paradigm. These factors concern not the structural causes of the internal war, but the insurgents themselves: how they emerged, what choices they made and on what ideological dispositions these choices were based.

The general thesis of this book should already be apparent. The insurgency was not merely the charismatic embodiment of structurally determined processes, but the expression of a distinct and forceful political will. A political will conditioned by ideas that, for all their grounding in the Salvadoran experience, were nonetheless shared by many people at a certain time in sundry countries and cultural environments. I shall look at this more specifically.

First, although a structural approach may wield superior explanatory power when analysing the causes of successful national revolts, a focus on the specific mobilisation of the insurgents is indispensable to understanding the *emergence* of insurgency – a stage that in most instances does not lead to full-fledged national revolt, let alone to the collapse of the old regime and the seizure of power by insurgents.

Second, in El Salvador, pressure for radical change – that is, political and military pressure – came initially and primarily from a dissenting faction of the urban, middle-to-upper stratum of society. This group can be singled out as one of the few beneficiaries of the unprecedented economic growth and social mobilisation of the 1950s and 1960s. University actors (students and faculty members) and actors located at their periphery (students and teachers in high schools and colleges) were the core elements of this dissenting faction.

Third, the emergence of insurgency in El Salvador appears to have been caused largely by a crisis affecting three key institutions: the universities (that is, the public and Catholic universities), the Catholic Church and the Communist Party.

Although the crisis took different forms in each of them, one can detect some common ideological dispositions. Among the key actors in the three institutions one can find a certain voluntarism, an impatience *vis-à-vis* both the perceived political immobility of society at large and the prudent indulgence of the old guard in their respective institutions. There was also a strong dose of elitism or 'vanguardism', which shielded them from input from the 'rearguard' (or the famous masses).

Finally, radical ideologies and the romanticisation of armed struggle, as featured by the initial nucleus of insurgents, were not merely a last resort response to injustice, exclusion and repression, as most analysts have asserted. They were pivotal elements of a *new post-developmentalist and countercultural disposition*. From the 1960s until the recent emergence of powerful countertrends, this disposition was shared by political activists – primarily university-based – all over Latin America and beyond (for instance among the North American social scientists who took to studying them) in heterogeneous social, economic and political environments. They usually had a more powerful political impact in countries where political opposition was banned or restricted (Latin American and Eastern European countries), although the exceptions are by no means negligible (France, Uruguay, probably Chile). All the same, the ideological shift towards the centre of the political spectrum (observable on both the left and the right) at the end of the 1980s, in spite of little if any variation in the socioeconomic environment, contributed decisively to ending the war and prompting democratisation.

Again, these four propositions and the dominant paradigm need not be understood as mutually exclusive – or at least not entirely. In the absence of a cross-national and comprehensive study of the etiology of internal wars in Latin America, it is safer to suggest that the focus on insurgents presented here is an invitation to recognise some significant weaknesses in the dominant paradigm, and to make the case for a reappraisal of the fundamental role played by them in the emergence of internal wars in Latin America and beyond.

2 From Causes to 'Causers'

> In addition to comrades who were coming from the Communist Party, others came from the social-Christian movement, which was quite developed at the time.... Finally, there were revolutionaries without party attachment who were coming from the most advanced sectors produced by the popular movement at that time. Practically, most were students, fundamentally university people and teachers. There was only a few workers. These were the three currents who came together to form both the FPL and the ERP. (FPL leader, quoted in Harnecker, 1993)

According to Michael Radu, 'one of the most amazing things about the abundant bibliography on Latin America's revolutionary traditions and movements is the almost total absence of a serious analysis of the revolutionaries themselves'.[1] This is a striking assertion. The muse of revolution has always animated philosophers and social scientists. Most insurgents are talkative and inclined to make their wisdom available to the widest possible public. Indeed there is no shortage of books and pamphlets devoted to radical insurgencies in Latin America.

Radu obviously means that self-proclaimed revolutionaries *are not studied as a relatively autonomous group of actors*, with a specific ideology, tactics and strategies. For in the literature radical insurgents are pictured as *interpreters* of an historical, structurally determined trend towards change. It is not easy to renounce the political enchantment of social revolution.[2] Insurgents are usually presented as trend-surfers who, emulating Hannah Arendt's (1984) 'men of the revolutions', strive to ride the top of the latest insurgency wave. Or they are amongst the interchangeable members of an eclectic coalition

– along with peasants, workers, the 'social subject of the revolution' and so on. Finally, and more frequently, they are merely pictured as someone else's voice: the voice of those who have no voice.[3]

The dominant paradigm espouses the 'evolutionary vanguard's' self-perception, which in turn replicates the typical self-perception of intellectuals. Latin American intellectuals share with their counterparts all over the world a propensity to deny or exorcise their attachment to the upper strata of society. They generally prefer to hide behind (or more precisely, above) the 'universal class' of the moment. Intellectuals are not 'unattached', to use Alfred Weber's famous adjective.[4] They are constantly attempting to attach themselves to whichever group is, theoretically, ready to be conducted by them to the commanding heights. All this is especially true of radical intellectuals, who are this century's intellectual vanguard *par excellence*.

In short, we have a case of intellectuals denying intellectuals' denial: that is the intellectuals' (perfunctory?) denial of their own existence as an elitist and pushy segment of the population is condoned by social scientists. A beautiful case of false consciousness!

The connection between revolutionary vanguards and intellectuals is loose but still meaningful. Of course, not all intellectuals are activists, let alone insurgents. But one can certainly assert that the Latin American insurgencies of the past thirty-five years have been led by intellectuals, with the following proviso: as Jorge Castañeda and many others stress, 'in Latin America, where societies are polarized, and knowledge and social recognition are rare, almost anyone who writes, paints, acts, teaches, and speaks out, or even sings, becomes "an intellectual"'.[5] The reason why performing such activities is deemed sufficient has to do with both the distinct culture inherited from Spain (the Don Quixote syndrome) and the cultural insecurities of nineteenth-century Latin America (the Ariel syndrome). The status of the intellectual is less defined in terms of the production and deconstruction of ideas than in terms of what is done with them, how one behaves according to certain ideas. François Bourricaud aptly emphasises that the typical Latin American intellectual is 'generally uninterested in pure learning or theoretical knowledge'. As a group, 'their interest focused almost exclusively on problems such as dependence and national identity, leading them to question the social mission of the intelligence, rather than the critical function of intelligence'.[6]

Three additional comments must be made before discussing the specificity of 'causers', or insurgents, in El Salvador. First, it must be emphasised that *from the mid 1960s to the mid 1970s virtually all Latin American governments, in the wake of the Cuban revolution, confronted insurgencies*. Mexico, which had retained diplomatic relations with Cuba, was the only exception to this rule.[7] And few scholars would now dispute that all these insurgencies were overwhelmingly led by urban, middle-class, university-educated young men.[8] Most of the leaders of Latin American insurgencies (and arguably, of insurgencies in all developing nations) became politically active as university students (more on this in Chapter 4). They often remained connected to university institutions after graduation as teachers or professors, while some became journalists, union leaders, lawyers, priests, engineers, doctors and the like. If this is the general rule for Latin America, it portrays perfectly the cases of El Salvador and Nicaragua, where virtually all the leaders of the FMLN and the Sandinista Front were originally mobilised as students, teachers or professors.

Second, *foco theory's (or the Bolsheviks' or Blanquists') basic premise, at least implicitly embraced by the kind of insurgents I am looking at here, is seldom taken seriously in the literature*. That is, virtually no one buys the argument that a small group of professional revolutionaries can trigger and sustain military opposition to a given regime without first meeting the supposedly 'objective' conditions of revolt, including mass support. Consequently most observers miss the opportunity to study the genuine political sociology of insurgency in the region.

As Arendt points out in her seminal work *On Revolution* (1984), the insurrectionist pattern of revolutionary mobilisation, featuring a small army of professional revolutionaries, has been the rule in the century of Lenin. Latin America is far from being the exception. In elitist, developing city-states, revolutions are not only performed by vanguards, they are typically 'revolution in the family'.[9] Behind the revolutionary and counterrevolutionary rhetoric, it is not difficult to find 'class-enemies' from the same social milieu, the same neighbourhood or even the same family. Few of these dissenting members of the urban elites are bereft of relatives in government or the economic establishment. This facilitates their reinsertion in the ruling class at the outset of the war (unlike their followers from lower strata), namely through the most recent and burgeoning coffin of revolutionary movements: the non-governmental organisations and the research institutes.[10]

The concept of 'ruling class' is obviously understood broadly: a radical student is not equivalent to a reactionary oligarch. Nevertheless in a poverty-ridden, still largely illiterate country, educated priests, university students, intellectuals, national union leaders and professors are awarded sufficient social deference and political authority to be considered members, or aspiring members, of the narrow club of elites.[11] This comment is especially warranted in periods of crisis, when the more conventional channels of political mobilisation are impaired.[12]

All this is consonant with the logic of power in Latin America since the conquistadors: struggle for power at the top, among elites vying to impose their agenda and political authority on the essentially disintegrated, excluded masses. Most elites in Latin America regard the countryside as the repository of uncivilised masses (Sarmiento's barbarians), held in reserve to be enlightened and mobilised.[13] During the exalted 1980s in El Salvador, the countryside was the 'promised land' where radical priests, Christian union leaders, student *guerrilleros* and gringo political activists competed with conservative priests, US-sponsored unions, fascist militias, multitudinous counterinsurgency agents and Agency for International Development (AID) clerks for control, *concientizaçao* (raising the awareness) and mobilisation (or demobilisation) of the peasantry. The French intellectual Régis Debray, well-known for his pamphlet *Révolution dans la révolution* and for his revolutionary immersion in Cuba and Bolivia during the 1960s, suggests that:

> An historian focusing on the long term would probably consider the contemporary revolutionary movement, third-worldism included, as another step, more convulsive than others, in a long tale involving peasants being taken over by city dwellers, oral culture by print culture; as it were, as a cunning of capitalist modernisation.[14]

In the late 1970s, Salvadoran sociologist Rafael Guidos Vejar was very perceptive when he observed that indeed 'the peasant problem is becoming urbanised!' (el problema campesino se urbaniza).'[15] It is sad and ironic that in the 1980s, this assertion took a fresh significance as hundreds of thousands of inhabitants of small villages in the northern and eastern parts of the country emigrated to Washington DC, Los Angeles and other North American or Australian cities.

The logic of power is not 'top-down' merely in the sense that ordinary citizens find themselves at the receiving end of the decision-making process; this is the fate of most citizens in any country. The logic of power is one, to put it bluntly, of conquest and colonisation; that is, one that involves not only the use of force but also a cultural/ideological mission, an attempt to change mentalities, to win hearts and minds, to found a new political order stretching from the civilised city to the barbarian countryside. This logic is conspicuously absent from the literature on political change in El Salvador.

This ties in with my third comment: *the insurgents' vanguardism is in part consonant with the time-honoured tradition of elitism and exclusionary politics in El Salvador*. The Salvadoran oligarchs, some of whose forebears emigrated to the country in the second half of the nineteenth century, consider themselves pioneers of a sort, a truly national vanguard who developed the country single-handedly (without foreign help), turning it into one of the most industrialised and economically successful countries in the region. According to their own self-image, the oligarchs did not take away from the people, and consequently are not obliged to give anything back through agrarian reform or other 'communist' (foreign) inspired, policies. According to the oligarchs, they created whatever resources the poor country has to go around. Even in the 1970s a member of the oligarchy was still someone who, by virtue of his or her social and economic position, was above the law and could dispose of people with very few legal, moral or cultural restrictions.

Similarly, the Salvadoran army likes to depict itself as the armed arm of the people, the backbone of the nation; not merely as the personal militia of the oligarchy. From the early 1930s onwards the military challenged the oligarchy every fifteen years in the name of the people. It enjoyed impunity, just like the oligarchy. The war in the 1980s allowed the military to modernise and expand itself in an unprecedented way, while individual officers enriched themselves to the point where they can now be considered as members of the country's new economic establishment. In short, over the past five or six decades the army has been successful in imposing itself as a true vanguard of the Salvadoran nation.

Military vanguardism has had incalculable consequences, not only for the political development of the country, but also because it has generated what Castellanos Moya calls a 'cultura del gorillismo' in the country. That is, it has been instrumental in creating the impression that political assassination and the survival of the cruel are fair rules of the political game.[16] Until the emergence of the insurgency, the army was the undisputed super-*caudillo*, bringing 'order', 'discipline' and 'progress' (that is, arbitrariness, corruption and authoritarian modernisation) to the nation.

The formation of the ARENA Party on 30 September, 1981, following the demise of the military party (the PCN), triggered by the coup of October 1979, is another instructive illustration of how the right-wins Salvadoran mind-set operates. All the ARENA officials encountered by the author have pointed out that they, not unlike the praetorian rulers of the 1930–80 period, are not *políticos* (politicians). Extraordinary 'circumstances', combined with an overpowering sense of 'national duty', have diverted them from their productive activities to serve the nation's utmost interest. *Arenistas* do not engage in petty politics, unlike other vulgar politicians. They are more like an interest group, but one that represents the whole nation. ARENA presents itself as a vanguard of the best elements of the nation, the saviour against international communism.

The history of ARENA is indistinguishable from the life of its charismatic leader and founding father, a young officer with popular background named Roberto D'Aubuisson.[17] D'Aubuisson supplied the three essential guiding principles of the party: 'first, El Salvador; second, El Salvador; and third, El Salvador'. ARENA is nationalistic in the way the military used to be: in a monistic, authoritarian, exclusionary way. In its manifesto of 22 October, 1981, addressed to 'the Salvadoran people, its army and all peoples who are friends [to the Salvadoran people and its army]', one can read a list of 'ideological principles' that are common to conservative parties: family, nation, free enterprise, God and so on. More interesting are the eleventh and thirteenth principles, devoted to two key leitmotifs of the Salvadoran extreme right: loyalty to the army, and all-out war against international communism in El Salvador:

> We recognise the Salvadoran army as the genuine armed arm of the people; consequently it deserves total support and gratitude in the accomplishment of its constitutional duty... We reject all doctrines that advocate class struggle; we defend our democratic, republican and representative system of government before the ideological penetration and the permanent aggression of international communism.[18]

For all the reconstruction the party has undergone during the 1980s and 1990s, these objectives have remained unchanged.[19] ARENA's communiqués are always succinct, which is not surprising given its mistrust of 'ideologies' and intellectual discussion. ARENA prefers to reaffirm its guiding principles and to act on them, especially its principle of unwavering faith in the 'Salvadoran Armed Forces, a universal formula to achieve security, tranquillity, order and justice, and an indispensable instrument in overcoming the current political, economic, social and military crisis.'[20] ARENA is the closest thing to a fascist party that El Salvador has ever had.

In the late 1970s and 1980s the right contested the left on its own turf, producing a rather explosive and epic melange. Heroic vanguard of the people, it resorted to violence to expurge the communist virus from the body politic. The left had its theology of liberation; the right manufactured its 'theology of counterrevolution', as Jean Meyer suggested, by fighting the atheist, anti-Christian, foreign elements that were surreptitiously inseminated in the brains of beleaguered and naive young men and women. Both ARENA and the FMLN launched some of their harshest attacks against the PDC, a common obstacle to full-fledged polarisation and *pistoletización de la realidad nacional.*[21] Attacks were also launched against the US, a meddlesome superpower that micro-managed such un-Salvadoran/counterrevolutionary policies as the agrarian reform, as well as organising a coup (1979), a coup attempt (1981) and elections (from 1982 onwards).[22]

In sum, a tendency towards self-righteous elitism was a dominant feature of Salvadoran politics for decades before the emergence of radical insurgency. Needless to say, all this does not mean that the radical left is indistinguishable from the right in any respect, nor that the insurgents' agenda never enjoyed popular support in Central America, nor that the insurgents were wrong in thinking that the poor had a raw deal and must revolt. One cannot help but side with the poor, especially in the countryside where the population has withstood centuries of contempt and repression from the government, the oligarchy, the army and the security forces. But our reading of the situation does not make the masses revolutionary. Whenever one witnesses the emergence of some urban radical insurgency in a Central American country, it is doubtful at best to assume that it must logically have been generated by the aggrieved popular sectors, regardless of how much we, social scientists, think (or wish) that the the popular sectors chose that option.

THE INSURGENTS

When insurgency emerged in El Salvador it appeared to be caused largely by crises in three overlapping institutions: the universities (that is the public and Catholic universities), the Communist Party and the Catholic Church.

The contributions of each institution to the insurgency were complementary, but unique. The Communist Party provided some organisational skills, ideological dispositions and what Charles Tilly called a 'cultural repertoire'.[23] Universities, colleges and often secondary schools provided resources and opportunities for the radical political mobilisation of the middle classes. The Catholic Church provided the bridge to the masses when necessary, and the Church was involved in one important university, the Central American University 'José Simeón Cañas'. Consequently it can be said that the Catholic Church operated on many fronts.

All three organisations have many common features that were enhanced during the critical period when insurgency emerged. They were all undergoing a severe crisis of identity; they were all subject to politicisation, often manifesting itself as a clash of generations; they were increasingly critical of the *status quo* in El Salvador; and they all had a strong tendency to picture themselves as the moral, cultural and political vanguard of the people. What is more, all three institutions have been politicised since their very foundation. The commitment to social change has been constant within the Communist Party, although the strategy and tactics adopted to achieve this goal have fluctuated dramatically according to mostly exogenous factors (that is, Soviet foreign policy). As will be discussed in the next chapter, the insurgencies of the

1960s and 1970s, along with the emergence of the 'new left' in Western countries, were largely revolts in the family; that is, revolts against the PC's (Communist Party's) moderate politics.[24] It was also a serious matter of concern in both the universities and the Catholic Church for decades. In that sense the seeds of the 1970s insurgency in Central America had been germinating for a very long time.

The 1960s and 1970s brought new generations of leaders who were ideologically stimulated by events unfolding within and beyond the national borders (primarily the Cuban Revolution, aptly called the 'Cuban crucible' by Jorge Castañeda, 1994). They consequently radicalised their forebears' discourses, and above all acted on these discourses.

Through its mobilisational work in the civil society, the Catholic Church, after Medellín, offered to the emerging revolutionary coalition a bridge to the excluded masses, mainly through the colleges, universities, unions and Christian Base Communites (CEBs). The Communist Party provided ideological and organisational skills, as well as useful connections with sundry left-wing organisations at home and abroad. The universities were, rallying points, the milieu in which most of the politico-military organisations were conceived. The university-based sectors of the opposition were the most radical and the most readily keen to advocate violence.

This does not necessarily mean that the Farabundo Marti Front for National Liberation (FMLN) was exclusively a university guerrilla organisation, as the Mexican intellectual Gabriel Zaid (1988) has suggested. Regional and local leaders of the FMLN were also recruited from unions and popular organisations. This being said, union leaders or 'delegates of the word' were often educated and converted politically either directly at the university or indirectly through contact with university actors. By 'the university' we mean primarily the National University – the University of El Salvador, UES – which until the foundation in 1965 and expansion in the 1970s of the Jesuit-led Central American University 'José Simeón Cañas' was the unique institution of higher education in the country, frequented by all Salvadorans with a college education. It was also one of the key breeding grounds for political – and Masonic![25] – recruitment and mobilisation, especially in the traditionally elitist faculties such as law, engineering and medicine.[26]

Teachers' unions, for instance, have been among the most powerful and radical organisations in the country. They have close links with universities, if only because they are all part of the education sector, or because their members were educated at the university, and so on. This explains why in El Salvador – and especially in Nicaragua – high schools supplied so many of the insurgents' rank-and-file.

Teachers' unions can also boast more intimate relations with the general population due to the nature of their clientele – there are more poor children in primary and secondary schools than poor young adults in universities. As a matter of fact they precipitated one of the defining moments in the history of vanguardism in El Salvador. In February of that countercultural year *par excellence*, 1968, the National Association of Educators of El Salvador (ANDES, founded in 1965) launched a strike to dispute the developmentalist-oriented education reform being pushed by the military government. The action eventually unleashed a general strike, with a huge demonstration in San Salvador. This conceivably boosted the union's and allied organisations' self-confidence for years to come. In a country traditionally dominated by oligarchies and the military, the teachers demonstrated that from the emerging middle class a new vanguard for change was born. General Jaime Abdul Gutiérrez (a member of the civil–military junta from 1979 to 1982) was perhaps right to consider this strike as the turning point in the unfolding of the political crisis of the 1970s and 1980s.[27] FMLN leaders readily acknowledge ANDES' contribution to the radical political mobilisation of the early 1970s.[28]

This last example is also indicative of one overlooked dimension of the internal war in El Salvador: to a significant extent, insurgency was, *a by-product of economic growth and reforms*. Change bred more change.[29] The period of authoritarian reformism in El Salvador (the 1950s and 1960s) produced a mixed record: it was successful in fostering economic growth and some social mobilisation, but it failed to modernise the state apparatus, to democratise the political system and to foster the inclusion of the many. Insurgency in El Salvador was the product of both these successes and failures.

The economic achievements of El Salvador in the 1950s and 1960s have been documented and analysed in some of the best works available on this country.[30] This process took place under the guidance of an authoritarian, developmentalist and moderately mobilisational military regime.[31] and was made possible by the relative success of the export-led economic model after the Second World War. During the 1960s, a decade that is noteworthy for the formation of the Central American Common Market (CACM), the annual average growth rate was around 6 per cent. This fantastic growth was more or less sustained in the 1970s (until the end of the decade), in spite of the CACM's collapse. In the last four decades the agricultural share of GDP has declined, while other sectors (manufacturing, services and so on) have expanded. Moreover there have been massive investments in infrastructure.

As Sara Gordon has demonstrated, this period saw a significant increase in both the magnitude and the depth of state intervention in the economy.[32] Clearly this dynamism of the economy did not equally benefit every segment of the population. Even considering the trickle-down effect – primarily with regard to job creation – vast sectors hardly benefited at all. Nevertheless it clearly had a positive impact on the urban middle strata, for whom the expansion of state bureaucracy and spending in elitist patterns of social development generated an unparalleled increase in the amount of social, economic and political resources available. In addition it undeniably benefited the capital of the country, which was firmly in the hands of the political, economic, military, ecclesiastic and intellectual powers.

Progress was significant in the composition and characteristics of the population. Partly due to advances in health and hygiene, the population swelled from 1.9 million to 4.8 million between 1950 and 1980. This is not without recalling Jack Goldstone's contention that 'revolution and rebellion in the early modern world' were caused by 'the broad-based impact that sustained population growth (or decline) had on economic, social, and political institutions of agrarian-bureaucratic states'.[33] The growth rate was particularly significant in cities, where the share of the total population went from 36.5 per cent in 1950 (or 693 500 inhabitants) to 44.2 per cent in 1980 (or 2 121 600).[34]

As they became more urban the Salvadoran people became more educated than they had been a few decades before. According to official statistics the illiteracy rate fell dramatically from 61.0 per cent in 1950 to 33.1 per cent in 1978; that is to say, from 76.5 per cent to 46.2 per cent in the countryside and, significantly, from 35.6 per cent to 16.6 per cent in the cities.[35] This extraordinary metamorphosis again occurred in only three decades, in a country known for its conservatism and resistance to change.

Meanwhile the political situation presented some timid signs of openness in the 1960s, but deteriorated sharply after the 1972 coup. Indeed the developmentalist military regime tolerated limited pluralism during the 1960s. It did not prevent the emergence of the typically middle-class political party, the Salvadoran Christian Democratic Party, whose leaders were individually elected as mayor of the capital for seven terms (of two years) in a row.[36] But this limited pluralism faded away in the 1970s, to be replaced by the mutually reinforcing phenomena of government repression and left-wing urban violence.

The coup against the dictatorship of Carlos Humberto Romero in October 1979 made possible a real democratisation of the country, but armed groups from both ends of the ideological spectrum made sure that this would not happen. In the 1980s the political dynamics in the country revolved around two pillars: the internal war, or as the FMLN would say the 'correlation of forces' between the FMLN and the government, and the death-defying attempt by civilian

Table 2.1 Political and civil rights in El Salvador, 1972–85

Years	*Political rights*	*Civil rights*	*Years*	*Political rights*	*Civil rights*
1972	2	3	1979	5[2]	3+
1973	2	3	1980	6–	4–
1974	2	3	1981	5	5–
1975	2	3	1982	4+	5
1976	3–	3	1983	4	5
1977	3	3	1984	3+	5
1978	4–	4–	1985	2+	4+

Notes
[1] 1 + = best score; 7 – = worst score
[2] Change in status since the previous year owing to reevaluation by Freedom House; this does not imply any change in the country.

Source: Freedom House, *Freedom at Issue* (Jan.–Feb. 1973–86), quoted in *Statistical Abstract of Latin America*, vol.15, table 1003.

politicians and their infamous US sponsors to put together a pluralist, Western-like political system (or at least some facade of it) in El Salvador.[37]

THE DOMINANT AND GENERAL PASSIONS

> The socialist and revolutionary impulse derives initially from moral and political, rather than economic, considerations. (Malia, 1994)

The emergence of the Salvadoran insurgency cannot be understood without taking into account what de Tocqueville once called the 'dominant and general passions' of the time. Over the past, say, forty years, two successive, though not entirely exclusive, political passions have dominated the intellectual milieu in Latin America: *developmentalism and Marxism–Leninism*.[38] The 1990s is likely to become the decade of critical revision of Marxism–Leninism, with the emergence of a new dominant passion blending ingredients borrowed from various sources: social democracy, immortal populism, even neoliberalism, understood as an elite-led march towards modernity. The new vogue of 'civil society', in a continent where both the left and the right have prevented society from engaging in autonomous social mobilisation, is probably an NGO-financed respite, a pause in the state-led chorus.

Developmentalism and Marxism–Leninism, which were the two successively dominant passions during the period under study, have some key common features. Both express an element of political voluntarism and a faith in progress, in its most basic Western version. Both advocate strong state intervention in order to foster socioeconomic progress. Both subscribe in a paroxysmal way to the central feature of modern ideology: its scientific claim.[39] Both assert that previous ideological discourses were subjective, detached from rational calculus and reality, and retrograde. Both have greatly stimulated the *libido dominandi* of technocrats and intellectuals by advocating a new historical fusion between power and knowledge.

On the other hand they differ in some essential ways. Theoretically, it is well known that developmentalists promote progress through reforms, whereas Marxist–Leninists champion radical change. In addition the developmentalist passion enthralled virtually all the political classes, including most of the intelligentsia, from the early 1960s until the 1970s. The Marxist–Leninist passion was primarily embraced by the intelligentsia, in an unprecedented bid not merely to participate politically, but to capture power. Developmentalism was compatible with the building of a consensus amongst the elites (government, the business sector, colleges and universities, social engineers); Marxism–Leninism spelled the advent of an eschatological duel between the enlightened and scientific vanguard and the unreconstructed members of the establishment. Finally, Marxism–Leninism is more than a recipe for change: it is, as Régis Debray asserts, the *last religion of the book*, seeking a quasi-feudal pattern of status-based, patrimonial access to resources.[40]

Developmentalism and its Discontent

It would be superfluous to expound in detail how and why developmentalist optimism emerged and flourished in Latin America in the 1960s as this has been done before.[41] Suffice to say that, in the name of progress, its exponents supported a multifaceted agenda of reforms, including regional economic integration (for example the Central American Common Market), agrarian reform and modernisation of the education sector.

Clearly the developmentalist approach to progress was imported from the developed democracies of the North, primarily from the US. The kind of technical knowledge needed for 'development' was mostly produced in the developed countries of the West, hence the proliferation of cultural exchanges and technical assistance in the 1960s and 1970s. This import was mostly deemed compatible with authoritarianism by both the local elites and their foreign sponsors. The first wanted to modernise the economy, even at the expense of some of the oligarchy's interests, but without attacking the oligarchy at its core and without putting into jeopardy their own exclusive access to the central levers of power.[42] The latter crossed their fingers, hoping that, down the road, economic and social progress would lead to democratisation and its corollary: stability and the convergence of values and interests with the North.

Education was a key component of the programme in the sense that a modern economy and a modern state apparatus required an educated working class and a pool of technocrats.[43] The need to modernise the economic structure was made urgent by the unique demographic situation in El Salvador: being a tiny, overpopulated country, technological advance and overall modernisation of the economy was perceived by government officials as 'a more urgent necessity than for any other nation of the continent or the world'.[44] Even big landowners, few of whom were thrilled about the prospect of change, conceivably saw the necessity to relieve the social and demographic pressure on land, an objective only achievable through emigration or transformation of the economic structure.

Modernisation through education was attempted through university reform in 1963, followed by overall education reform in 1968.[45] Substantial modernisation was sought in all aspects of the educational process, including rationalisation of administrative operations and above all democratisation in both accessibility to and the nature of higher education. The Central American University (UCA), a Jesuit-led private university founded in 1965, was not impermeable to this intellectual atmosphere. The UCA official handbook stresses that 'the UCA was founded in the context of the 1960s developmentalist optimism, centred almost exclusively on growth in per capita production and industrial development'.[46] Typically, developmentalism remained the dominant ideology at the UCA until the early 1970s.

As the former secretary-general of the *Facultad Latino Americana para las Ciencias Sociales* (FLACSO) and sociologist Edelberto Torres-Rivas point out, the development of social sciences and the foundation of new institutes and programmes related to development was made possible in Central America by a significant injection of funds from foreign governments and institutions, primarily from the US.[47] The short period from the end of the 1960s to the beginning of the 1970s saw the foundation of the Consejo Superior Universitario Centroamericano (CSUCA–1968), the Central American Universities Publisher (EDUCA–1969) and the Central American Program for Social Sciences (1971), all university-based institutions but with a scope that went far beyond scholarly activities. Faithful to the developmentalist dogma, they were all in the business of social change, a venture that – as the military found out – was essentially political. Universities became the wellspring of cultural (or more precisely, countercultural) activity as well as the repository of resources for dissident political mobilisation.

For Beverley and Zimmermann, EDUCA was 'perhaps the single most important institution in the development of [this] counterculture among the intelligentsia... EDUCA became the main publisher of the new generation of left-oriented writers and literary critics represented by figures like Claribel Alegría, Roque Dalton, and Manlio Argueta in El Salvador; Otto René Castillo in Guatemala; and Sergio Ramírez in Nicaragua'.[48] The paradoxical outcome of US-sponsored developmentalism was that the Agency for International Development (AID) and the Ford Foundation ended up being the main sponsors of a countercultural industry built around national universities (that is, relatively autonomous from the state) that were notoriously devoted to the denunciation of US imperialism.

The institutional development of universities in the 1960s in part resulted in the formation of what could be called a politico-intellectual market covering the entire Central American region. Indeed the rapidly growing number of students and former students provided an immediate market for many publications that were more political in nature than scholarly. Indeed the number of books and journals published in the region increased dramatically during that period.[49]

This development mirrored a pattern unfolding in the North. Most 'development studies' programmes in North American universities were initiated by the passage in 1958 of Title VI of the National Defense Education Act (NDEA).[50] Young Americans were sent around the globe as members of the Peace Corps; many of them returned with an interest in the Third World; and some subsequently pursued graduate studies, motivated by the prospects of a career in a university, a private foundation or the civil service.[51] The Democrat-led 1960s was a decade of globalisation of communication, technologies and ideas.

The 1960s and early 1970s were also the years of the Vietnam War and the Woodstock pop festival. Most of the Western world was undergoing a period of countercultural rebellion, in the wake of two decades of unprecedented improvement in the living standards of almost everybody.[52] A genuine 'universality of protest' (Paz 1993), flourished, with university students playing a central role in the production and reproduction of new countercultural totems and taboos.[53]

In Latin America the Beatles, the Rolling Stones, Jimmy Hendrix, Jack Kerouac and other icons of the 1960s had an enduring impact on the educated militant class of an entire generation.[54] Interestingly enough, the end of the internal war in El Salvador was soon followed by the appearance in San Salvador of bars and discotheques such as 'La Luna' and 'El Quinto Sol', hangouts where the 1960s atmosphere is still palpable and where, incidentally, most former revolutionaries, engagé's (committed) gringos and this author choose to obtain their evening's entertainment. The ambiance is one of freedom and liberation; here there is no futurist bowing to the ever-developing productive forces.

In a sense the athmosphere in the 1960s was similar to the one created by *modernismo* at the turn of the century: a cosmopolitan communion, celebrating the present – *el incesante advenimiento del ahora* (Paz, 1993). Darío and Che: two rebels against time, two apostles of birth and death. In Latin and Central America, the universal protest took a much more political tone. The students' environment in San Salvador, Managua and Guatemala City had little in common with the not so discreet charm of the prosperous bourgeois environment surrounding Dustin Hoffman in 'The Graduate'. Rather it was marked by rapid change, and the promise of more change to come, but it remained hopelessly remote from the level of development reached by countries in the North. V.S. Naipaul, in his usual iconoclastic way, suggested that in the Third World, the students' and intellectuals' motivation for joining insurgencies was not only to embrace a foreign current, but in fact to push it somewhat further. One more effort, if you want to be there, inhabitating your time:

> What had driven them to their cause? There would have been the element of mimicry, the wish not to be left out of the political current of the '60s. 'What the students say in America, they want to make concrete here' – I was told this in 1972 by a woman whose guerrilla nephew had been killed by the police: the young man had taken his revolution

> more seriously than the American students whose equal he wanted to be.[55]

More importantly, Central American students were putting their lives on the line. No other segment of the population, with the important exception of civilian victims in the countryside, paid a heavier 'quota of blood' to the messianic internal wars of the time.[56]

It is possible to make the case that, with the triumph of developmentalism, which meant an attempt to modernise *par le haut* agrarian, 'traditional society', post-secondary institutions became the midwife of development and the cradle of cultural renewal. In this scenario it was the enlightened military who gave birth to progress and development. This is a key element in explaining both the insurgents' vanguardism, since most of their leaders were the sons and daughters of those taking part in the social mobilisation of the time, and their relative frustration *vis-à-vis* a process that was granting them prestige, resources and influence, *but no real political power*.

Marxism–Leninism as a Dominant Passion

During the 1960s and the early 1970s developmentalism was replaced by Marxism–Leninism as the dominant ideology in universities, colleges and the various radical organisations of the militant class.[57] 'Marxism–Leninism' is an unfashionable term in this post-Cold-War period: nowadays virtually all those who attack liberal values, from the Catholic or Leninist left to the antihumanist right (a strong German tradition rooted in Nietzsche and Heidegger, posthumously gallicised by Foucault and Derrida), are simply called 'critical' or 'progressive'. Without unearthing the old debate on the connivance and antinomy between the two branches of the socialist tradition (that is, Marxism and Leninism), it is fair to say that the Leninist interpretation of Marxism was clearly dominant in Latin America during that period. And of course most insurgents had no qualms about identifying themselves as *Marxista–Leninista*.

Leninism is characterised by four political dispositions: (1) a focus on the 'subjective conditions' for revolt; (2) a typically 'Blanquist' impatience to seize power; (3) a Jacobinic propensity to bloom in periods of war (as in 'war communism'); and (4) a totalitarian and military conception of the state. These features are compatible with Marxism. A case could be made that they represent Marxism's inevitable political expression. Nevertheless, these defining attributes of Leninism are *not* the essential tenets of Marx's philosophy of history.

Carlos Fonseca, a radical Nicaraguan university student and one of the three founders of the FSLN, baptised his generation of rebels the 'generation of the Cuban revolution'.[58] Fidel Castro was the Kerensky and the Lenin of the Cuban revolution, as Huntington once suggested in *Political Order in Changing Societies* (1968). As far as the Latin American left was concerned, he was clearly the latter.

Based on Salvadoran rebels' testimonies and experience, it would be difficult to exaggerate the impact that Fidel Castro, Ernesto Che Guevara and the construction of socialism in Cuba had on their political orientation. The first attempts to mimic the *barbudos* (bearded) occurred in the early 1960s with the ephemeral existence of the Frente Unido de Acción Revolucionaria (FUAR) and the Movimiento Revolucionario Abril y Mayo (the latter mimics the name of the Cuban insurgency: the Movement of the 26 of July).[59] In a manifesto published in May 1980, the joint command of the radical military organisation (then called Dirección Revolucionaria Unificada, DRU) made it perfectly clear that 'the Salvadoran people, its democratic and revolutionary organisations, admire the example of steadfastness and sovereign dignity portrayed by Cuba, and recognises in her the vanguard of all Latin American peoples in the struggle for social justice, liberty, development and true national independence'.[60]

Castro shipped arms and monitored the shipping of arms to almost all the countries of Latin America. In El Salvador, 'in the course of 1980 and through 1982 . . . perhaps upward of

10,000 weapons with ammunition were brought into El Salvador. So much arrived that some fighters had two arms each, though they didn't necessarily know how to use every one.'[61] He also forced competing factions in both El Salvador and Nicaragua to stop fighting (and killing) each other and to unite against their respective governments, or else arms delivery would stop.[62] Nevertheless, as author and 'witness' Jorge Castañeda points out' 'It was not so much a question of the Cubans exporting revolution or supporting these groups' activities in other countries. Rather, the Cubans' most important contribution...was one of *ideology and example*.'[63] Indeed 'for more than a decade, the urban, middle-class, university-educated, politicized youth of an entire continent was mesmerized by the armed struggle'.[64] Havana, he recalls, became a sort of Mecca where 'every Latin American intellectual worth his pen, canvas, or songbook made the journey... at one point or another'.[65]

Although Cuba was at times the subject of, or the pretext for, bickering among the FMLN's various factions – discord on the distribution of arms, quarrels over the apportionment of money, and so on –, it remained, '*foco*' theory or not, a model for young middle-class radicals impatient to capture power and subvert the established order. The Cuban model did not have to be fully understood or emulated. What mattered was the overall cultural repertoire provided by the bearded heroes, a repertoire that had more than a few themes in common with the European and North American 'new left' of the 1960s (or even with the misguided perception of the Chinese 'cultural revolution' that spread throughout the Western countercultural milieu at the end of the decade).[66] In all of these instances, university students were not only taking over from the working class as the new enlightened advance guard; they were overtaking the old materialistic agenda, elevating liberation and *gemeinschaft* as the new overarching goals.

Marxism–Leninism became a much more dominant ideology than any that had held sway in the past. Developmentalism, for one, was more eclectic. There were reformist developmentalists, conservative developmentalists (many of the theorists of 'modernisation' for instance) and some quite radical developmentalists (in the CEPAL for instance). Moreover, developmentalism was never dominant at the exclusion of any other ideologies.[67] In the first decades of this century, to go back even further, Latin America consumed a wide variety of ideologies, including modernism, positivism and anarchism, followed by fascism, personalism and existentialism. From the mid nineteenth century until the late 1960s it was possible to find a liberal current in most Latin American countries. But from the late 1960s onwards Marxism–Leninism truly became, to use Sartre's snappy expression, *l'horizon indépassable*, of the time.[68]

It goes without saying that to talk about Marxism–Leninism as the dominant ideology among intellectuals does not mean that the works of Marx and even Lenin were carefully studied and understood. The Marxism–Leninism taught at the UES during the late 1960s and 1970s (and the 1990s for that matter) was at best rudimentary.[69] The intellectual framework used in the manifestoes and declarations of radical organisations was mostly simplistic, using and abusing wooden formulas that betrayed an essentially binary structure of argument: objective versus subjective conditions of revolt, vanguard versus rearguard, quantitative verses qualitative steps; scientific materialism versus utopian or plain erroneous, contradiction versus solution to the contradiction, objective ally versus objective enemy, *la* realidad versus some smoke screen manufactured by the enemy, and so on. Virtually every possible situation involving a variation in time, or simply a confused situation, deserved the adjective 'dialectic'. This wooden political discourse was at once rigid, in the sense that just a handful of concepts were used in virtually all intellectual contexts. But it was also very flexible, because none of these terms were very well defined, thus lending themselves to all kinds of linguistic manipulation.[70] Omnipresent in written material and intellectual discussions, this glossary easily yielded to the neoclassical cum revolutionary fixation with the 'the heroic death' and the eschatology of 'liberation' in situations of social fusion (festive or mobilisational).

Theory and Praxis

In academia, Marxism–Leninism took many different forms. Dependency theory, an approach closer to Lenin's work (especially his *Imperialism, The Highest Stage of Capitalism*) than Marx's, was certainly the most sophisticated and successful one. In a passage consonant with the general approach to the ideas and ideologies defended in this book, Packenham remarks that:

> it was in Latin America's least dependent country, Brazil, where *dependencia* ideas had their most powerful initial expression. It was precisely during the period of intellectual preoccupation with *dependencia* that Brazil did more to reduce its dependency than at any previous time in its post- colonial history. It was in Brazil where the most important and enduring intellectual currents had nothing to do with the dependency fashion. And it was in Brazil during the last fifteen years or so where the trend away from the dependency way of thinking has been strongest.[71]

The president of Brazil, Fernando Enrique Cardoso, who was one of the fathers of this theory in Latin America, is currently championing neoliberal policies. Brazil is still Brazil, but other times, other ways!

The most conspicuous consequencc of the new hegemony of Marxism–Leninism in university campuses was the striking confusion between scholarly and political activities.[72] Marxism–Leninism, and Marxism *tout court*, are especially suited to this kind of confusion since they present themselves as a science, even a science of praxis. University members were called to strive for social change, not to embrace science for its own sake. The National University (UES), emulating (probably unconsciously) the cultural revolution in China, sacrificed many competent professors on the altar of the correct political praxis – or at least the correct position on the moral superiority of praxis over science. Non-Marxist–Leninist political stands were *de facto* 'non-scientific'.[73] In the early 1980s, one of the insurgency factions with the closest links with universities, (the LP-28), routinely called for a more 'scientific society', meaning a society moulded according to the tenets of scientific materialism.[74]

Edelberto Torres-Rivas deplores the 'anti-empirical syndrome' of the Central American social sciences of the time: 'construed as a 'dissident science'...our short tradition is closer to a logic of vindication [or political action] than to a logic of discovery'.[75] He continues: 'We don't find in our milieu this empirical tradition that focuses on the importance of techniques [of research].... Consequently there has been no polemic concerning rigour, objectivity, ideological contamination and the political or emotional values of the researcher.'[76]

Typically, in a special issue of a scholarly social sciences journal in Central America, various Central American scholars presented the history not of their respective academic institutions, nor a survey of the methods and approaches that had been used in their country. Instead social science was confounded with the historical praxis and intellectual production of unions, popular organisations and radical political organisations.[77] For Miguel De Castilla Urbina (on Nicaragua): 'Carlos Fonseca Amador is not only the founder of the Sandinista Front, but also [the founder] of revolutionary and scientific social sciences in Nicaragua.' After the Sandinistas seized power in July 1979, it was therefore logical that 'researchers and university professors had undertaken to advise or to rule the apparatus and organisations of propaganda and the political education of the FSLN, as well as the new ministries of the emerging bureaucratic apparatus. It was [and is] the moment of social sciences in the exercise of its favourite theme: power.'[78] In Guatemala, 'revolutionary organisations' supplied '*through their political praxis*...an extremely important contribution to the issue of social classes' articulation, class struggle and the ethnic question'.[79] In El Salvador, Mario Lungo maintains that 'the bulk of the social analysis was developed from 1978 onwards, in the publications and internal documents of the Salvadoran revolutionary organisations'.[80] As usual Costa Rica was the exception to the rule. But for all the ideological passion on their campuses, the universities remained largely faithful to their primary academic duty and never sacrificed their autonomy and *raison d'être* to radical political organisations.[81]

One can understand why, in El Salvador, young radical militants entirely discarded the social analysis of earlier thinkers such as Francisco Gadivia (1863–1955), Alberto Masferrer (1868–1932), Carlos Bustamante (1891–1955), Pedro Geoffroy Rivas (1907–80), José Simeón Cañas (1767–1835), Manuel José Arce (1787–1847) and José Matías Delgado (1765–1833). They were a world apart. And indeed the emergence and expansion of social sciences programmes in the region and even in the North coincided with the appearance of radical ideologies in campuses. But the fundamental points are these: (1) Marxist–Leninists viewed the exponents of other ideologies as simply non-scientific, and (2) the ultra-left version of Marxism–Leninism advocated political activism and armed struggle – not research. This leads to one of the most interesting paradoxes of the ultra-left activism of the time: in spite of being born in university campuses and vindicated with ideological constructs requiring a certain level of education and a capacity to manipulate abstract concepts, this activism was in fact, like most totalitarian political mobilisations, profoundly anti-intellectual.

This hyperpoliticisation all but eradicated the distinctions between the different disciplines and discourses on 'reality'. For Torres-Rivas, 'during this period [the 1960s and 1970s], history, political science and sociology made their disciplinary distinctiveness disappear, converting themselves in a large field of intellectual experience'.[82] In fact it is preferable to talk about a process of intellectual homogenisation, stemming from the will to crush all discourses and approaches, whether academic or artistic, into one single petition for change. The Nicaraguan writer and politician Sergio Ramírez aptly alludes to a 'claim to totality' in Central American intellectual production since the 1960s. According to Ramírez, this claim had become 'a genuine habit' and 'a manifestation of the writer's political consciousness, who wants to put it all in a book in order to get the message across'.[83]

Passions and Contingency

The predominance of the social reformer, even the political activist, over the scholar in most universities of the Central American region (that is, all public universities plus a score of private ones) is partly understandable given the prevailing situation. As Torres-Rivas points out, 'the crisis pulls social scientists away from their tasks... It obliges them to improvise and to renounce balanced thinking.'[84] A certain tradition of resistance and, over the ages, a long call for change corresponds to the permanence of the objective conditions of revolt. According to Gabriel Zaid, 'ever since the early nineteenth century, poets, priests, lawyers and students have taken up arms against imperialism (Spanish, French, North American) in all Spanish-speaking countries'.[85]

Nevertheless, this accounts neither for the timing of the emergence of such radical, ultra-leftist insurgencies (born in the 1960s and early 1970s, declined and disappeared in the 1980s and early 1990s), nor for the remarkable capacity of this generation of insurgents to detach themselves from the contingencies of the environment on the one hand, and to embrace wishful abstractions on the other (more on this in Chapter 3). The kind of radical agenda pursued by the insurgents during the 1970s was neither an obvious answer to the problems of the country, nor has it been, historically and virtually everywhere on the face of the Earth, an option that has enjoyed much, or any, mass appeal.

THE IDEOLOGY OF *LA REALIDAD*

> Very soon the UCA aimed at supporting the process of liberation of the Salvadoran people... Hence its mission

> consisted of being the critical and creative conscience of the Salvadoran reality. ('Los Jesuitas ante el pueblo salvadoreño', *Estudies Centroamericanas (ECA)* June 1977).

Nothing better encapsulates the nature of the intellectuals' political engagement in Central America (and possibly in Latin America) than their use and misuse of the notion of 'reality'. '*La realidad*' is arguably the notion that Central American and Latin American intellectuals use most frequently (Incidentally this magic notion has found a sanctuary: in April 1996 the Zapatista rebels in Mexico organised a forum against 'free-market economics', involving about 400 militants from around the Americas and beyond, in a tiny village and rebel stronghold baptised '*La Realidad*'!)[86]

A puzzle of ill-fitting parts, *la realidad* is both a description and a promise; a passive victim of events and the engine of history.

It is both conservative (part of the problem) and revolutionary (part of the solution).[87] Originally *la realidad* may have meant some 'truths' censured by the dictatorship. But look more closely: the 'real' message conveyed by 'reality' is hardly accessible to the many. Even the intellectual elites constantly compete, sometimes violently, for exclusive access to *la realidad*. For whoever understands *la realidad* must logically be elevated to power, so that they can interpret and execute *la realidad*'s will in a superior way. Or at least, those who speak on behalf of *la realidad* can be excused for thinking they rightfully deserve this promotion.

In a nutshell, this notion is essentially a trick that allows intellectuals to deceive the people and possibly themselves in two complementary ways. First, the use of *la realidad* allows intellectuals to obscure their social status and navigate freely from one class to another in accordance with political contingency. As Daniel Pécaut – the only social scientist who, to the best of my knowledge, has paid any attention to the phenomenon of *la realidad* – pointed out in an excellent book on Brazilian intellectuals: 'ideology [of *la realidad*] allows them to be part of the elite when necessary, or part of the people when it is more convenient'.[88] The radical intellectual of the past decades has sought communion with the people; to 'dissolve' him- or herself 'as an untouchable, and integrate with the people to which he or she belongs'.[89] Nevertheless, he or she has had few links with the lower strata – with the possible exception of priest–intellectuals, by virtue of their first function. As the Guatemalan writer Arturo Arias recognises, the intellectual's primary contacts are with the ruling class:

> Central American writers see their function as a social one; they carry the burden of their people, and they do not write to change the people's way of thinking. The people can't read what they write, in any case. The writer writes to collect the people's thoughts in order to press their views upon the ruling elites, and to try to change the consciousness of those elites.[90]

Second, the use of *la realidad* allows intellectuals to conceal the ultimate frontier between the realms of the political and the scientific, a phenomenon we discussed earlier. Only with difficulty can one renounce the power and prestige of science, in spite of the fact that, as Tolstoi understood very clearly, 'science is meaningless because it gives no answer to our question, the only question important for us: "What shall we do and how shall we live?"'[91] *La realidad*, if manipulated properly, allows one to explain, with the pseudo-authority conferred by science, what people should do and how they should live.

In sum, to mention but one example, thanks to *la realidad* the subjective and partisan point of view of an upper-middle-class student of, say, theology, at the Central American University can be presented as the translation of the people's objective interests, scientifically conveyed by the indispensable student.

The two general functions of *la realidad* (blurring the dividing lines between science and politics on the one hand, an the elite and the masses on the other) are not always apparent and clearly distinguished in the many possible uses and misuses of the notion. To single out but a limited sample, first, *la realidad* is understood as an objective situation recorded by the intellectual. According to Miguel de Castilla Urbina, Carlos Fonseca founded the Nicaraguan social sciences by elaborating a 'theory on *la realidad nicaragüense* of his days'.[92] Intellectuals have privileged access to *la realidad*. In a UCA manual containing preparatory readings for the admission tests (Lecturas para el curso de admisión a la UCA), one can read that '*no one* should know better the *realidad nacional* than the University.... Through the rational and scientific development of this reality, we try to know it better and to create a viable theoretical alternative that others will have to put into practice.'[93] For both Castilla Urbina and the UCA, knowledge of *la realidad* renders 'a theory' or the 'theoretical alternative' almost free of intellectual origins, as though they have simply emanated directly from reality. Interestingly enough, since *la realidad* occupies all the theoretical space, it means that it does not have to occupy it *practically* – the contradiction between the two dimensions being totally blurred. For instance Jon Sobrino (Jesuit and leading intellectual of the UCA) explains the meaning of the university's orientation in favour of the poor: 'What it means is that the world of the poor has entered into the university, that its real problematic is taken into account as a central theme, and that from there one can tackle the *social reality and define its legitimate interests*, which are the interests of the poor.'[94] In comparison with students in other universities in the country, UCA students are often the most privileged, enjoying the material and cultural advantages of the middle-class, and often the upper-class, milieu. But this does not really matter, for the 'real problematic' of the poor has entered into the university.

La realidad is slightly less passive when it is presented as follows: '*la realidad* of the past two years *demonstrates* that a maximalist solution is no longer possible, whether in its conservative or revolutionary version'.[95] Here the UCA is not merely interpreting *la realidad*: the latter is manifesting itself through the UCA,[96] which is radically different from saying that the UCA considers that a maximalist solution is no longer possible, a mere opinion in a sea of subjective opinions.

Often, *la realidad* is presented as hanging between the present and some point in the future. For instance, during a round-table organised by the very 'scientific' and 'dialectic' national university (University of El Salvador, UES), one of this institution's positions was that 'the truth [truth being synonymous with reality in this context] of the Salvadoran people remains to be built, just like the truths of the Guatemalan, Nicaraguan, Honduran and Costa Rican peoples. To conform ourselves to a positivist reflection of reality is tantamount to accepting [the current situation].'[97] No doubt the UES has a positive role to play in reaching this historical goal.

La realidad can also designate an actor (the people, the social subject of the revolution, the majority, the masses and so on) under whose penumbra the reality specialist can veil his or her *libido dominandi*. As an objective situation, *la realidad* breeds *la realidad* people, who in turn, stimulated and enlightened by its vanguard, build a *realidad* that is more 'real'. For Ignacio Ellacuria: 'The national reality, that is, the Salvadoran people, taking into account the way it is structured into social classes and its historical problems, as well as its social institutions, traditions, customs, and potential, is the natural place of the university and the invigorating origin outside of which [the university] has no roots'.[98] The UCA manual champions a curriculum that would be true to 'the demands of the *realidad nacional*... The *realidad nacional* not only shapes all subject matter, it also unifies it and endows it with its authentic interdisciplinary character.'[99] *Realidad cum* people, according to Ellacuria, are fundamentally anticapitalist: 'The real situation of Latin America denounces prophetically the intrinsic mischievousness of the capitalist system and the ideological lie of the democratic facade that legitimises it.'[100] Whether Ellacuria is anticapitalist or not is obviously irrelevant here; *la realidad* is anticapitalist. In this particular case *la realidad* vaguely refers not to people as they are, but as they were prior to the fall, as in a state of nature *à la* Rousseau. The *ECA* has routinely denounced the 'militarisation of *la realidad*' and called for its demilitarisation.[101] Of course *la realidad* people do not have a very clear awareness of its existence *pour soi*. Hence the indispensable presence of intellectuals – professors, guides, and a vanguard of individuals in particular – who remain the humble interpreters of *la realidad* in general.

Thanks to *la realidad*, intellectuals are scientific and political, elite and of the masses.[102]

* * *

In sum, much has to be learned about the insurgents before one can speculate on the roots of revolt in El Salvador. They had their own distinct environment, and they responded to intellectual stimuli from their own milieu and far beyond their national borders. Their ideological dispositions were also the product of a complex interplay of factors, some emanating from various dimensions of the national formation, some from a generational politico-cultural repertoire, and some from specific conjunctures in the three organisations identified at the beginning of this chapter. The following chapters are devoted to exploring more specifically the particular organisational and ideological context into which insurgency was born.

3 Revolution within the Revolution

> Paradoxically, the appearance of previously unknown spokesmen and the challenge which they have thrown down to the titular heralds of the major political and above all trade-union organizations have concealed the fact that there is doubtless no situation more favorable to professional public speakers of the political variety than the situations of crisis apparently totally abandoned to the 'spontaneity of the masses'; and, in fact, just as the prophets of ancient Judaism were often defectors from the priestly caste, so the majority of the leaders thrown up by the 'popular ferment' had in fact been trained in the various political organizations, those of the students or the lecturers or the revolutionary 'sects' where a specific competence is acquired, usually comprising a set of linguistic and postural instruments, enabling exploitation and control of the institutionalized places of speech. (Pierre Bourdieu, *Homo Academicus*, 1988)

The crisis in the Communist Party – or more precisely, the crisis of the communist movement – deserves the honour of going first in our discussion for two reasons: (1) because of its seniority in the business of internal war and radical change in El Salvador, and (2) because of its unparalleled contribution to the formation of the insurgents' ideology.

Most of the insurgency groups that coalesced in 1980 to form the FMLN can be situated along a chain of scissions and parallel developments. The 'foundational' schism occurred in 1970, when the PCS's secretary general, Salvador Cayetano Carpio, left the party founded in 1932 to create an organisation that would be truly devoted to armed struggle: the Fuerzas Populares de Liberación (FPL).[1] Two years later, disgruntled members of the newly created FPL reached out to radicalised renegades from the Christian Democratic movement (the PDC, Catholic unions and lay organisations, the UCA and so on), in order to create yet another 'revolutionary vanguard': the Ejercito Revolucionario del Pueblo (ERP). Following the infamous assassination of the most notorious leader of this organisation (the poet Roque Dalton) by fellow ERP leaders in 1975,[2] the ERP provided the Salvadoran left with yet another historical schism, this one giving birth to the Resistencia Nacional (RN).[3] According to the former insurgent Marco Antonio Grande, yet another of the five vanguards of the people, the Partido Revolucionario de los Trabajadores Centroamericanos (PRTC), was created in 1975 by a group of dissident members of the RN named the 'group of Central Americanists'.[4]

Finally, in 1979 the Communist Party, under the new leadership of Secretary General Jorge Shafik Handal, looped the loop by joining (but not merging with) its boisterous offspring. This family reunion, after nearly a decade of revolt against the father, took institutional expression with the creation of the FMLN in October 1980. But the 'revolution within the revolution', to put a new spin on the famous Régis Debray (1967) expression, never quite ended: the five factions comprising the FMLN never really managed to build a 'new type of Marxist–Leninist party', a problem referred to by insurgents themselves as *el cinquismo* ('five-ism').

Their inability to unite once and for all in a single, homogeneous organisation, with all the different groups – including the father-turned-brother PCS – blending themselves into a single Marxist–Leninist Party, is routinely explained by former insurgents as the result of problems of 'leadership', problems that were characterised by personal rivalry between the five leaders, compounded by rivalries that pitted national leaders against regional, or even local, military commanders. In most textbooks on Latin American politics, this widespread problem is referred to as 'caudillism', a phenomenon whose roots go back to the aftermath of the wars of independence, or even further back, the conquest, the *reconquista* in

Spain, and the Arabs (who occupied Spain). In short, an old practice from which the left proved incapable of departing.

There was arguably some strategic and tactical divergence as well. Nevertheless it seems clear that *el cinquismo* was not caused by substantial and permanent ideological discord between the rebellious offspring of the Communist Party.[5] As Ferman Cienfuegos (the *nom de guerre* of Eduardo Sancho, leader of the RN) points out: 'From the point of view of the construction of the party, we were born as a negation of the PCS, with an antiparty position, but within the conception of the historical PCS of the Communist International. We were seeking to develop an organisation that would also be based on the tenet of democratic centralism, which is the axis, the fundamental building block of the party.'[6] The objective was to be more Marxist–Leninist than the dull and petrified Communist Party (once described as 'right wing' by Poet and Activist Roque Dalton). Similarly, radical Catholics wanted to be better missionaries for the Church, closer to the primitive Christians. And university activism was nothing but an *encore un effort* prolonging the post-Second World War agenda of regional integration and social change. The rebellious children, in a way, just took the argument a step further.

The point here is not to present yet another exhaustive history of the FMLN and its various components, a challenging undertaking given the sometimes widely differing recollections of the insurgents.[7] After a brief portrait of the insurgency, our interest is to provide evidence for the propositions outlined at the end of Chapter 1, especially the ones dealing with the insurgents' ideological disposition and their relations with each other and the outside world.

THE FMLN

> In the FMLN we don't have five parties, but six. Thus works the single party in formation, five plus one; this is dialectic. (Cienfuegos, 1993)

The FMLN was formed on 10 October 1980.[8] Until the peace agreement of 1992, these groups were usually viewed as 'political–military' organisations, or small vanguards of 'professional revolutionaries', as Lenin would have said.[9] The 'rearguard' of the 'revolutionary army' was 'built' up by the insurgent groups in the mid 1980s. Cienfuegos refers to this period as one of 'great extension' of the insurgency, the goal being 'to generalise the guerrilla warfare to a superior stage with the creation of an army'. As he recalls, 'during the 1970s we expanded the urban guerrillas without having an army. This was the great change of direction of the years 1984, 1985 and 1986.'[10]

The FMLN, though the vanguard of the Salvadoran people, apparently needed more direct links with the people. Hence the formation of 'popular' or 'mass' organisations.

The Popular Organisations

Originally, the primarily military organisations were linked to popular organisations that had formed in the mid 1970s. The People's Revolutionary Bloc (BPR–1975) was linked to the FPL; the People's Leagues of the 28th of February (LP28–1978) were linked to the ERP; the United People's Action Front (FAPU–1974) was linked to the RN; and the Popular Movement of Liberation (MLP–1979) was linked to the PRTC. In January 1980 the Revolutionary Coordination of the Masses (CRM) was created to unify these groups. None of them were still active in the mid 1980s, as a result of massive repression in the early 1980s and the FMLN's narrowly militaristic orientation.[11]

Basically, the popular organisations were federations that mobilised some fifteen unions and student's organisations. Their loosely controlled and elusive membership (estimates range from 50 000 to 100 000!) cannot be automatically equated with a precise degree of popular support for the insurgents' political agenda. For it was the organisations' leaderships that were recruited, not directly their constituent bases.[12] The process is well summarised by Cienfuegos:

> We undertook a struggle to achieve hegemony in the masses, seizing the unions' executive branches [arrasando las directivas sindicales]... This was a period of accumulation of forces for each [of the insurgency groups] and a period of quest for hegemony between the different popular organisations. All of us [the different insurgency groups] were building our own mass organisations and defining their particular areas, even outlining quotas [for each organisation] where other organisations had no right and could not interfere.[13]

What is more, these federations were mostly created and controlled by the competing military organisations; they were not, strictly speaking, grass-roots organisations, as is usually implied. An FPL leader put it bluntly: 'The mass movement constituted a group of organisations *that we created*'.[14] Another leader of the same organisation referred to the BPR as a 'project of revolutionary front of the masses, including masses exclusively organised by the FPL'.[15]

These mass organisations were not immune to the sectarian and vanguardist compulsion that, as will be discussed later, impaired the whole insurgency. A repentant FPL leader recalled the following: 'what we were trying to do was to make the other fronts recognise the BPR as the vanguard, based on the fact that it was very powerful and consequently had the "right" to hegemonise'.[16]

Since internal wars are never exclusively internal, some additional links with the outside world soon became an urgent necessity. Hence the creation of the FDR and the CPD.

The FDR

The Democratic Revolutionary Front (FDR) was created in 1980. It was also a 'front of fronts', regrouping the CRM, the Social-Democratic Party (the National Revolutionary Movement, MNR–1965), the Social Christian Popular Movement (MPSC–1980), the General Association of Salvadoran

University Students (AGEUS), the National Conference of the Popular Church (CONIP), some unions and union federations, and other less significant groups. With the rapid extinction of the CRM and its constituent parts, and given its diplomatic function within the radical coalition (Cienfuegos dubs them 'quasi ministers of foreign affairs', – though 'ambassadors' seems a more appropriate term),[17] the FDR soon became the personal vehicle of two talented politicians: Guillermo Manuel Ungo of the MNR and Rubén Zamora of the MPSC.[18]

Ungo had an upper-middle-class background, and as a key asset he assumed high functions in the Latin American branch of the Socialist International – ideal for an insurgency hungry for international recognition. He had also been among the founding fathers of the PDC back in the early 1960s and the UNO vice-presidential candidate in 1972. Zamora, perhaps the smartest politician in the country, came from a prominent Christian Democratic family, and he led the radical wing of the Christian Democratic Party out of the party in 1980 to form the MPSC. Both had been student activists and had occupied teaching positions in national universities.

The FDR and the FMLN were often presented as a single front: the FDR–FMLN (or FMLN–FDR.) The FDR was linked to the FMLN through a Politico-Diplomatic Commission (CPD), created in 1981, though it officially remained an 'autonomous' organisation.[19]

The attitude of the military vanguard towards the FDR did not seem to differ much from its overall attitude towards all non-military (that is, non-vanguard) organisations. As an FPL leader put it: 'we used to consider the FDR as a strategic ally, but not as part of the vanguard'.[20] The revolutionary movement may have been very broad, but make no mistake: the ones with the guns, to use Régis Debray's formula, were the 'vanguard of the vanguard'.[21] For as Max Weber remarked, 'the bearer of arms acknowledges only those capable of bearing arms as political equals. All others, those untrained in arms and those incapable of bearing arms are regarded as women, and are explicitly designated as such in many primitive languages.'[22] Whether the FDR leaders were fully or even partially aware of this quasi-law of history has yet to be ascertained.

This portrait is undoubtlessly sketchy. The picture could also include, chronologically, the many military groups that emerged prior to the abovementioned 'politico-military' organisations[23], and even the fairly autonomous brigades and 'urban commandos' of the 1980s.[24] A thorough description would have to take seriously the problem of overlapping organisational structures, the inflated projection of organisational coherence and strength, and other conundrums deriving from the 'revolutionary inflation' of the 1970s.[25] In any case, one has to acknowledge the following: in a country of less than five million inhabitants, where two individuals could not be standing more than 200 kms from each other, and where the whole militant and radical class was certainly smaller in the early 1970s than its sister solidarity organisations in Mexico and the US during the 1980s, there were more enlightened vanguards of the people than in any other Latin American insurgency or radical movement. Salvadorans have the reputation of being hard-working and smart, and no doubt they were more than a little zealous in representing their people.

The achievements of the Salvadoran insurgents were remarkable. For all its constant fragmentation, the FMLN armed and trained between 6000 (in 1980) and 15 000 (in 1992) men and women during the internal war, an increase from only several hundred during the 1970s. This was achieved mostly without resorting to forced recruitment.[26] It launched massive national military offensives in 1981, 1983, 1988, 1989 and 1990, two of which drew worldwide attention (1981 and 1989). It was publicly recognised as a legitimate political player by Mexico and France in a joint declaration in July 1981. It not only won the support of the socialist bloc – which countries most of the FMLN leaders and scores of mid-level commanders visited before and during the 1980s – but also the sympathy of many political, religious and human rights organisations all around the world.[27] After the peace accords of 1992 it converted itself into a fairly successful political party.

In short, the FMLN achieved everything short of seizing power in San Salvador.

A LENINIST VANGUARD

> We were all consistent with this sectarian, incorrect and hegemonist line. (Cienfuegos, 1993)

Cienfuegos contends that 'from the very beginning, the FMLN has sought inspiration in Marxism–Leninism'.[28] 'Inspiration' here cannot be interpreted in terms of 'among other sources of inspiration'. Rather it means that Marxism–Leninism provided the basic ideological disposition to which a variety of radical styles and sensibilities could be attached. In their various publications the insurgents refer to an apparently broad but actually homogeneous body of practical and theoretical influences. Frequent reference is made to the Tupamaros in Uruguay and the experiences of other insurgents in Latin America, for example the MIR in Chile, the FAR in Guatemala and of course the M-26 in Cuba, as well as to foreign models obtained when FMLN leaders made political pilgrimages to Cuba, North Korea and Vietnam. 'Nevertheless', recalls Cienfuegos, 'we did not know much about the Sandinistas, even though the Frente Sandinista de Liberación Nacional (FSLN) was founded in 1961'.[29] The insurgents read the books of Lenin and his populariser in Latin America, Marta Harnecker, as well as the writings of Mao (who was particularly appreciated for his simplicity), Kim Il Sung, Castro and Guevara, and some 'manuals' by obscure Russian authors. In common with most Marxist–Leninists, few of them seem to have read Marx.

The Leninist influence is visible in the distinctive wooden style chosen by insurgents in their communiqués. For instance the communiqué the FPL issued after the kidnapping (and eventual assassination) of Foreign Minister Mauricio Borgonovo Pohl in 1977 -- an operation baptised 'The 11th of October's revolutionary heroes Eva-Francisco-Antonio' – proclaimed that the objectives of the operation were:

> to bring out, before all the peoples of the world, the heroic struggle of the Salvadoran people who, in the context of the Central American revolutionary struggle, are increasingly implicated in the various levels of the people's protracted popular war, a war that is primarily based on revolutionary armed struggle and indissolubly linked to other forms of struggle of the popular masses in their march towards Popular Revolution and Socialism.[30]

The insurgents' ideological agenda hinged on three basic assumptions that were easily adaptable to a variety of radical socialist agendas. First, capitalism, being both condemnable and doomed in all respects, must be abolished. Second, a small army of professional rebels must trigger the anticapitalist revolution, defeat the old regime's army and capture the state apparatus. This stands in glaring contrast with the more patient and pragmatic stand adopted by official communist parties. Third, once in power, professional rebels must mobilise the population to rally behind the scientific construction of an anticapitalist, antiimperialist (that is, anti-US) Leninist polity.

One can find no departure from this hard-line position in any of the insurgents' proclamations during the 1970s and early 1980s; a position, as it were, that has been traditionally espoused by intellectuals, not by illiterate peasants or even urban workers ('who were we?' an FPL leader asked rhetorically; 'at the level of the command structure, we were bourgeois or petit-bourgeois, not proletarians').[31] Few would challenge the view that the Salvadoran insurgents, from the time of their emergence until the late 1980s, were more radical, at face value, than either their Cuban (pre-1959) or Nicaraguan (pre-1979) counterparts during the insurrection stage.[32]

This radicalism did not manifest itself merely through the insurgency's espousal of Marxism–Leninism, a choice made by a whole generation of rebels and intellectuals in Latin America.[33] It was also expressed through a heightening of certain dispositions associated with Marxism–Leninism, namely problems of vanguardism, sectarianism and dogmatism. This indicates the insurgents' propensity to misread the 'objective' structure of the opportunities before them, opportunities to be cut from the political 'reality' in their country. The FMLN's inability to embrace publicly a more moderate and flexible political agenda during the 1980s prevented it from building a broad opposition coalition against the old regime, which has been a prerequisite for national revolution in the Third World since the Second World War.[34]

Vanguardism

From their formation in the early 1970s until the end of the 1980s the different factions of the FMLN openly proclaimed themselves as the vanguard of the Salvadoran people. For tactical reasons the insurgents could have formed an alliance with civilian sectors, or even with dissident members of the army,[35] but they remained dogmatically convinced of their privileged status as *the* vanguard of the people. This is probably the most resilient feature of Leninism, and the FMLN, even at the expense of increasingly evident political costs (permanent fragmentation and uneasy connection with the masses), stuck to it until the end of the war. In its year-end message transmitted on Radio Venceremos in January 1990, the FMLN was still emphasising its leading role, and not just in the Salvadoran struggle:

> Comrade militants, leaders, and combatants, our struggle is at the vanguard of the social changes that will continue to be made around the world through the struggle of the masses. Victory in El Salvador is guaranteed by an exemplary heroic people, whose most faithful representatives are the FMLN fighters... our struggle, which is essentially for self-determination and democracy, is in the capitalist world the spearhead of the struggle of all Latin American and

> Third World countries, which demand these transformations.[36]

In the 1970s the newly created politico-military vanguards competed with their first model, the communist party, and with each other, for the exclusive role of the people's revolutionary vanguard.[37] Leaders of the FPL, interviewed by Marta Harnecker, openly criticised this early display of political immaturity: 'this evil [*este mal*] of the organisation called vanguardism; we did not accept that others could take the initiative'.[38] One recalls that the same rule applied to the FPL's 'mass organisation': 'It was never contemplated that the BPR could enter into alliance with other fronts during the first phase of its development... In addition, what was attempted was to get the other fronts to recognise the BPR as the vanguard, based on the fact that it was the most powerful mass organisation and consequently it had a "right" to seek hegemony.'[39]

Closely related to this vanguardism was an indulgence in radicalism and sectarianism, each vanguard trying to appear more anti *status quo* than the other – or more accurately, trying to portray the others as objectively less representative of the real interests of the Salvadoran working class and peasants. An FPL leader admited that 'dogmatism was impregnated into the marrow of our bones... We felt that we were the "owner of the truth", of the purity and firmness of the proletariat.'[40] This dogmatism, for him, 'was not a theoretical dogmatism, like the one that possibly affected some parties in the Southern Cone. It was, as it were, a more underdeveloped dogmatism, with much less knowledge of the theory.'[41] More testimonies corroborate this affliction:

> The evil of sectarianism and radicalism, the FPL has carried it in its blood since its formation.[42]

> During all these years [the 1970s], we had a generalised weakness associated with the left, consisting of a defence, more emotional than rational, of a particular political line;

this conduct was linked to a wrong-headed form of party loyalty, translated into sectarianism . . . and it was combined with a political orientation where we would proclaim ourselves as the only alternative [to the current regime], or we would place ourselves beyond the others . . . postponing self-criticism and rectification.[43]

We fell into a great radicalism. There was a lot of ultra-leftism [*izquierdismo*]! The watchword was socialism from above; many went for beyond first than what was objectively achievable in this country, and second much beyond what the non-radicalised masses, who were essential for the process of change, were able to comprehend and assimilate. True, the masses, and not only a handful of militants, responded to these slogans, but at that moment . . . what slogans did we put forth to appeal to the backward masses [*la masa atrasada*], to those sectors with democratic, patriotic positions? None.[44]

[Were the masses receptive to the slogans?] . . . the masses that we mobilised, the FAPUs, the LP-28s, the UDNs and the MLPs, yes. But the other sectors, the middle strata, started being afraid [of us] since their interests were not at all represented in the alternative that we were putting forward.[45]

Our Marxist–Leninist formation in the clandestinity was intense, but deficient. The first person in charge had received, sixteen months before, one of those theoretical courses in the Soviet Union and was formed by the old Communist Party, and then got into an environment close and as secretive [*cerrado*] as the clandestinity of the 1970s . . . during the first period [of insurgency] we did not have political relations with other parties in the country, and with those abroad, no relations at all. Many factors contributed to a dogmatic assimilation of the Marxist theory.[46]

Little by little, inadvertently we became invaded by a sort of scholasticism.[47]

In the countryside, where the competition between the different vanguards started to take place in the 1970s (for control of the few existing peasant organisations), 'we had to demonstrate...the correctness of a specific [political] line. We considered that the others were not "correct" [*consecuente*] revolutionary organisations and that they had to embrace the FPL line in order to be so.'[48] All the same, in the cities 'our politics with the working class was very sectarian'.[49]

This dogmatism and sectarianism was certainly nurtured by the very nature of this kind of political mobilisation (conspiracy), which required faith in the dogma of the group and some form of paranoia *vis-à-vis* the outside world. As an FPL leader admitted, 'a party by itself is a very small world of its own and if you do not raise your eyes to look around you, you loose touch with reality [*te desfasas*]'.[50] Nevertheless it was doubtlessly ingrained into the ideological disposition of the insurgents, thus imposing 'its own limitations, especially in the policy of alliances'.[51]

THE CLASH WITH *LA REALIDAD*

The radicalism of the Salvadoran insurgency is often interpreted as an indicator of the nature of the internal war itself; that is, a war of 'class struggle' as opposed to a broad 'war of liberation', such as the one in Nicaragua.[52] As the argument goes: the more radical the opposition, the deeper the class conflict must be. (As routinely happens in class analysis, the effects demonstrate the causes.) The insurgents were unable to build a strong multiclass coalition against the regime because they were locked into a polarised, class-based conflict. As one author suggests, 'the hardening of class warfare radicalized both sides in the Salvadoran struggle and left precious little space in the middle of the political spectrum'.[53] This mainstream argument, consonant with the summary presented by John Booth (see Chapter 1), does not hold up to scrutiny, for the following reasons.

First, the insurgents were more radical and extremist *before* sporadic violence turned into full-blown internal war. The Salvadoran insurgents did not try to tone down their radicalism or reach out to the leaders of the moderate opposition until the very end of the internal war. Even their contact with the people was apparently impaired by their propensity to favour the application of 'scientific' ideology at the expense of a more popular bid for national liberation.[54] Some FPL leaders are quite clear on this:

> In 1977 this [dogmatism] started to affect negatively the work we were doing in the organised and non-organised sectors of the countryside.[55]

> Erroneously, we attempted to establish an alliance policy by levelling off and by force, without taking into account the other sectors' interests. We were only considering our own interest as a party and as a revolutionary movement. We totally ignored the other forces, meaning not the other forces in general but the actual mass organisations, in addition to all these small and medium business leaders and democratic elements, and the Christian democratic militants, who were dissatisfied.[56]

Second, the constant reference to the 'polarisation' of Salvadoran politics in the 1980s, as though only the political extremes were effectively mobilised, conceals a much more interesting phenomenon: *political inflation struck the entire Salvadoran political class*. Though the Salvadoran extreme left and extreme right were indeed stronger than their Central American counterparts, one could say the same about most other forces on the ideological and political spectrum. The 'centre', namely, the Christian Democratic Party, was, from the late 1970s to the late 1980s, stronger in El Salvador than in Nicaragua, Guatemala and Honduras. Politicised social forces such as the Catholic Church, the unions and the student movement were arguably more active politically in El Salvador than in other countries of the region. The army itself went further than its regional counterparts in building a political vehicle (the PCN) to mobilise the population. More than any other military regime in Central America, the Salvadoran PCN tried to emulate the example of the Partido Revolucionario Institucional (PRI) in Mexico by attempting to institutionalise a reformist authoritarian regime. Overall El Salvador has had more vanguards, spokespersons and 'representative forces' of the people, ranging from the extreme left to the extreme right, than any other country in the region.

Third, it is not so evident that the 'popular movement' was stronger and enjoyed more widespread support in El Salvador than, for instance, in Nicaragua before the downfall of Somoza, or in Cuba before the collapse of the Batista regime. This kind of grass-roots mobilisation is arguably a prerequisite for the emergence of class warfare, but there is no evidence that this happened. In, 1972 during the period of emergence of the Salvadoran insurgency, the country went through a major crisis when the military blocked the likely electoral victory of a reformist coalition. But no national revolt occurred then. In the late 1970s there was some consensus in the political class that the military dictator Carlos Humberto Romero should be ousted, but there is no strong evidence of massive popular support for (or against) the military coup. For several months after the coup, numerous demonstrations were successfully organised in San Salvador, but they occurred in a context of institutional confusion and ministers sometimes demonstrated outside their own offices. At that time the insurgents did not seriously try to build on the general movement for reform since the priority was to preserve their vanguard position and to polarise the political competition, not to democratise the country. Then massive repression stifled further mobilisation in the cities. In the 1980s the FMLN did not put together, or enjoy the tacit support of, a broad coalition of forces opposed to the juntas (1980–82) and the governments of Alvaro Magaña (1982–84), José Napoléon Duarte (1984–88) and Alfredo Cristiani (1988–94).

The contrast between the cases of El Salvador (insurgency/counterinsurgency and confrontation) and Nicaragua before 1979 (national revolt) is instructive. Each case hinged upon such variables as the capacity to build a broad opposition movement against the current regime, and the nature of the regime itself. In El Salvador the absence of a single undisputed nemesis figure (El Salvador had no Somoza or Batista) rendered the task more difficult than in Nicaragua.[57] But the generally overlooked factor is that the insurgents' extremism rendered broad mobilisation virtually impossible. All in all, the importance of understanding the insurgents' profile and ideologies is perhaps even greater in El Salvador's case than in other cases where internal war was characterised by heterogeneous and widespread social protest.

As Peter Berger once suggested, 'Revolutionary warfare ... is very largely *not* a matter of "winning the hearts and minds of the people", but rather a competition as to which side can make more people afraid of it.'[58] Insurgents (and their supporters) have some solid reasons for objecting that it is consonant with their strategy and with their disposition to frighten the masses. Nonetheless one is also justified in wondering how 'anybody who approaches with gun in hand is going to get an honest answer to any question'.[59]

A top FMLN leader, Salvador Samayoa, went a long way towards recognising the (political) limitation of popular support during the war:

> I believe that the people have different motivations for fighting than those acquired by a more sophisticated leadership. Politically, people have more rudimentary motivations: often *they simply have no choice*, like in the case of the peasantry, such an important component of the struggle in El Salvador, which joined the guerrillas *because it couldn't be on the other side, because their families were simply murdered*. They know since they were born that the Army is evil and that the guerrillas are against the Army. That's about it; the rank and file have a great deal of political vision, but as far as elaborating much more with

regard to socialism or Marxism, this has never been its strong suit. That is more a problem for the elite.[60]

Many, perhaps most, incentives to join the insurgency, from the people's point of view, arose as a *consequence* of the internal war. They may have contributed to its consolidation, but they could not possibly have 'caused' it in the first place. To say that the peasants were 'radicalised by the war'[61] is probably accurate. However, to assume that the insurgency became radical and turned into a class struggle because pressure for change from the popular sector was invariably met with rejection and repression, thus radicalising the aggrieved and contributing to the formation of revolutionary coalitions, is little more than an academic leap of faith.[62]

An Agrarian Revolution?

In the countryside, evidence of a pivotal contribution by peasants, agricultural workers and the agricultural semi-proletariat to the emergence of insurgency is sparse at best. The presence of peasant unions and some 'Christian base communities' (see Chapter 5), along with a certain tradition of resistance, does not prove *ipso facto* that the countryside was ripe for revolt, or even for sweeping political, social and economic change.

All the evidence and the subsequent testimonies of insurgents tend to indicate that during the 1970s the peasants responded to incentives for 'small-scale mobilizations around local problems, such as road repairs, transportation to medical facilities, and community insurance schemes'; rather than to abstract political ideologies produced in the 'First World' and revisited in the Salvadoran universities.[63] Once the insurgency had moved into the countryside, *after* the failure of the January 1981 'final offensive', some support in the countryside did indeed became pivotal. But then the peasants were exposed to a new series of incentives to revolt, some of them perhaps as decisive, or even more so, than historical factors of grievance: self-defence, obedience to the *de facto* authorities in their region, forced recruitment and so on.

It would have been convenient to explain why the peasants revolted and provided the initial impetus for insurgency in the western part of the country (the departments of Ahuachapán and Sonsonate), where a famous peasant rebellion – followed by an infamous massacre – took place in 1932, and where most of the large coffee estates are located. Only, it did not happen: this region was the one that was least hospitable to insurgency during the entire internal war.

Perhaps the most plausible countryside-based explanation of the emergence of insurgency is the 'proletarianisation' hypothesis, which commands quite a bit of academic respect since it rests on the Marxist postulate that (roughly) workers do revolt; but peasants – who are like 'potatoes in a sack' (Marx) – are backward and politically useless unless they are 'proletarianised'). This century has seen various waves of *urbanisation* and proletarianisation of the workforce in the Salvadoran countryside, necessary factor, according to this approach, in rebellion.[64] This logically leads us to conclude that the cotton region (the departments of La Paz and Usulután) ought to have been the hotbed of revolt, but this region did not become a zone of conflict until well *after* the FMLN's 'final offensive' of 1981.[65]

After the insurgency moved from the cities to the countryside, the first 'liberated zones' (1981–82) were located in the northern parts of the departments of Morazan and Chalatenango and around the Guazapa volcano. The most logical explanation of why these particular areas were chosen is that, for wearied insurgents escaping brutal repression, the obvious move was to seek refuge in the most underpopulated, isolated and mountainous region of the country. It was also a region characterised by minifundium (small landholding), not by large estates. If guerrillas in the countryside are like fish in water, it is best to be in water where fishermen have no easy access. In the countryside they could regroup, seek new recruits from a politically enticing population, cultivate relations with foreign countries and organisations, and prepare militarily for the real objective: a successful military confrontation in the cities located in the south, especially San Salvador, the seat of all power and the natural environment of the *comandantes*.[66]

Compounding the Differences

The evidence strongly suggests that during the 1970s and early 1980s the radical insurgent groups strove to compound their differences (that is, to become more polarised) because their overall ideological dispositions and strategies were consonant with political polarisation, not with some broad-based struggle for reform.

This was hardly a new phenomenon. French historian François Furet discusses this issue at length in a recent book. He quotes a resolution of the Executive Committee of the Communist International (reproduced in *L'humanité* – the organ of the French Communist Party – on 1 April, 1933), stating that 'the installation of an outright fascist dictatorship [in Germany], *dissipating all the democratic illusions of the masses and hence liberating them from the social-democratic influence*, accelerates Germany's march towards the proletarian revolution'.[67] We all know the consequences of the German Communist Party's all-out attack on the 'social fascists' (the Social Democratic Party), the number one enemy according to the communists.

In El Salvador, as the former insurgent Marco Antonio Grande rightly points out, 'the Salvadoran problem was seen by the left as a problem of class struggle and seizure of power, not as a problem of how to democratise the system'.[68] Incidentally, the extreme right always preferred to deal with the extreme left militarily than with some moderate reformist party in the ballots. In short, the two extremes objectively conspired to marginalise the centre and to retain violence as the paramount resource in the political competition.[69] Any liberalisation and democratisation of the regime was considered a more powerful counterrevolutionary device than military repression itself, the latter having at least the benefit of clearly displaying the 'contradictions' in the country.

To mention some historical examples, Ferman Cienfuegos points out that the insurgents' position on the 1972 elections – when a coalition comprising Christian democrats, social democrats and closet communists presented candidates for president (José Napoléon Duarte) and vice-president (Guillermo Manual Ungo) – was one of clear rejection and denunciation:

> We had already pronounced ourselves against the elections. We published something called 'Is the vote your weapon?', written by Rafael Arce, where one can find the first Marxist–Leninist analysis of political parties in the country, locating the different sectors of the bourgeoisie to which each of them belonged.[70]

They may have been right in foreseeing the farce that would take place, but their position can hardly be seen as the result of an *a posteriori* radicalisation, once all the peaceful avenues had been explored. One can easily speculate that the insurgents' position would have been the same, or even more blunt, if there had been a prospect of fair elections. The argument for late, incremental radicalisation may apply to some Christian democrats, a handful of social democrats or perhaps even the Communist Party before its adoption of armed struggle, but it does not apply to the politico-military organisations that emerged during this decade and eventually formed the FMLN.

In 1976 President Molina's attempt at 'agrarian transformation', a timid reform opposed by the private sector but supported by reformist sectors such as the UCA, the Christian Democratic Party and the Communist Party, was immediately denounced by the BPR as 'a politico-economic, counterrevolutionary measure of imperialism in our country'.[71] The position *vis-à-vis* the coup of 1979 and the reformist[72] civil–military junta that emerged from this successful coup is even more enlightening. An FPL leader recalled that

> during the first months of 1979, some young officers [*elementos de la juventud militar*] came to talk to us, given the strength of the BPR, in order to find together a solution to the critical situation the country was going through at that moment. Our position was to reject their offer... It was not consequent with our alliance policy because it resulted in allying ourselves with forces that were not working class and peasants.[73]

The FMLN actually formed an alliance with the *juventud militar* in 1981, when it was agreed that the former was the vanguard, an agreement that presumably could not be reached in 1979.[74] The question, therefore, was not one of working-class and peasant support, but one of leadership. In any case, immediately after the coup and the progressive Proclamation of the Armed Forces[75], the turn of events was unanimously condemned (after some brief hesitation by the LP-28 who probably thought – mistakenly – that, being the only radical organisation in the broad-based opposition coalition called Popular Forum, it would be offered some degree of power in the new government) as an 'auto-coup' of the oligarchy, the army and the US. The reformist, apparently progressive nature of the coup and the ensuing junta was doubtless the core feature of the counter-revolutionary plot, as Villalobos (leader of the ERP) explained:

> Perhaps one of the boldest steps we have taken is the insurrection of October 16, 1979, the day after the fall of General Carlos Humberto Romero's government. For 12 hours and [in] some cases longer, we maintained the military occupation of various towns... Why did we proceed in this manner? Because the situation was a guise of imperialism to deceive the Salvadoran people: to have united behind it would have signalled a defeat, passing, if you like, but defeat nonetheless, of a revolutionary alternative...the necessary risks had to be taken, beginning with the loss of our cadres.

> ...notwithstanding the good intentions of those who joined the first ruling junta, our policy consisted of applying a line of constant pressure, so that the military sectors that held the real power would thus be forced to assume the defense of the true scheme devised by imperialism, the oligarchy, and their allies. The combative pressure of the masses plus the revolutionary actions of a military character hastened the crisis of the first ruling junta; the democratic officials resigned, and the tactics of their enemies stood revealed to the people[76]

With hindsight, one of the FMLN leaders, Fermán Cienfuegos, recognised that 'with the coup of 15 October, 1979 what was put forward was our own agenda [*las banderas que veniamos levantando*]. The Armed Forces' proclamation of October 15th was the programme of the left.'[77] But it was not the programme *implemented by* the radical left. This position, in addition to the insurgents' military response, aimed at provoking the army (and the new government) into showing its 'true face', is the subject of self-criticism by former leaders of the FPL as well:

> I think that the characterisation of the coup was absolutist and hasty. Naturally this position was influenced by a rejection of the counterinsurgent powers that operated behind some of the forces driving the coup, *but it was primarily determined by an oversimplified politico-ideological position*, since we were so used to coming up with pre-determined conclusions, especially when we had to analyse the different forces in power.[78]

This compounding of differences and deliberate polarisation served the interests of extremists at both ends of the ideological spectrum, and this at the expense of groups seeking incremental reforms and democratisation. As the UNO deplored in 1977, 'the tireless repressive and bewildering efforts of the regime, *and... the sectarianism propagated by leaders of some popular groups*, who persist in not seeing the *obvious favour that their divisionist actions do to the oppressors and scourges of our people*'.[79]

Can this position be explained as the result of some popular demand, after many unsuccessful attempts to reform the system? Certainly not. Although it was not the only factor explaining the explosion of violence and the bankruptcy of the reformist agenda in 1979–80, it seems clear that the maximalist position adopted by the FMLN was not only consistent with the insurgents' position from the very outset, but it was specifically meant to destroy any prospect of peaceful transition and incremental change in El Salvador. Villalobos' recollections of the period strongly suggest that the savage repression perpetrated by the army, though tragic and reprehensible, was an integral and necessary part of the insurgents' strategy. Again, all this radicalisation did not happen because the people asked for it, regardless of how legitimate progressive social scientists might think it was, but rather because it was consistent with a particular mind-set, born and nurtured in the rarefied air of the insurgency's dogmatic, sectarian, almost fantastic world.

The Clash

Insurgency is always understood to be both the product and the most lucid interpretation of 'reality'. The insurgents' attitudes and actions are seen as having emerged from the deepest recesses of Salvadoran history, but the evidence strongly suggests that it is a mistake to underestimate the insurgents' capacity to create and live within their own ideological and political world. It apparently took a long time before they could evaluate how removed they were from political inputs generated outside their immediate environment.

During the emergence of the insurgency, the intellectual debate that took place among the different radical and rebel organisations was not merely a logical and timely response to the unfolding events. It was a private and sectarian dispute among opposing extremist factions. This occurred in a period of Latin American history when, as Castañeda points out, 'Marxists sought to build orthodox working-class parties where there were no workers, to distribute wealth that did not exist, and to lead revolution on behalf of a sector of society that constituted the smallest of minorities.'[80] The slow and painful process by which insurgents came to terms with the aspirations and ideological disposition of people outside the vanguard was aptly described by an FPL leader as a 'clash with reality' [*choque con la realidad*].[81]

In El Salvador, as Rodolfo Cardenal (a leading Jesuit from the UCA) recalls, the political language at the time

> was functioning like a syntactic ideology, that is, it was operating as a series of clichés and not as though it was resulting from analytical processes. Words had become almost magical, having power in themselves, and therefore *it was possible to disregard reality*. For example the word socialism was understood in a utopian way.... [At] many important junctures one could notice the *predominance of ideology over reality*, which had negative consequences for the revolutionary process in general.[82]

Likewise, Edelberto Torres-Rivas claims that 'in the 1970s there [was] a radicalisation of the means employed, and sometimes this occurred in a way that appeared independent from the ends. The point was to valorise the rifle for its capacity of expression, this being reinforced by the conviction that the problem was not one of "forms of struggle" but one of "revolutionary paths".'[83]

Though 'reality' was constantly invoked (each faction claiming exclusive access to it), the capacity to juggle with outlandish doctrines in close, clandestine surroundings was paramount. The insurgents' intellectual and ideological atmosphere was not simply dictated by necessity. By dismissing this early stage of ideological development as an infantile but normal step in the apprenticeship of revolutionary struggle, most observers missed a pivotal element in the emergence of insurgency in El Salvador.

THE SIREN SONG OF ELECTIONS

At the time of the Chapultepec peace accord in January 1992, most of the political leaders and military officials involved in the negotiations were the same ones who had fought the war. Social injustice and poverty were certainly more acute at that time than at any time in the 1960s and 1970s. El Salvador was still a poor Central American country, dependent on the US and the contingencies of the 'world economy.' And yet compromise and peace proved to be feasible in 1992 whereas it had not been in 1972 or 1982. What was so different in 1992?

At first glance many things had changed: world politics had changed dramatically with the end of the Cold War; the Sandinistas had lost the elections in 1990; George Bush had proved to be less ideologically driven than his predecessor, Ronald Reagan; and the Central American nations, led by Costa Rica, had joined the UN and, belatedly, the US to put their weight behind a negotiated solution to the conflict. On the domestic front, observers have pointed to a general sense of exhaustion in the population, and some have noted an ideological shift in both the extreme left and the extreme right, both falling prey to what a Salvadoran sociologist has called a new 'fascination with the centre'.[84]

The international factors are well-known, but their ideological impact on El Salvador is usually overlooked. Events such as the collapse of the Soviet empire and the Sandinista's electoral defeat in neighbouring Nicaragua were paramount in causing some FMLN leaders to turn away from Marxist–Leninist orthodoxy. As for the general exhaustion of the population, polls conducted in El Salvador, as well as plain common sense, suggest that it was already obvious in the early 1980s. The whole idea that the war was driven by popular demand, with millions of average Salvadorans applauding the FMLN's military feats and economic sabotage, is an intellectual construction based on academic wishful-thinking, not on solid evidence.[85]

The phenomenon that remains to be explained, in keeping with the general propositions presented in this book, is the

FMLN's famous ideological 'shift to the centre'. Indeed much has been written on the FMLN's shift from Marxism–Leninism to a more moderate social-democratic stance at the beginning of the 1980s.[86] The most conspicuous shift was by two factions of the FMLN: the ERP, rebaptised 'Expresion Renovadora del Pueblo', and the RN.[87] Both joined forces to create the Democratic Party, a still relatively undefined party (at the end of 1996) whose leaders actually signed a pact – the 'Pact of San Andrés' – with the right-wing party ARENA in June 1995.[88] This pact sealed a common agreement on such things as respect for private property, which was presented as a building block for development and a fundamental right of the population; a subsidiary role for the state, which should intervene only when problems arose that the citizens themselves could resolve; and other neoliberal ideas.

Whether these words genuinely reflected the Democratic Party's (PD's) ideological disposition, as opposed to its immediate tactical objectives, is open to question.[89] The power and significance of rhetoric was not lost on that old master of obfuscation, and arguably the father of all political parties in El Salvador: the PCN. One should keep that in mind when reading the FMLN communiqué that advocated a common effort to negotiate together 'integration into the international market under conditions acceptable to everyone'.[90] After all, as the always perceptive Horacio Castellanos Moya has commented, the left, more than any other political force in the country, was used to manipulating political ideas.[91]

The FMLN's ideological shift, whether genuinely felt or prompted by the circumstances, was no doubt influenced by the collapse of the socialist bloc and what Fukuyama, after Hegel and Kojève, has labelled the 'end of history'. But the *desideologización* (de-ideologisation) of both the left and the right was probably brought about in large part by an institutional mechanism that had been introduced during the war and had proved increasingly efficient in deflecting ideologies towards the centre of the political spectrum: elections.

As correctly pointed out by most observers, the elections in El Salvador were mostly imposed by the US. Former insurgents and most observers agree that the US-sponsored elections in the 1980s and early 1990s were an unqualified failure. An element of sophistication was added to this judgment by political scientist Terry Karl, who maintains that the US-imposed elections did worse than fail: they impaired pact-making and democratisation.[92] Being somewhat artificial, these 'demonstrative' elections postponed the achievement of a real, firmly grounded pact, achieved through negotiations, a breakthrough that presumably could have occurred at any time in the 1980s if only the Salvadoran belligerents had been allowed to work out a deal among themselves. In short the US-imposed elections ended up adding fuel to the internal war.

For this hypothesis to be validated, two counterhypotheses, strongly related to the relative autonomy of the insurgents, first have to be falsified. First, there is no definite evidence to warrant the assumption that a peaceful agreement is always possible between armed, and therefore extremist, factions; that there has never been such thing as incompatible ideologies or agendas.[93] Belligerents can so to speak, make a pact not to make a pact, at least in the short run.[94] In the early 1980s the Salvadoran extreme right set out to destroy the communists and emasculate the opposition movement. This policy was implemented in a spirit of crusade, to save the country from the 'evil' of communism. The ARENA party thrived on this anticommunist fixation and in just a few years became the most popular party in the country.[95] On the other side, the different factions of the FMLN were able to weather the centrifugal tendencies because of their overriding commitment to military struggle and revolution.[96] Military struggle and revolution were in fact so intertwined – 'means' becoming 'ends' – that without resorting to armed struggle the rest of the agenda would have rested on shaky ground, as the FMLN's ongoing crisis of unity illustrates.

Moreover, observers who dismiss the electoral process because of the exclusion of the FMLN are missing a fundamental point. To be excluded from a polity, one either has to have been included in it in the past, or one has never been in but aspires to be so.[97] As Juan Linz has suggested, 'the exclusion from political competition of parties not committed to the legal pursuit of power – which in reality is limited to enforceable exclusions... is not incompatible with the guarantee of free competition in our definition of democracy'.[98] While the elections were certainly not sufficient to bring about democracy in El Salvador, it was not insufficient merely because the system would not accommodate the insurgents and its desire to destroy the system.[99]

The exclusion argument also blurs the fact that full- fledged internal war can only come about with a certain degree of insurgent activity. Between this point and the moment when the spiral of violence starts (the late 1960s in El Salvador), conspiracy, exclusionary measures and violent rebellion are all mutually reinforcing. This makes the initial causal explanation (repression begets radicalisation) a commonsensical but uncorroborated assumption. Again, as Juan Linz points out: 'political violence is both an important indicator and a contributing cause of breakdown, but the line between cause and effect is blurred'.[100]

Of course this is not to say that ideologies and dispositions never change. To the contrary, recent breakthroughs in the Middle East, South Africa and El Salvador teach us that the political arena is more fluid and changing than the socio-economic structure. This fluidity can breed anything from war to peace, even in a context of relative social and economic stability. In El Salvador, the recent rapprochement between archenemies is inextricably tied to a significant ideological shift on both sides, away from their extremist positions. Nobody has clearly demonstrated that the introduction of election, was not a major factor in this shift. Hence the second counterhypothesis to the dominant 'demonstrative elections' thesis: the elections created a new political dynamic where the extremists, in order to win votes, had to moderate their ideological stance.

After the electoral defeat of 1984 and 1985, the party of Roberto D'Aubuisson strove to cloak itself in the mantle of political respectability. A self-composed businessman, Alberto Cristiani, was designated by D'Aubuisson to be the new leader.[101] ARENA comfortably won the 1988 and 1992 legislative elections, and the presidential election in 1989. Adam Przeworski's comments on the radical left and elections in Europe could be applied to the extreme right as well. He claims that in periods of democratisation, once a competitive democratic mechanism is more or less in place, radicals can hardly resist the 'siren song of elections'. According to Przeworski 'they tend to be wary of democratic institutions, distrustful of their chances, and skeptical that their victories will ever be tolerated. Yet the attraction of an open-ended democratic interplay is irresistible, and radicals find that to abstain is to forsake popular support.'[102] At the other end of the ideological spectrum, the two top leaders of the FDR (Rubén Zamora and Guillermo Ungo) returned from exile in November 1987 (*before* the end of the Cold War) in the wake of the Esquipulas II accord, whereupon they founded a new party and participated in elections. After some contradictory signals, the FMLN finally decided not to obstruct the electoral process through intimidation and sabotage. During the March 1994 elections the former insurgents toyed with the idea of asking a mainstream Christian Democrat (Abraham Rodríguez) and even a businessman close to both the Christian Democrats and the ARENA party (Roberto Murray Meza) to become their presidential candidate. Indeed as Goodwin and Skocpol correctly maintain, 'the ballot box may not always be "the coffin of class consciousness"...but it has proven to be the coffin of revolutionary movements'.[103]

There was no 'stunning' or foundational elections from 1982–only *repeated* elections. Gradually the US-imposed device began to affect the political actors' tactics and strategies, as well as gaining public credibility. Some of the actors who had condemned the elections as a counterinsurgent mockery started to have second thoughts. As early as 1985, for example, the generally pro-insurgent Central American University qualified its stance on elections.[104] The 1988 legislative elections were seen as a 'breach', likely to 'introduce new dynamics' and 'broaden, or perhaps break, dominant structures'.[105] At the same time the FMLN's usual sabotage of the electoral process became the object of adroit criticism by influential Jesuit intellectuals:

> The resort to violent action to prevent or disorient elections bestows on these elections, in the first place, a great importance, which contradicts the position that they are not important; second, this indicates the FMLN's low expectation of attracting with its propaganda, through an effort of persuasion, a great number of Salvadorans; and third, it demonstrates the relative weakness of the FMLN when it comes to imposing a political platform to the population.[106]

The above counterhypotheses are predicated on the same idea: actors' dispositions, beliefs and ideologies *do* matter in politics. In a period of transition they are key factors in the pact-making equation. Thus elections, though imposed from above and abroad (and therefore quite distinct from Booth's (1982) socioeconomic domino theory of revolt) can be instrumental in ending internal war, for elections do affect the actors' ideological disposition.

4 The University Vanguard

> One must take into account that the Salvadoran student movement of that time was moved by what happened in France in May 1968, by the events in Mexico... It was in this context that the thesis of the university reform movement from Córdova, Argentina, was reintroduced. All kinds of tendencies coexisted, from Marxism to existentialism. There was a group called the 'mathematics students', and another called the 'metaphysicists'. They were dissidents from the Christian Democratic Party, the Communist Party... [T]he university served as the crossroads where all these people converged and united. ('Salvador', an FPL leader interviewed in Harnecker, 1993)

> For a certain period of time, students must be the force that leads the popular movement. (Carlos Fonseca, founder of the FSLN, Nicaragua)

Latin American universities have been highly politicised throughout their history, and their political activism has often had a significant impact on the polity as a whole. For instance most if not all the guerrilla movements of the 1960s and 1970s in Latin America were born in universities (As mentioned earlier, Gabriel Zaid coined the term 'university guerrillas'). Nevertheless, relatively little has been written on the subject since the 1960s.[1]

A university is a composite but in many ways integrated organisation. It brings together at least three groups of actors: the administrative executive (rector or president, directive junta), professors and students. For all their particularities and potentially conflicting interests, these groups share a number of values and ideological viewpoints, in addition to common interests (the university's budget, autonomy, academic prestige) and other factors that derive from their common location in a single 'university city'. Finally, the university is linked to, and exerts authority over, the lower levels of the education system (especially high schools, if only because many teachers have some university education), and often considers itself the cultural vanguard and critical conscience of society at large.

To talk about 'the university' as a political force does not mean that it is politically homogeneous. Even in highly 'politicised' universities most actors abstain from taking part in any kind of political mobilisation.[2] It is therefore useful to distinguish between *intellectuals*, who are outward-oriented and engaged in the promotion of political ideologies, and *professionals*, who are inward-oriented and not specifically interested in the promotion of ideologies. As regards the students, they may be considered as novices of either type.[3]

It is important to point out that although not all university actors are intellectuals, it is hard to find in modernising Latin American countries an intellectual who is totally 'unattached' to a university institution (unless he or she has attained world-wide fame).[4]

EXPLAINING THE POLITICISATION OF UNIVERSITIES

Three specific and interlocked variables can be identified when explaining the politicisation and political impact of universities in Latin America: the pattern of elite reproduction, the 'critical' status of Latin American countries in historical perspective, and the mobilisational structures of universities.

First, there has been a distinctive pattern of elite reproduction in the region, where the patrimonial/oligarchic state lasted roughly until the 1920s. Elites in Latin America have typically been less differentiated and 'functional', or more homogeneous than, for instance, in North America.[5] They form a fairly exclusive club before the 'invertebrated' masses, to use Ortega y Gasset's terminology. The early institutional convergence between the state, the Church and the universities has shaped the latter's mission in an essentially political way: creating a 'nation', forming the elites, 'modernising' state bureaucracy and so on. Ivan Vallier's comment on the early contradiction of the Catholic church in Latin America applies equally well to universities, if one substitutes the Church's mission with the university's mission, and religious-moral foundation with academic-scientific foundation:

> By virtue of their image of the Church's mission and by reason of their various ties, involvement, and subordination with secular society, Catholic elites failed to create and institutionalize a religious-moral foundation for the growth of an agreed-upon system of values. The bishops' and clergy's potential capacities to symbolize, foster, and demand conformity to a higher moral order were constantly weakened by their maneuverings and inconsistencies bred, for the most part, by the institutional features of the society.[6]

The legacy of patrimony, joining together a distinct monistic and corporatist tradition, helps us understand why the typical role of Latin American intellectuals is closer to their continental European than their North American counterparts. In France, for instance, the most centralised and statist country of the European continent, elites tend to be *cumulard*: they cumulate social, political, cultural and often economic roles. Politicians who aspire to the highest positions must display some mastery of art, literature and philosophy, reminiscent of the Middle Ages' trivium of grammar, rhetoric and logic. All the same, in Latin America, where power not wealth is the pivotal resource, the low differentiation of elites is salient among cultural and political elites. Disciplines such as art and science have not been fully milked if their mastery has not been converted into political (or 'public') capital. Latin American universities, with their emphasis on the liberal professions, are more suited to forming *homo politicus* (the 'surrounded man', as described by Glen C. Dealy) than solitary scholars and technicians, seeking private rewards.[7]

Latin American elites are not a loose collection of interconnected but distinct heads of 'functional groups'. They form a fairly homogeneous and selective club of rulers. Cultural, political and economic resources command social deference, but these resources come with membership of the club, rather than being a prerequisite for membership of the club. Latin American intellectuals are largely defined by the nature of their relations with this club, to which many belong or aspire to belong. This explains why the category of intellectual is so unspecific in Latin America: as Jorge G. Castañeda (1994) and many others have pointed out, 'almost anyone who writes, paints, acts, teaches, speaks out, or even sings, becomes an "intellectual"'. A society that values what you are more than what you do, and where mastery of universal discourses commands more deference than instrumental reason and technical skills, is a society where, all things being equal, intellectuals are more likely to be rewarded for their talents.

Second, effective university political activism is more likely to emerge and have a significant impact in what Fernando Uricoechea has called 'critical societies'.[8] Critical societies have two components: belated and contradictory but rapid socioeconomic development (or social mobilisation), combined with resistance to change at the political level.

With regard to socioeconomic development, it seems that there is a bell-shaped relationship between effective political activism in universities and the level of development achieved in a given country. The degree of political activism and its effectiveness is low in highly developed countries, where both the social and the political structures are too diversified and institutionalised to provide intellectuals with influential and/or direct access to the central power. It is also low in very underdeveloped countries, where the university community and its potential audience are all but non-existent. On the other hand it is high in transitory societies such as most of those in Latin America.

Ignacio Ellacuria, a former rector of the UCA who was assassinated in November 1989, was perceptive enough to measure this phenomenon. Pondering on the university's capacity to shake the structure of power and have a progressive political impact on society, he said that

> this happens less and less as the social structure becomes more developed and diversified; then, it becomes very unlikely that a university revolt would generate even a military coup . . . And there are still countries where development of the productive forces has not yet reached a sufficient level; that is, enough to minimise the possibility that a university could become a political force and generate political change.[9]

In 'critical societies', social mobilisation engenders a growing educated stratum in the cities, particularly in the capital. This provides university intellectuals with a public to echo their ideologies. Through their intellectual influence, social prestige and sheer numbers, university actors occupy a pre-eminent position within this stratum, something that is unlikely in a more developed and diversified country. Lipset's comment on students applies to the university community at large: 'Because of the small size of the educated middle class, students in certain underdeveloped countries make up a disproportionately large section of the bearers of public opinion; their various affinities of education, class and kinship with the actual elites give them an audience which students in more developed countries can seldom attain.'[10]

With regard to political development, the case can be made that the university's political activism – and the influence of intellectuals – is also interconnected with political instability on one hand, and the capacity of the political system to respond to new demands on the other.[11] Thus another correlation can be established between effective political activism in universities on the one hand and the level of political openness permitted by the state on the other. In other words, effective political activism is likely to be weak if political openness is non-existent (case A) or if it is very high (case B). University political activism is, after all, a form of extra-institutional mobilisation, a rarity in case A and unnecessary or politically ineffectual in case B.

In El Salvador during the 1960s and early 1970s the regime was authoritarian but also slightly mobilisational. Until 1972 it strove to portray itself as a progressive, reformist, even revolutionary-like civil–military regime, where virtually everybody was welcome to 'participate'. Authoritarian reformists in power encouraged the development of the universities and their commitment to social change, but without democratising the country. In a way they produced the rope with which they were likely to be hanged. The 'critical society' equation is schematised in Figure 4.1.

A corollary to 'critical society' status is a relatively unsuccessful attempt to institutionalise political rule. In such cases political parties usually enjoy no monopoly in terms of political representation and mobilisation. In fact other seasoned 'representative forces' such as the army, students, the church or unions have as much, if not more, of a legitimate say in shaping policies than normal politicians. This kind of

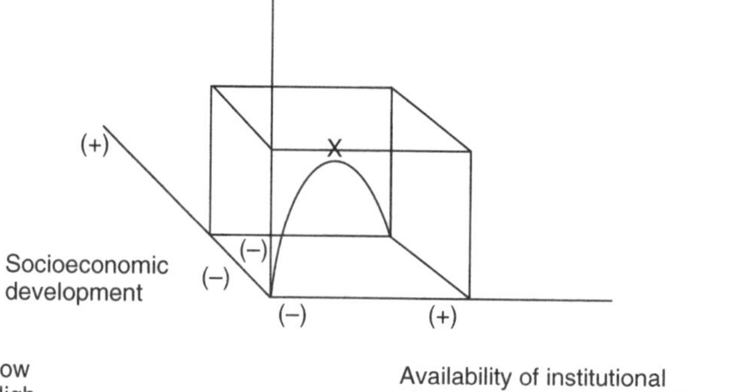

Figure 4.1 Effective political activism in the university

setting invites all actors who have mastered the art of political discourse (including, nowadays, social scientists) and who enjoy organisational resources to participate actively in politics.

This leads to the third factor: universities offer distinctive mobilisational resources in a critical society. Three factors are easily identifiable: the university's autonomy, the organisational configuration of the university community, and a specific disposition to act as society's vanguard in experimenting with new social and political formulae.

The university's autonomy means that it can provide a sanctuary for opponents of the state and a comparatively secure base to plan and conduct political activities. In El Salvador this autonomy has been recognised, more or less formally, numerous times since the end of the nineteenth century, but it was enshrined for the first time in the political constitution of 1950 (Article 205). The political advantages stemming from autonomous status are contingent upon the government's goodwill. As in most Latin American countries where the rule of law is not solidly established, university autonomy in El Salvador has never been a right; only a privilege, very much like the *fuero* (privilege) of the colonial period. This privilege can be removed at any time by the state or ignored by political and military actors, especially during times of extreme political tension. In El Salvador, autonomy was respected most in the 1950s, when all parties openly recruited on the campus, but in 1960, 1972–79, 1980–84 and 1989–90 the government despatched soldiers to occupy the campus, where they acted like a ragtag army from the Middle Ages, pillaging and looting everything in sight.

As regards the organisational configuration of the university community, it must be pointed out that no other organised community, with the possible exception of the army, possesses a greater degree of social density and such suitable conditions for the aggregation of political actors. As Lipset has observed:

> The ecological concentration of universities within a limited area, bringing together many young men and women in a similar situation in life, and isolating them for the most part from the motley routine of adult life contributes to the perpetuation of student restlessness. This is as true of universities in underdeveloped countries as it is of those in advanced countries... It is easy to reach students; leaflets handed out at the campus gates will usually do the job. These facilitate quick communication, foster solidarity, and help to arouse melodramatic action.[12]

This apparently invariant feature of the university community takes on a distinct tone in the Latin American environment. Glen C. Dealy suggests that in Catholic and caudillistic societies (such as the ones in Latin America), 'formal educational institutions do not exist to convey technical knowledge that will be economically useful, as in capitalistic cultures, but to provide a place where young men may begin to sort out and establish hierarchies of power'.[13] Hence his comparison with the army:

> National politics in *caudillaje* [from *caudillo* = chief] society is almost constantly in the hands of university graduates or the military. This has much less to do with a monopoly of coercive force than usually supposed. Rather, it follows from the fact that both university and barracks provide an ideal setting for the aggregation of a following which may sooner or later prove useful.[14]

Finally, there is a plethora of evidence to show the propensity of university actors in Latin America to appoint themselves as the engineers of the 'new society'. Of course this tendency can be observed in campuses all over the world. Nevertheless a number of specific conditions have arguably shaped the way cultural elites, university actors and intellectuals see themselves and their roles in society, in a way that mahes the Latin American case unique. First – returning to the Iberian matrix – as the Chilean historian Claudio Véliz has suggested, 'to understand the personality of Don Quixote is to take the first step toward an understanding of the Latin American intellectual.'[15] Several features come to mind: the difficulty of focusing anything that lies between narrow personal interest on the one hand and lofty, universal values on the other;[16] a certain inability to adopt a pragmatic, middle of the road approach to problem solving; a penchant for melodra, hierarchical deference, martyrdom and so on. All these features tie in nicely with the central cultural matrix of the Iberian culture; that is, Catholicism. Indeed a book that remains to be published, as Régis Debray once said, is one entitled 'Catholicism and the spirit of Latin American revolutionary ethos'. The current Protestant tide will soon help us to see how Catholicism shaped Latin America in even more ways than we realised.

The tendency initiated in the 1920s by the movement for university reform in Córdova, Argentina, held sway in universities all over the continent, including in Central America.[17] This somewhat utopian movement conveyed at least two general ideas to future generations. First, the university should run itself as an egalitarian and autonomous community of faculty members and students. Second, the university should be both a model and a politico-cultural vanguard *vis-à-vis* society as a whole. The model proposed by the Argentine students was archetypal: the university campus was to become a quasi-monastery, a relatively closed city where young, uncorrupted, principled individuals would construct the ideal *polis* in the midst of a corrupt, spiritually backward society. In El Salvador this propensity has been inordinately salient in the history of the National University, the only Salvadoran university until 1965.

THE NATIONAL UNIVERSITY OF EL SALVADOR: IN THE STATE ORBIT

Although some observers of Salvadoran politics acknowledge the importance of universities in the political development of the country, there is very little published material on the subject.[18] In El Salvador, such analysis must begin with the national university, the University of El Salvador (UES). It was the first and is still the most important university in the country.

The FMLN was tied to the UES from the very outset of the insurgency. In fact very few of the FMLN's top commanders did not begin their career as 'revolutionaries' at the UES. The overwhelming majority of the FMLN leaders, probably most of its intermediary cadres and a good many of the rank-and-file had previously been rectors, professors or students at the UES (or to a lesser extent, at the UCA or the Jesuit college Externado San José). Some of its various organisations were founded at the UES.

The five top *comandantes* of the FMLN – Joaquín Villalobos (ERP), Fermán Cienfuegos (FARN), Francisco Jovel (PRTC), Jorge Shafik Handal (PCS) and Salvador Sánchez Cerén (FPL) – had been student activists in the AGEUS, as had numerous other FMLN commanders and cadres. Sánchez Cerén had served as professor at the UES. Of the first seven members of the FDR-FMLN Political- Diplomatic Commission (CPD) – Guillermo Manuel Ungo (MNR), Mario Aguiñada (PCS/UDN), Rubén Zamora (MPSC), Fabio Castillo (PRTC), José Napoléon Rodríguez Ruiz (FAPU/ERP), Ana Guadalupe Martínez (LP-28) and Salvador Samayoa (FPL) – Ungo, Castillo and Rodríguez Ruiz had held professor ships at the UES, and Castillo and Rodríguez Ruiz had also served as rector. Ungo had lectured at the UCA, where he was director of the Institute of Research in the early 1970s. Samayoa had been a professor at the UCA and the Externado San José. About a decade earlier Dr Rubén Zamora, leader of the MPSC, the FDR, the CD (Democratic Convergence) and the most recent presidential candidate of the FMLN, had been the leader of the Social-Christian University Revolutionary Federation (FRUSC).

Among other prominent leaders of the Salvadoran left who were strongly identified with the UES were the following: Hector Dada Hirezi (member of the second junta – 1980 –

and leader of the FDR), was a former director of the Department of Economics at the UCA and former candidate for rector at the UES; Rafael Menjivar (a 'leading theorist of the BPR'[19] and leader of the FDR) served as rector at the UES in 1972; Melida Anaya Montes (founder of the magisterial union ANDES and second-in command of the FPL until her assassination in 1983 Salvador Cayetano Carpio taught at the UES; and Eduardo Calles (leader of MIPTES – the Movimiento Independiente de Profesionales y Técnicos de El Salvador – and FDR's vice-president) served as dean of the UES Faculty of Agronomy.

Since the FDR was 'constituted by university members and professionals', it is not surprising that the kidnapping and assassination of six FDR leaders, during a meeting at the Externado San José in November 1980, was presented in a UES publication as another episode in the 'anti-university campaign'.[20] The fact that most books and articles published during the 1980s on revolution and counterrevolution in El Salvador only briefly allude to the UES, while stretching over hundreds of pages the scant information about revolutionary peasants and workers, is a powerful indication of how a dominant paradigm can mould assumptions and distort the analysis of empirical evidence.

The increasing political activism of the UES and its contribution to the emergence of insurgency during the late 1960s can be explained by at least three factors: (1) the tremendous expansion of UES enrolment and resources; (2) the commitment of the 'developmentalist' military regime to placing the UES at the centre of its development strategy during the 1950s and 1960s; and (3) the new momentum instilled in the UES's time-honoured tradition of political activism by new countercultural and radical passions stemming, as argued in Chapter 2, largely from outside the national borders.

University and Nation Building

In his book on the political evolution of the UES until the early 1970s, Mario Salazar Valiente contends that it is 'correct, regarding the Salvadoran university institution, to lay down the historical and general postulate that it has progressed all along in accordance with the ebb and flow of forces present in the state orbit.'[21] Indeed the UES's attitude towards politics and political participation in El Salvador has been constant, in various guises, since its foundation in the nineteenth century.

The UES was created (along with the Colegio de la Asunción) only fourteen days after El Salvador's declaration of independence in 1841.[22] In a decision symptomatic of the clergy's influence in education, the university was first housed in the former Convent of San Francisco. The foundation of the UES represented one of the first attempts to create an educational structure in this illiterate, schoolless country.[23] Some timid attempts were made to develop elementary and secondary schools in the aftermath of the country's independence from Spain. Nevertheless it seems clear that educating the masses was not a priority for the *independentista* elite. Rather their goal was 'to forge a national identity and to create a national culture'.[24] The university was one part of a broader nation-building process (involving a state bureaucracy, an army, security forces and so on) where institutions were not meant to represent or reflect the nation, but literally to *create* one from above. During the first years of the institution the confusion between the different sectors of the elite, so typical of an oligarchic and patrimonial state, shaped university development as well. Article 10 of the UES decree of foundation states that 'all the doctors, licentiates [*licenciados*], college graduates [*bachileratos*] and citizens of the state are university native-members and have a seat in the faculty assembly [*Claustro*] when they happen to be in the capital'. On two occasions a rector usurped the presidency of the republic while retaining his position at the university. This occurred in 1846–47 with Eugenio Aguilar (rector from 1841 to 1847 and president of the republic from 1846 to 1848), and in 1852–54 with Francisco Dueñas (rector from 1848 to 1854 and president of the republic in 1852–54, 1863–65 and 1865–71). In 1866, when Gregorio Arbizú, the future president Rafael Zaldívar and Darío González were respectively rector, vice rector and secretary general, the university council granted the title of doctor to the current president of the republic, Dueñas, and even to Arbizú, who in addition to being rector, dean, professor and president of the university council, held the position of minister of foreign affairs and public education.[25]

From its foundation in 1841 to the positivist period at the end of the century, the university slowly evolved from a mere cultural club for the educated elite to an institution devoted to modernising the public administration. As Bradford E. Burns has demonstrated, it became 'much more than a showpiece of modernization or a cultural adornment. Its graduates and professors filled increasingly complex positions in the political and economic life of the nation in addition to providing loyal support for the institutional changes underway.' At that time, contends Burns, 'intellectuals enthusiastically embraced the modernization selected by the political and economic elite'.[26]

The UES did achieve some degree of administrative autonomy from the state during the last two decades of the nineteenth century, but its complete emancipation and its ensuing development into a modern institution received a major boost from the rapid diffusion of the university reform movement (initiated in Córdoba, Argentina, in 1928) in the second quarter of this century. This movement had far-reaching objectives, as a Salvadoran student organisation of the 1960s was keen to recognise: 'The reform does not end with a change in the university's structure, but must inevitably expand itself to carry out an integral change of the country's structures.'[27] The intellectual influence of this movement was instrumental in shaping the political orientation of Salvadoran students in their struggle for university autonomy in the 1920s and the 1940s, and then in their struggle for social change in general.

The idea that the universities of the region had an enlightening mission *vis-à-vis* society as a whole is clearly stated in the Declaration of Principles of the Central American

Universities' First Congress, held in San Salvador in September 1948:

> the Central American universities, because of particular environmental circumstances, cannot exactly follow in the footsteps of Europe and the United States.... [T]hey have a singular and profound mission on top of the three missions universally recognised – [scientific] research, the teaching of professions and the transmission of culture – that is, they should spiritually guide their people and build a Central American nationality in order to reconstruct the mother country [*patría*] and establish the conditions that will provide the spiritual force for the coveted unity and cultural, economic and politic renewal of this part of the world.[28]

During this congress, which resulted in the formation of the Central American University Confederation,[29] the focus was still very much on the necessity to create a nation (Central America) as a cultural, almost spiritual entity. Politics ensued from this necessity. This cultural approach, shared by many thinkers and modernist intellectuals, was gradually replaced, in little more than a decade, by more voluntaristic, politically oriented aspirations.[30] The Confederation's 'Fundamental Bases' and 'Declaration of Principles and Goals' were updated during the Confederation's Second Congress, held in San Salvador in 1968. The first basic principle was

> to fight decidedly along with social forces committed to social change [*fuerzas sociales transformadoras*], in conformity with the particular conditions in each country and national interests, in order to replace the current structures in the Central American region and to attain the economic, political and cultural independence of our peoples.[31]

The first goal of the Confederation was to 'promote a profound process of change and to create a mentality favourable to that, since the current structures in Central America do not respond to its inhabitants' aspirations for a life that allows them to satisfy their spiritual and material needs'. It was also affirmed that 'the university's task should not be limited to generating the cultural integration [of Central America], but also to aspire to the union of Central America'.[32] Once again, the university shared one of the aspirations of the political class as a whole.

The UES's political presence was particularly marked in times of instability and change. As early as 1932 the UES, through the actions of some of its communist students (for example Mario Zapata, Alfonso Luna and above all Augusto Farabundo Martí), was indirectly instrumental in the rebellion that ended in the massacre (the famous *matanza*) of thousands of peasants in the western part of the country. In April and May 1944 the university community played a central and successful role in mobilising urban populations against the dictatorship of Maximiliano Hernández Martínez (1932–44).[33] In a sense, students and faculty members spearheaded the rise of the Salvadoran middle class in politics.

Salvadoran students, as in most Latin American countries, have long been engaged in political activism. They fought for the autonomy of the university back in the 1920s. The Salvadoran General Association of University Students (AGEUS) was founded in the wake of this struggle, in 1927. It became one of the key mobilisational organisations of the radical left in the 1960s and 1970s, and many – conceivably most – of its leaders became insurgents during the 1980s.[34] In the 1950s, prior to the hegemony of Marxism–Leninism at the UES, radical groups had already established loose connections with universities: for instance the Literary Circle formed around such Leninist intellectuals as Roque Dalton García (1935–75) and the Guatemalan Otto René Castillo (1936–67).[35] From the early 1960s student organisations became firmly aligned with the Communist Party, and then with the various 'ultra-leftist' Marxist–Leninist organisations. During their first congress in 1969, Salvadoran university students proclaimed the necessity of a broad-based coalition of revolutionary groups, including workers, who would be directed by the 'most revolutionary and dynamic' sector of society: that is, the university students themselves.[36]

The growing influence of student organisations in the management of the university – sometimes leading to virtual *alumnocratismo* (or 'student*ocracy*'), as in early 1970s – was a key factor in the radicalisation of the university. The exclusion and/or withdrawal of non-ultra-leftist tendencies from the campus around 1970 left the university with an official ideology of sorts, behind which the mundane struggle for power could freely take place.[37]

In 1960 the UES was occupied by the army because of its leading role in the uprising against President José María Lemus (1956–60).[38] The rector (Napoléon Rodríguez Ruiz), as well as numerous professors and students, were brutalised by the army. After the downfall of Lemus on 26 October 1960, a six-member 'university–military' junta (three civilians and three army officers) came to power. The three civilians were Fabio Castillo Figueroa, a former student leader who had been involved in the mobilisation against the dictatorship of Hernández Martínez in 1944, rector of the UES from 1963 to 1966 after the collapse of the junta and presidential candidate for the Renewal Action Party (PAR) in 1966; Romeo Fortín Magaña, rector from 1955 to 1959 and former minister of the economy during Hernández Martínez's dictatorship; and Ricardo Falla Cáceres, known for his previous involvement in the university students' organisation.[39]

The fact that the three civilians were directly identified primarily with the UES is an indication of the clout wielded by the university during this period. At least two of them remained important political players after leaving their university positions: Romeo Fortín Magaña eventually became leader of the Democratic Action Party (AD), while Fabio Castillo Figueroa became a key FMLN supporter. What is more, the tiny opposition parties of the 1960s had significant links with the UES. In addition to the Communist Party, which had settled down at the UES since its formation in the early 1930s, the other parties with links to the UES were the April and May Revolutionary Party (PRAM), the

National Revolutionary Movement (MNR), the Christian Democratic Party, the PAR and the Nationalist Democratic Union (UDN, linked to the PCS). This suggests that the UES was the springboard from which elements of the emerging middle class and dissident members of the ruling class could mobilise and challenge the old elites' exclusive hold on power.

EXACERBATING THE CONTRADICTIONS

The political crisis of 1972 heralded the decline of both the military regime and the UES. In March the army rejected the validity of the presidential elections, won by the National Opposition Union (UNO), a reformist coalition headed by José Napoléon Duarte of the PDC and Manuel Guillermo Ungo of the MNR. The UNO victory revealed not only the exhaustion of the political capital gained by the military in the wake of its victory against Honduras in the 'soccer war' of 1969, but also the new strength of the middle sectors and their civilian-led political parties. The rejection of the electoral results and the ensuing repression unleashed a spiral of violence from which the country only escaped in 1992.

On 19 July 1972, a few months after Colonel Molina captured power, the army intervened once again at the UES, occupying the campus and rounding up many of its faculty members and students. The justification presented by the government, if not the means employed, resonated positively in many sectors of the population: the university had become totally chaotic following a strike in the overcrowded 'common areas' (*areas comunes*, part of a programme involving a common curriculum for all new students for one or two years). The common areas were created in 1965 in the wake of the 1963 reform. The idea was to save scarce resources while making sure that all students received the same basic formation in humanities. The programme had to cope with the rapid massification of higher education. It turned out to be a hotbed of 'perennial students' and professional activists.

In 1970, 61.5 per cent of UES students (including those at the regional branches in Santa Ana and San Miguel, created the year before) were registered in this programme.[41] Nearly two years later, in the midst of a revolt fuelled by ultra-leftist groups, the UES students openly challenged the restrictive admission standards, pressing the intimidated authorities to live up to their reformist principles and to 'open the door' of the university by removing restrictions (the so-called *puertas abiertas* principle). The revolt started as a strike in the increasingly packed common areas but rapidly evolved into a full-fledged student revolt, with all that entailed: the occupation of buildings, Maoist-like summary 'trials' of politically incorrect faculty members, permanent protests, and so on. In the Faculty of Law, students took over the building and replaced the professors and administrative body with a pseudo collective decision-making committee imposing a regime of ideological terror. The students' invasion of all administrative structures (the so-called *alumnocratismo*) proved successful: the administration quickly changed its position and approved the *puertas abiertas* principle in May 1972.[42]

The parallel with the successful strikes launched by ANDES during the same period is interesting. In both cases the students (UES) and teachers (ANDES) successfully challenged the authorities and articulated demands that went far beyond the immediate interests of their members.

By the turn of the decade student organisations were totally controlled by Marxist–Leninist groups, prone to 'assemblyism' (*asambleísmo*) and permanent 'mass mobilisation', and fully committed to the subversion of all national institutions – starting with the university. They manipulated the General Assembly and the University Superior Council, which led to reform of the UES's Fundamental Law that undermined democratic processes. For example the reform abolished the secret vote in the general Assembly.[43] The reform provided an excuse for military intervention, an action that the military government had been itching to undertake.[44] The election of leftist-oriented authorities in 1971 was finally repealed, as was the twenty-year-old Organic Law. Another Organic Law was adopted in October, in order to 'reinforce' the university's autonomy. The new law was officially designed to prevent the future use and abuse of democratic procedures by ultra-leftist organisations while respecting the university's autonomy, as enshrined in the constitution.[45]

The military intervention, in spite of its brutality, was apparently met with passivity, and even with relief by many groups outside the university.[46] The university ended up being managed by the state for the remainder of the decade. In a sense, abuse of the university's autonomy by radical students provoked its abolition by the military regime, thus producing the kind of political polarisation that suited extremists on both sides.

From 1972 to March 1977 the UES was supervised by a 'Commission of Normalisation' [*Comisión Normalizadora*], controlled by the Federation of Academic Professionals' Associations of El Salvador (FEPRO), an organisation that shared the government's view on how to 'normalise' the UES. From then until December 1978 it was ruled in a thoroughly authoritarian and centralised fashion by the infamous Provisional Administration Council of the UES (CAPUES).[47] The campus was given back to its proper authorities only in June 1979, just in time for political activism to acquire a new vigour at the peak of the anti-Romero struggle.[48]

The UES was one of the main victims of the spiral of violence and chaos over the next two decades. Two rectors were assassinated: Carlos Alfaro Castillo in September 1977 by the extreme left (FPL), and Félix Antonio Ulloa in October 1980, in all likelihood by the extreme right. On 30 July, 1975 at least 37 students were killed by security forces during a student demonstration in San Salvador. In late 1977 the Legislative Assembly decided to extend the CAPUES's mandate from one to five years, because 'the climate of disorder and violence' that had presided over the creation of CAPUES had 'increased'.[49] Security measures were tightened and the campus was permanently policed by special security agents. Persecution and repression also reached new tragic heights.

In September 1978 the dean of the Economics Faculty, Carlos A. Rodríguez, was assassinated by a death squad. Countless individuals were illegally detained, interrogated and tortured by the security forces. Many 'disappeared'.

According to Fernando Flores Pinel, it was during this period that 'the use of violence was established as the normal solution to the university's problems'.[50] This situation eventually caused the helpless rector, Eduardo Badía Serra, to resign during the summer of 1979.[51] Typically, the ensuing election for the position of rector – that is, for political control of the university – turned into a purely political showdown opposing the so-called FUERSA, a university front tied to the FPL/BPR, and the UR-19, and linked to the ERP/FAPU.[52] In line with the logic of polarisation, ultra-leftist gangs on the campus, far from receding, continued to expand and multiply as repression increased during the 1970s and early 1980s. In April the UES (and the UCA) acquired 'observer' status in the FDR, while the AGEUS opted for full membership.[53] The motive behind the UES's political engagement is explained by Félix Antonio Ulloa, rector from late 1979 until his assassination in October 1980:

> We believe that in this historical moment for the country, no Salvadoran can abstain from participating in this process of liberation. In this sense the university's involvement in FDR activities means that it is not engaged in an abstract way but with each and every one of its members: students, workers and professors...The institution can offer its infrastructure and its human quality alike, that is, the participation of each and every member of its community.[54]

The 1980s

The 1980s proved to be a decade of terror and intervention at the UES. The army seized the campus on 26 June 1980, to give it back only on 22 May 1984, after inflicting considerable damage to its facilities.[55] On 27 February 1981 the Legislative

Assembly issued Decree no. 603, which suspended remuneration to the top UES officials, that is, the rector, vice-rector, treasurer, secretary-general, external judge advocate, deans, vice-deans and directors of the regional centres.[56] After 1984, both political activism at the UES and state repression continued in fits and starts, like the internal war itself. Permanent demonstrations and civil disobedience by student extremists plagued the UES during the last years of the Duarte's mandate, which, even according to UES sympathisers, tarnished the university's image. For a year before the FMLN military offensive on 11 November, 1989, soldiers mounted guard at every campus gate.[57] Shortly after the offensive started, the army once again occupied the campus until 8 June, 1990, while the university authorities managed swiftly to resume classes and enrol freshmen for the forthcoming academic year.[58] Although the UES was no longer supposed to take a political position, its support for the FDR-FMLN and the Democratic Convergence (the electoral vehicle of the FDR, and therefore close to the FMLN) was unmistakable at the end of the 1980s. The students' (AGEUS), professors' (ADUES) and workers' (CCTU) unions coalesced to create the University Unity (UU) during the 1980s, and the UU became a member of the most pro-FMLN union in the country: the National Unity of Salvadoran Workers (UNTS).

VANGUARDISM

Although this book focuses on the emergence of the insurgency (roughly, from the late 1960s to the very early 1980s), it is useful to look once again at a more recent occurrence in order to demonstrate the UES's political disposition. In April 1988, the Superior University Council of the UES approved a 'Plan of Development' for the next five years that spelled out with unprecedented clarity its political mission. Arguably, the plan was never meant to be implemented (indeed it never was)[59] for it was more a blueprint for radical political change than a concrete agenda with a clear timetable. Nonetheless, it was approved – or rather it was not rejected – by the University Council[60] and the tightly controlled university community.[61]

The 'UES's mission in society' (Chapter 1) and the 'political project of the UES' were clearly the main themes of this plan, which was otherwise free of the type of details generally included in this kind of document (specific objectives and the means to achieve them, a timetable, an assessment of resources and so on). Education itself seemed relevant only to a larger totality; that is, the political totality.[62]

At least three interlocking principles, listed bellow as postulates, can be drawn from this document: (1) the current regime should be replaced by a socialist regime; (2) the UES was a component of the vanguard called by history to liberate the Salvadoran people; and (3) the UES, in its own management, should be a model for a new society. The first postulate was specific to the period dominated by Marxism–Leninism, described in Chapter 2. The others had been part of the UES's standpoint for at least four decades, perhaps since its very foundation.

The UES has been consistent and unambiguous in its diagnosis of the Salvadoran 'reality'. This is summarised in the following paragraph, drawn from the plan's 'Frame of Reference':

> El Salvador is a dependent, semi-developed capitalist country whose economy is in permanent structural crisis. This crisis consists in the impossibility of capital's broad reproduction, and in the presence of obstacles to the development of productive forces. The possibility of developing productive forces and incorporating the products of the scientific–technical revolution is hindered by its own built-in structure; that is, by the system of social relations of production and the global subordination of the country's economy to the world capitalist market, and above all to the economic interests of the United States of America.[63]

According to the plan, there were two ways out of this predicament. The first would be to 'step forward to a superior phase of dependent capitalism'. This solution had been favoured by Salvadoran governments since 1979, in conformity with the 'North American counterinsurgency project'. The second would be to implement the 'democratic–revolutionary project promoted by the FMLN-FDR'. The latter was emphatically supported by the UES, for the FDR-FMLN's solution 'possesses historical viability' and 'proposes to bring about a profound transformation of society's economic, social and political structures; to create the material for a social regime of authentic democracy for the people that will fully express national sovereignty and the Salvadoran people's right to self-determination'.[64]

While strongly supporting the FMLN-FDR, the UES highlighted its own theoretical contribution through its 'political project'. This contribution revolved around four guiding principles: the university must be *popular*, *democratic*, *free* and *humanist*. These principles, and indeed the political project they would inform, would be valid for both the new university and the new society. The former would be to be to the latter what the monastery had been to the Christian world: a model for social planning; a small, organic community living 'by the book'.[65] According to the plan:

> From the UES' Frame of Reference and Political Project, a national political project must be identified and formulated, containing basically an economic regime with the following principal characteristics: a mixed economy model implemented by a planning, investing and caring state, which defines the basic premises of national reconstruction; and a political regime with the following fundamental characteristics: a popular, democratic state, with a foreign policy of non-alignment. These principles are ruled by the economic, social and political aspirations of the broad majority [of the people].[66]

In another declaration in the same period, the UES talked explicitly about how its political project confirms its 'guiding role' in society, for with this 'historic vision', the UES is engaged in a process of '*constructing scientifically* the criteria that must provide society with orientation'.[67]

The '*popular*' principle was clearly the central postulate, for it defined all the others: 'The popular essence of the UES is based upon full identification with the fundamental interests of the popular majority, to which the fundamental interests of the minority must be subordinated.'[68] Hence 'the main social foundation of the popular [principle] in the UES consists of the workers, craftsmen who will bring about a new society where social wealth comes from and is for the majority'.[69] The other principles are hardly distinguishable from the first: democracy, liberty and humanism are simply variations of the popular principle; that is, variations of the basic idea of social equality.

First, '*Democracy* for the UES is conceived as a form of political organisation for a society where the interests of the majority are preeminent, and which is based upon the production and distribution of goods generated by the productive apparatus for these majorities... Hence democracy in the UES passes by the development of productive forces in order to increase the national wealth and provide a superior standard of living for all citizens.'[70] Likewise 'the essence of *Liberty* for the UES is to provide man with the possibility of conscientiously utilising science in its practical activities, and to support efforts to make scientific advances and productive forces part of the universal heritage'.[71] Finally, '*Humanism* is conceived by the UES as paying respect to human dignity, caring for human welfare and development, creating favourable social conditions and liberating man from all forms of oppression and exploitation and from the horrors of war, and furthering peace, liberty, equality and fraternity among men and nations.'[72] This should not be confused with 'formal humanism, which denies the permanent search for better material conditions of life for the immense working masses'.[73]

These principles have to be comprehended within the UES's intellectual mind-set. By 'popular', the UES meant the 'authentic and legitimate aspirations' of the people; that is, not their inauthentic or illegitimate aspirations, promoted by enemies of the UES.[74] The principles of democracy, freedom and humanism would not be based on individual rights but on those of the 'majority', according to ideological criteria. Democracy and freedom would not be extended to those actors who did not acquiesce with the UES's vision of the new university and the new society. 'University freedom' meant 'the political liberty... to organise inside the different sectors of the university community, but on condition that the university's popular and democratic character [is respected]. The UES cannot tolerate in its premises any organisation that would spoil its proper specificity and nature.' 'Academic liberty [*libertad de cátedra*] would be recognised, but only as long as it was consonant with the framework outlined for political liberty. As a consequence 'diverse intellectual movements [*corrientes de pensamiento*] are not prohibited, but they must contribute to the university's fulfilment of its stand for the majorities'.[75] It is hard not to notice a conspicuous feature of the UES since the early 1970s: the virtual absence of any other political current than the ones represented by the ultra-left, including even those of the moderate left.

The nationwide discussion of the 'project for building a new society' would be limited to those groups and actors 'who represent the majorities' interests'.[76] The project explained the UES's relations with external organisations such as unions, 'popular organisations', corporations and above all the state. Here the UES stood firmly:

> the nature of the state... defines the possibility... of UES participation in its plans. In order to define the nature of the state, the interests it fundamentally represents must be identified; if they are those of the majority, the state's and the university's interests converge and the possibility for cooperation are real... [W]ith the current state, which denies liberty, violates human rights and disregards the interests of the broad majority, a relation of confrontation

> unavoidably exists because the UES's relations are determined by its Political Project.[77]

Of course there were no objective criteria that would enable any citizen or university member to single out the friends and foes of the 'majority', and therefore no criteria objectively to ascertain the proper foundations of the new university and the new Society. In implementing the political project, the intellectuals in charge of 'analysing the reality' and identifying the 'authentic and legitimate aspirations' of the 'majority' would doubtless be in a dominant, even autocratic position.

Yet the link between the new university and the new society is somewhat ambiguous, in spite of their common foundation. The difficulty lies in the university's limitations with regard to its specific political mission as a university. To what extent could the university be a political force without ceasing to be a university? According to the plan: 'joining the people in its struggles [*luchas reivindicativas*] does not mean claiming for oneself an inappropriate vanguard role, let alone for the university to seek political power. But it means that the university should... [assist in] these struggles by means of its main instruments: science, culture and art; and with its specific missions: research, social projection and teaching.'[78]

This position is very moderate by UES standards. In other publications the UES's involvement in 'popular struggles' seems a much less distant venture.[79] In fact a more professionally oriented approach took hold later, after a profound internal debate. As the then secretary general of the UES (René Mauricio Mejía Mendez) said, many faculty members realised that sometimes the 'university's interests clash with the interests of the Revolution'.[80] In any case this was a relatively new phenomenon; the UES was firmly in favour of armed struggle from the time that the insurgency emerged and during most of the internal war.

In sum, it was thought that the UES and the FDR-FMLN should combine their efforts to further the liberation of the Salvadoran people. The UES would move forward with the people. The UES would fight side by side with the people.

The UES might sometimes present itself as a 'part' of the people, but thanks to its insight into the people's fundamental interests, the UES clearly belonged to the elite. The UES was part of the revolutionary vanguard of the people. But since, as Régis Debray (1967) has pointed out, the bearers of arms should be 'the vanguard of the vanguard' in a Latin American revolution, the UES's contribution should be complementary, on even somewhat subsidiary to the defining politico-military struggle.

That does not mean that its role would be negligible. Indeed, 'at the cultural and artistic level, the university has as a first priority to redeem, transform, conserve, promote and diffuse the cultural values of the Salvadoran people, and to give the people access to science, culture and art'.[81] The UES would be nothing less than the 'critical conscience', almost the brain of the Salvadoran people. In presenting its position on current political events, the tone employed by the UES was pedagogical, even arrogant. Concerning the elections of 1984: 'the UES considers it vital to indicate to the Salvadoran people that the current electoral process *can only be correctly interpreted* within the minimal framework of these political events'.[82] The same year, referring to the first round of negotiations between the Duarte government and the FMLN: 'Before the announcement of a dialogue between the Government of the Republic and the FDR- FMLN . . . the UES, *assuming once again its function as the critical conscience of the Salvadoran people*, presents the following reflections.'[83] In 1988, announcing its stance on the elections: 'The UES, in keeping with its function as society's critical conscience, considers incontestable its obligation to pronounce its views on the current electoral process; it does this so that the *citizens can orient themselves and analyse critically the country's reality*.'[84] And in January 1989, commenting on the political situation in the aftermath of an FMLN peace proposal: 'The UES [is] aware of its utmost responsibility as the *nation's moral and cultural guide*, as an integral part of the Salvadoran people, and with the full moral capacity and intellectual soundness to discuss and pass judgment upon the great and serious problems that burden the Salvadoran society.'[85]

The roots of the UES's political disposition are manifold – and too complex to be addressed in this limited essay. The early convergence between the university and the state has been highlighted, as has state dominance over cultural activities in El Salvador and Latin America. Iberian political culture is often cited by commentators to explain the recurrent quixotism of intellectuals, their concern for social issues, their elitism and their readiness to use arms against intruders or tyrants. Beyond the Iberian and/or Latin American political culture, the presumption of being the omniscient guide of humankind is shared with varying degrees of intensity by all manner of intellectuals around the world.

THE RADICAL LEFT IN POWER

The political situation is changing rapidly in El Salvador, but certain practices seem slower to change. Ever since its foundation, the UES has been, a mirror and an extension of the political scene. Since the 1960s it has grown more rigid and more politicised. While still reflecting some of the tensions that have torn Salvadoran society apart, it has been more and more a mirror, during this period, of the traumas that have distressed the radical left. True, the UES is still, four years after the signature of the peace agreement, the object of contempt and mistrust by the government and broad sectors of Salvadoran society. The recent scandal involving the selling of diplomas (summer 1995) did nothing to lesson this perception. Nevertheless the institution is doubtless ill at ease with the new values of openness and pluralism that have made some inroads in other sectors of society, including the FMLN and the army. The UES is a special and interesting case study because it is, after all, the only organisation in EI Salvador where one can observe the radical left *in power*.

Based on numerous interviews conducted from 1990 to 1995, both inside the university and outside (with former UES faculty members and students), it is possible to conclude that in the 1990s, virtually everybody has been aware of a malaise at the UES. This malaise is multifaceted, though it is based on a single overarching factor: the fact that the university is, and has been for many decades now, the site of endless power struggles, involving groups or factions who hide their personal rivalries behind arcane ideological struggles. All positions of power in the university – meaning the administration and the unions (representing faculty members, students, staff) – are held by people who are not only Marxist–Leninist, but who have an extremely low level of tolerance for people of other ideological persuasions. Moreover, during my interviews, countless individuals, including people who work at the UES and still defend its reputation, have alluded to a certain negative correlation between the level of politicisation and academic competence. Many faculty members have left the UES over the past fifteen years, primarily to escape the uncertainty and insecurity resulting from constant harassment, persecution and repression by the government. Many of them have found employment in the newly created private universities, where salaries are higher. Those faculty members who were not very politicised were the first to go, often with the encouragement of the UES authorities, for whom political commitment was more important than competence. The best professors, arguably, were recruited more quickly. It is logical to conclude that beyond a handful of exceptional cases, the administrators and faculty members who are still at the UES, in spite of low salaries (probably the lowest in the country for a professor) and after decades of hard-core political dogmatism, are the most politicised and least competent, hyper-politicisation being part of a strategy to compensate for lack of competence. This sounds terrible, but all the available evidence suggests that it is probably very close to the truth.

Take for instance the annual report produced by the former rector, Fabio Castillo[86] (a presidential candidate in 1967 and still a distinguished leader of the radical left). The words used by Castillo indicate how relations at the top were rife not only with frustration (a rather normal situation in universities), but also with anger.[87] According to Castillo, the vice-rector launched a vendetta against him almost immediately after taking office. She, according to Castillo, 'was out of her mind' (*se encontraba fuera de control mental*).[88] Both of them, needless to say, supported the FMLN; the issue in question was not ideology, though it was sometimes dressed up with ideological overtones. Opposition to Castillo involved the kind of electoral tactics that were used and abused in Stalinist regimes (or in regimes in the process of Stalinisation). The vice-rector's strategy consisted in mobilising the university's workers' union (ASTUES) against the rector, so that the revolt would seem to come from 'below'. The university's workers (that is, those in the workers' union) were granted, through a reform of the electoral system, 20–25 times more electoral power than the students, and almost twice as much as professors.[89] It may seem odd that the university ended up being administered by its blue-collar workers, most of whom had a very low level of education. But of course, the true story is merely that a certain group within the administration, together with leaders of the workers' union, conspired to get rid of the rector and the group he represented.

Castillo hints at administrative and academic problems that are usually dismissed by UES officials as reactionary propaganda. He presents data that leaves little doubt about problems such as the extraordinary time it takes to graduate (the UES seems to have many 'professional students' who never graduate), poor teaching and mediocre research. According to him, the UES 'despises... studies in both social sciences and natural sciences'.[90] What is more, 'the UES, as the people's and the state's institution of higher education, ought to be a model of efficient administration for the country. Unfortunately it isn't; instead it features a highly inefficient administrative apparatus.'[91] In a situation of budgetary crisis, for instance, 'the faculty of agronomy has the lowest number of students of any faculty... an average of three students for each administrative or service-oriented worker, as well as the highest ratio of workers to professors'.[92]

Castillo's report strongly suggests that these problems have plagued the university for a long time, and he does not sound optimistic about the chances of finding workable remedies with the current staff in the near future.

The group that fought Castillo and finally won the 'election' was the Movimiento de Concertación Universitaria (MCU). Its manifesto was short on concrete measures to improve the situation at the UES. There is no evidence that the MCU even recognised the magnitude of the problem.[93] Typically, it was rather long on its denunciation of neoliberalism, on the necessary relations between science and the objective development of productive forces, and other abstract and ideological matters. According to the MCU, the 'political project' of 1987 is still valid, although it will need some 'revision'. The style of the MCU is still confrontational, but one key statement indicates that beyond the rivalries there is room for common ground at the UES: 'now, more than ever before, the university will need to be the critical conscience of society in order to prevent any deviation from its integral democratisation'.[94] A bit of auto critique is clearly necessary if the UES is ever to overcome its deeply entrenched vanguardism and dogmatism.

* * *

The particularity of the UES's disposition lies in internal and external factors. The conviction that it is the people's critical conscience has been strengthened by (1) more than a century of virtual exclusivity as an institution of higher education; (2) successive generations of politicians entrusting the university to create or develop the nation; and (3), more recently, Marxist–Leninist ideology, which grants its believers a 'scientific' and exclusive access to 'reality'.

Two parallels can be drawn here. First, there is the obvious parallel between the UES's and the FMLN's ideological dispositions. Both have been marred by exactly the same brand of dogmatism and vanguardism. Second, the parallel between the events at the UES and the ones that shook the national political scene is striking. Both the UES and the military regime faced new demands and new institutional challenges in late 1960s and early 1970s. The state's response was both simple and counterproductive: it used repression. The UES allowed itself to be overwhelmed by its 'base', which resulted in a violent state reaction. Both the UES and the state proved incapable of flexibly responding to the challenges produced by decades of rapid and multifaceted social change. Underlying the ongoing confrontation between the state and the UES one finds a common and deeply rooted antipluralist (or monistic) and elitist disposition, as well as a congenital incapacity to conceive politics other than in a Manichean, eschatological and ultimately authoritarian way.

Clearly there is no justification whatsoever for the repression that took place at the UES throughout the internal war. But acknowledging this does not imply that scholars interested in understanding the dynamics of the internal war in El Salvador should disregard the fundamental contribution made by the UES in shaping both the insurgency itself and the messianic confrontation that terrorised the country for almost fifteen years.

5 The Catholic Church, Social Change and Insurrection

> Underlying any theological argument and, at the very roots of any polemic on God, one almost invariably finds men's interests and, very clearly, interests of power. (Cabarrús, 1983)

> Very soon the Central American University 'José Simeón Cañas' attempted to participate in the process of liberation of the Salvadoran people; that is, liberation from its situation of structural oppression. Hence its mission to attempt to be the critical and creative conscience of the Salvadoran reality. (Salvadoran Jesuits, 'Los Jesuitas ante el pueblo salvadoreño')

Observers agree that the Catholic Church has played a pivotal role in the recent political development of El Salvador.[1] More specifically, what is now known as the 'Popular Church' is widely viewed as a force, if not *the* force, behind the political mobilisation of the poor to support the insurgents' agenda. Thanks to radical priests and theology students, hitherto apathetic and conservative peasants and urban poor learned to identify the 'structural sin' of capitalism and started to yearn for a politico-religious version of the 'promised land'.[2] Alain Besançon once made the distinction that Moses and Saint John 'knew that they believed', while Marx and Lenin 'believed that they knew'.[3] By blurring this distinction – radical Christians know that they believe *and* believe that they know – the 'Christianisation' of the revolution conceivably produced an explosive mixture.

The hypothesis that the Church has been a significant force behind the political mobilisation of the poor makes a lot of sense for at least three reasons. First, it is well known that the Church has played a key role in the political development of the whole region over the past five centuries. Chapter 4 highlighted the early convergence of the state, the university and the Church in a common project of nation building.

Second, priests are natural leaders in popular communities, where lay intellectuals have little access or authority. 'Intellectual priests' (such as Jesuits at the UCA and the Externado San José) are, as historian Jean Meyer points out, 'the only intellectuals who are close to the popular masses', by virtue of their priestly function.[4] An FPL leader readily recognised that, 'because many of us came from the Social-Christian sector… it was easy for us to reach out to the peasants'.[5] To formulate the argument in Gino Germani's sociological terms, the Church was one of the few organisations able to bring about a 'primary' political mobilisation in Latin America: that is, a mobilisation favouring the political inclusion of social sectors previously excluded from the polity (roughly, the poor).[6] The Church has also, to continue with Germani's terminology, been one of the most efficient catalysts of 'secondary' political mobilisation: that is, the mobilisation of sectors at one time included in the polity but displaced or destabilised by social change (the middle sectors, unionised workers and so on).

Third, the Church's time-honoured practice of participating in the ruling of Latin American societies and its unique mobilisational capabilities were conceivably stimulated by yet another factor: the propagation of the Theology of Liberation in the late 1960s and 1970s. This latter factor allowed the Church to bridge the gap between the insurgents of the time: Marxist–Leninist students and radicalised activists in unions and other grass-roots organisations.[7] Interestingly enough, the radical Church's trajectory of activity paralleled that of Leninist activism in the universities: emerging during the 1960s, radicalisation levelled off during the 1970s and declined during the 1980s; and this happened simultaneously in most Latin American countries.

Those on the Catholic left never relinquished their premodern longing for a 'civilisation of poverty'. The realm of necessity is not an alienating though necessary step towards abundance and liberty. Rather it is a constraint on human nature and an invitation to spiritual values. These values must be the foundation stone of the new society. Clearly a priest-led *gemeinschaft* geared to an economy of subsistence was not exactly – at least not in theory – compatible with the aspirations of the Catholic left's 'atheist' allies, for whom economic progress was a sacred cow. Nevertheless they easily found a common mind-set, a sort of theology/theory of antiliberalism that clearly overrode any discrepancy in their images of the shape of future society.[8] As a matter of fact, it turned out that Catholics in the FMLN were the most reluctant to shift from an agenda of 'liberation' to electoral politics.[9]

MOBILISING THE PEOPLE

Surprisingly little is known about the Church's impact on the emergence and development of the insurgency. Assumptions are made about the Church's role in the masses' 'conversion' to a radical ideology and a disposition to rebel, but supporting evidence remains scant. One must certainly accept the possibility that the influence of the Church was a pivotal factor in the emergence and development of insurgency among the masses. But after fifteen years of attention to this aspect of the internal war, it is certainly revealing that the scholarship is still so poor on the subject.

Perhaps, as Jorge Castañeda remarked, 'the importance of the grass roots religious movements in Latin America has been both *idealized* and *exaggerated*'.[10] Which brings me back to the 'dominant paradigm' and its impact on scholarship. To be sure, part of the Church became radicalized in the late 1960s, and it is true that in the late 1970s Archbishop Oscar Romero became an advocate of social and political change, leaving behind the anti-Marxist disposition he had displayed in the first half of the decade.[11] It is also true that the 'Christian base communities' (or CEBs) probably converted a number of poor to radical politics. Most of the insurgents who were demobilised in 1992 were Catholic and religious. And it is true that the leaders of some (Catholic) unions and peasant organisations joined the leadership of insurgent or semi-insurgent groups in the mid-1970s.

However most Salvadoran peasants were (and still are) both Catholic and religious, so it is hardly an independent variable that can explain why just some, and not most of the others, joined the insurgency. None of the above mentioned factors constitute evidence that the Church and/or the popular sectors played a leading role in the emergence of insurgency in El Salvador.

In order to address the problem systematically, one should distinguish between at least two categories of Church influence: (1) the Church's influence in the politicisation of the poor; that is, the urban poor as well as countryside-based actors such as landless or land-poor peasants and agricultural workers; and (2) the Church's influence in the politicisation of the urban middle class – mostly students.

Mobilising the Poor

The politicisation of the poor is most certainly overemphasised (again, not only from the point of view of the Church's influence), as Castañeda (1994) has perceptively pointed out. The revolutionary poor, even the ones mobilised primarily and initially on a religious as opposed to a strictly political basis, find a niche in the dominant paradigm. Revolutionary students and other middle-class militants can only be tagged as the coattail of the 'real' agents of history.

Most analysts who emphasise the radicalisation of the poor, and the influence of the Church in encouraging such radicalisation, seem willing to limit their investigation to a cursory review of second-hand literary evidence. The existence of radical priests in El Salvador is unquestionable. They even achieved some institutional status during the war, with the creation of the Conferencia Nacional de la Iglesia Popular (CONIP) in 1980.[12] But first-hand research material on the radical mobilisation of the poor in the cities during the 1970s and the early 1980s is all but non-existent, and first-hand research material on rural insurgency in general (that is, mobilised by the Popular Church or not) can be found in only a few books and articles. One looks in vain for a comprehensive study showing how, when and to what extent the Church and/or the poor from the countryside contributed to the emergence of insurgency in the 1970s, or even to the spreading of insurgency in the countryside during the early 1980s. No work goes beyond an extrapolation of particular cases that are limited in both time and space. What one almost invariably finds is the same cursory emphasis on the CEBs and the Christian Federation of Salvadoran peasants (FECCAS), a Catholic peasant union whose organisational and political strength *fell* during the mutually reenforcing cycle of radicalisation and repression of the early 1970s.[13]

One of the few presumably comprehensive publications on the 'genesis' of the internal war in El Salvador is the oft-quoted book written by a priest: Carlos Rafael Cabarrus.[14] He emphasises the role of the CEBs and the peasant union FECCAS, but looks at only a few municipalities or municipal agglomerations: one in the west (the coffee region, virtually impermeable to insurgents throughout the war), one in the south-east (the cotton region, virtually impermeable to rebels until the mid 1980s), and the suburban region of Aguilares, located a few kilometers north of San Salvador. Aguilares is the favourite example of all observers, for it was the scene of the most famous – indeed one of the few – CEB experiments in El Salvador. Officially led by a Salvadoran priest (Rutilio Grande), which in itself was a departure from the rule,[15] the experiment ended tragically after only few months, when the army assassinated Grande and two of his aides on 12 March 1977.

In one of the few serious works published on 'revolutionary peasants' in El Salvador, Douglas Kincaid contends that a 'community-solidarity' approach helps elucidate why peasants do or do not engage in rebellion and radical politics, and he explores the few case studies that do exist. According to Kincaid, 'what made the sugar belt a fertile zone for the

Catholic left was the persistence of localized peasant solidarities, around which the Christian Base Communities could be organized'.[16] Unfortunately it is no easier to find convincing evidence to support this hypothesis than for any other in which the basic assumption is that revolt comes initially and primarily *from* the countryside.

By and large, virtually none of the most commonly quoted books on the Salvadoran internal war have strayed away from the relatively meagre information found in *Génesis de una revolución* (Cabarrus, 1983), a few publications on the development of unions proposed by Salvadoran social scientists and/or militants, and the few first-hand testimonies on the pilot project of Aguilares. Even in the limited number of cases that were seriously documented, it could only be *assumed* that (1) a significant number of grass-roots members of the CEBs and FECCAS (later the UTC) did seize arms, or at least supported the insurgency in a significant way during the 1970s and early 1980s; and (2) that the political mobilisation triggered by these organisations was sufficiently self-sustainable over time to have more than a fleeting impact on the initial development of the insurgency.

Mobilising the Middle Class

The first locus of influence, and in my view the most significant – the Church's influence in the politicisation of the middle class – is overwhelmingly neglected by most analysts. However, the *indirect* influence of the Church in the politicisation of the urban middle class sectors *through political parties* is fairly well documented. One of the best books available on modern politics in El Salvador deals with the creation of the Christian Democratic Party (PDC).[17] The PDC split in 1980 as a result of a compromise made by the PDC leader, Napoleon Duarte, with the military (he accepted a leading position in the civil–military junta after most of the civilians had resigned). What was first known as the Popular Tendency (TP) in the PDC became the Social Christian Popular Movement (MPSC), one of the two major components of the

FDR.[18] The MPSC leader, Rubén Zamora, was (and is) one of the most able and articulate politicians in the country and the FMLN presidential candidate during the general elections of 1995.

Of these two parties – the PDC and the MPSC – only the latter was involved in the insurgency. Its very existence testified how some sectors of the political class had indeed been radicalised by the conflict, while the reconstructed PDC under Duarte feruently espoused the counterinsurgency plan (including socioeconomic reforms) promoted by the US. Nonetheless the MPSC remained a small political vehicle for disenchanted Christian Democratic *politicians* – it was never a mass party, let alone a social or political movement. There is no evidence that it ever mobilised significant sectors of the population in support of the insurgency project. Its main function in the FDR was, as pointed out in Chapter 3, essentially diplomatic. It was supposed to bridge the gap between the insurgency and the political class. Both the FDR and the FMLN failed to achieve this important task.

Far more important for the politicisation of urban middle class was the mobilisation of students and youths through the UCA, the Externado San José, and the various Catholic youth and lay organisations (such as Justice and Peace). Because these youths – and quite a few professors – tended to be much more militant and radical than, say, dissident Christian Democratic politicians, they had much more of an impact on the emergence and development of insurgency, something that is typically overlooked by analysts.

* * *

In sum, the available evidence does not allow us to assert much more than the following propositions: (1) the countryside was the scene of the expansion of the insurgency, not the scene of its emergence; (2) only a tiny minority of rural dwellers joined the insurgency, mostly young men and teenagers, and this as a result of a multiple set of incentives, most of which probably resulted from the war itself; (3) all the insurgents' testimonies attest to the influence of Catholic institutions in the political mobilisation of middle-class youths, but there is insufficient evidence (in spite of towering paradigmatic interest in that direction), to prove that Catholic institutions or lay organisations contributed *decisively* to shepherding the poor in a radical and insurrectional direction; and (4) the idealised and exaggerated importance that most analysts bestow on grass-roots participation in the emergence of the insurgency and the Church's role in prompting this participation, stems from dogmatic application of an ideologically stimulating but empirically flimsy dominant paradigm.

One more dimension of the insurgency deserves our close attention before the specific case of the UCA can be discussed: that is, the nature of the relations between Catholic and Marxist–Leninist elements on the one hand, and the nature of the relations between radical Catholic leaders and the people on the other.[19]

VANGUARDISM

Tommie Sue Montgomery contends that, 'given the large number of Christians in the revolution, *one must assume* that there is a dialectical process by which the ideology of the revolution is being formed and that it is incorporating many of those principles'.[20] The 'dialectical process' is a grass-roots, bottom-up process of mobilisation in which the Popular Church plays a subsidiary though fundamental role. Still, evidence suggests that for years the insurgent groups viewed the Catholic left with a great deal of mistrust.

During the 1970s, Catholic popular organisations (in fact *most* popular organisations) were hijacked by the emerging politico-military vanguards, who were not particularly respectful of either the autonomy of these groups or their distinct set of ideologies.[21] In itself, this does not invalidate the probable contribution of these sectors to the emergence of the insurgency, but it casts doubt over the dominant paradigm's assumption that insurgents were the political manifestation of simmering grass-roots' trends.

What is more, there is certainly a correlation – though for lack of evidence it cannot be called a relation of causality – between (1) the radicalisation of grass-roots Catholic organisations; (2) their rapprochement with the politico-military organisations; (3) the repression to which they were the victim; and (4) their organisational decline during the 1970s. Repression is conceivably the single-most important factor in explaining the decline of the CEBs at the end of the 1970s. Nevertheless the whole experience of the Popular Church in Latin America, especially if analysed in a comparative perspective (with the rise of Protestant churches for instance), suggests that the radicalisation and politicisation of the religious discourse, with heavy borrowing from the discourse of social sciences, probably made contact with the popular sectors *more*, not less, difficult.[22] Far from coming *from* the aggrieved (the poor), radical ideology was brought *to* them. The attitude of the FPL towards the FECCAS during the 1970s provides a telling illustration of this disposition. According to one of its leaders:

> Concerning our work in the countryside, our organisation started to have an influence on the FECCAS, at that time led by the Christian Democracy and the Catholic Church, although the FAPU already enjoyed some ascendancy in it. The FPL's effort consisted in reorienting the FECCAS. This was meant to liberate it from the influence of the Christian Democracy and from the Catholic Church, in order to assume it as an FPL project, and at the same time to take it away from the FAPU.[23]

Another FPL leader remembers that in the 1970s 'there were many good conditions that were met in order to appeal to sectors of the population influenced by Christian Democracy or deceived by it, but our politics were very sectarian…we accepted only our option as the true revolutionary alternative'.[24] The FPL welcomed Catholics but they had to put their religiosity on the back burner and follow a 'scientific line' – that is, the Marxist–Leninist line.[25] Neither the FAPU, the ERP nor the RN, all of which purportedly blossomed from the stalwart Catholic left, produced communiqués where Catholicism was conspicuous in either content or form. Their manifestoes were always indistinguishable from the ones produced by other radical organisations, as though a single mould was uniformly adopted. This, far from suggesting that the insurgency emerged as the ultimate rallying point of sundry popular organisations and movements (ideologically syncretic by definition), clearly implies that the logic of insurgency building was top-down and commanded by a homogeneous faction of ideologically articulate individuals.

The CEBs

One more comment should be made about the relations of power within the Popular Church. If during the 1970s the relations between the politico-military organisations and the grass-roots movement on the one hand, and between the former and the Catholic organisations on the other, were marked by verticalism, paternalism and caudillism, a similar pattern can be identified within the Catholic movement itself. Most relevant testimonies on religious and political missions among the people highlight the journey of uplifted missionaries who, forsaking the comfort of their homes, set out to discover the impoverished masses, their language and traditions, creating an atmosphere of mutual trust that was vital to their mission: that is, converting the poor to a new set of religious and political ideas. For this delicate operation, according to an FPL leader:

> [the work of Paulo] Freire influenced us a lot. We really put his method into practice in the countryside as well as the method used by the Church in its social projection work through *Justicia y Paz*, and with the CEBs. What happened exactly? They would go there, in a community, and they would immediately give you a course on becoming a

> promoter, on learning the group's dynamic, for instance initiating a discussion on a record, a book or a movie. This would force one to understand what was going on in the place and what were the people's thoughts.[24]

A good example of paternalism can be found in the CEB experience. Although CEBs are portrayed by their promoters as essentially grass-roots organisations, what is missed is that the 'resocialisation of the people' undertaken by priests in the CEBs was essentially a top-down enterprise, rooted in the time-honoured tradition of the Church's (and elite's) penetration of the 'peripheral', unintegrated sectors of society.[27] This should not be understood as a criticism of CEBs: they were certainly beneficial in many ways, namely in uprooting the political apathy that too often characterised the marginalised sectors of Latin American society. The point here is to understand the *logic* of 'CEB building' from a mobilisation of resources perspective.

Much has been written about the CEB experience, attempted in many Latin American countries in the late 1960s and 1970s. A CEB usually involved a group of individuals, mostly from the poorer strata of the population, being mobilised by one or several animators (mostly educated priests or middle-to-upper-class students). The purpose of the CEB was to discuss religious, and often social and political issues.[28] The perspective was shaped by the recommendations of the Second Vatican Council and Medellín, and by dominant discourses in social sciences (essentially, during that period in El Salvador, dependency theory and Marxism–Leninism).[29]

For most of these animators the countryside was a *terra incognita*, where they literally 'landed' as missionaries.[30] Not all the CEB experiments in Latin America were particularly 'politicised' and left wing,[31] but the Salvadoran CEBs were. For as Carlos Rafael Cabarrús asserts, 'religious conversion' remained incomplete if it did not include the 'political conversion' of the poor.[32]

The first CEB in El Salvador were launched in Suchitoto in 1969 and in the region of Aguilares in 1972.[33] Two Salvadorans,

José Alas and Rutilio Grande, both recently graduated from a seminary in Quito, Ecuador, were among the initial pioneers. Grande was named parish priest at Aguilares on 22 September 1972, the village were he had been born and raised in a prominent family (his father was a member of the military government's official party, the PCN). Later some other priests (nationals and foreigners), as well as theology students from the UCA, flocked to Aguilares to help set up a CEB pilot project. The Jesuit Ivan D. Paredes describes the initiation of the first CEBs, in the following terms: 'Originally, they [the CEBs] were born out of the initiative of many priests, whose intention was certainly to *raise the communities to adulthood* [*dar la mayoría de edad a las comunidades*].'[34] With regard to the *conscientización* (raising the awareness) of the peasants, Cabarrús explains that 'all the elegant and complicated words were explained slowly [to the peasants], pretty much in the way that the catechism was taught to the Indians during the conquest. In a very short period of time the peasants started to use continuously and with ease words that were not previously part of their vocabulary.'[35] The attitude behind this approach parallels the innate sense of authority and paternalism felt by urban middle-class insurgents when in contact with the masses.[36]

According to Salvador Carranza, who participated actively in the setting up of CEBs in Aguilares, the immediate task of the missionaries was to familiarise themselves with the targeted community. An 'anthropological data-base of the place' (geographical, social, economic, political and religious data) was put in place – a strategy that conjures up memories of the Council of the Indies. This data-base was then used to identify 'the basic themes... to which one had to find the corresponding decoding in the New Testament'.[37] Based on this data collection, the population of Aguilares was classified as 'dependent, alienated and oppressed'.[38] It was also incumbent upon the missionaries to visit the people in their homes and to organise public meetings, in order to create 'an ambiance of trust'. During these meetings the missionaries took notes on attendance and participation, in order to identify 'delegates of words' who 'would emerge as locally born leaders'.[39] After the first contacts and some preliminary meetings it was necessary to 'reach a certain uniformity in the scheme and the stages followed in the celebration of the Word'. Hence the missionaries and their delegates were required to take what the author calls an introductory course [*curso de nivelación*].[40] The delegates' training ended with a training session in San Salvador, coordinated by priests and students from the UCA. This kind of training session was also encouraged for the leaders of other organisations such as the FECCAS.

The themes of the CEB discussions can be summarised as follows:[41] 'announcing a new man who is the denouncer of the exploiter and the consciousness of the exploited'; 'the evacuation of established ideas...in order to receive new ones'; 'consciousness [awareness]: constant critical attitude in a dialectical unity of "action-reflection"'; 'to give priority to the marginalised and to the communities over the individual'. Carranza also lists the CEBs' tangible results: 'great discovery of the Gospel'; 'they [the people] soon learn to associate the Gospel with the situation in which they live'; 'they progressively realise that the way things are is not the result of God's will'.[42]

To celebrate the Aguilares experiment the missionaries organised a popular festival, the 'festival of the corn'. The basic organisation of the festivities was entrusted to the grass-roots, but several criteria had to be respected: everything had to be related to the community, not the individual; money ought not be an important factor; the festival should be one of 'protest and hope'.[43] In a way this festival engendered an atmosphere that was analogous to that in the 'liberated zones' of the insurgency. In both cases there was an element of utopia, a general rehearsal for the 'new beginning', a controlled social fusion involving a 'community' organised according to strong principles and authoritative leadership. The utopia of the egalitarian community, with neither avarice nor *luxuria*, led by charismatic lower-order priests was hardly new in the history of Christianity. One can find evidence of this in the Spanish Catholic Church in the sixteenth and the seventeenth centuries, and of course in the famous Jesuit-led religious communities (*reducciones*) in Paraguay in the seventeenth and eighteent centuries (which incidentally were praised in the 1930s by exponents of one of the dominant antiliberal currents of the time: fascism). As Gerald Brenan has indicated, this Jesuit- led communitarian and theocratic experiment could be seen as the 'first communist state founded by Europeans'.[44]

Daudelin and Hewitt encapsulate the nature of the new relationship between the Popular Church and the masses by calling it a transition from the 'authoritarianism of fear to the authoritarianism of love'.[45] One could take issue with this, but they are certainly right to question (from a sociological point of view) the grass-roots romanticism that has surrounded the Popular Church in Latin America. What is too often overlooked is 'the weight of the Vatican's history, tradition and hierarchical structures', from which CEBs never really departed.[46] The romantic position, so consonant with the dominant paradigm, also typically underestimates the nature of the mobilisation commanded by the Popular Church. For all the participatory and populist style of the CEBs and other Catholic popular organisations, one invariably finds a clear sense of leadership, in addition to a manifest division of labour between the mobilised masses on the one hand and the urban-born, ideologically harmonious, activist leaders on the other. This certainly doesn't imply anything reprehensible from a moral or political standpoint, but it contradicts one of the dominant paradigm's basic assumptions about the roots of revolt in El Salvador.

If one had to locate the leading insurgents, the Catholic left and the masses on a mobilisation scale, the dominant paradigm would certainly place the masses as the driving force, the Catholic priests and lay organisations second, with the leading insurgents closing this bottom-up process of 'reflection-action' (thinking and action). For the seeds of revolt came from the aggrieved who, after fruitless attempts to promote radical change through non-violent means, finally resigned themselves to radical politics (even Marxism–Leninism) and urban insurgency. The evidence demonstrates that the leading insurgents considered themselves the vanguard of the vanguard, poaching on the *cúpulas* (leadership) of the Catholic left to 're-socialise' them in a 'scientific' way, and attempting through them (with relatively little success) to mobilise the masses according to arcane (from the illiterate masses' viewpoint) and dogmatic ideological principles.

We shall now look at the Catholic Central American University 'José Simeón Cañas' as one more example of how the Popular Church's verticalism, paternalism and desire for power influenced the recent political evolution of El Salvador.

THE CENTRAL AMERICAN UNIVERSITY 'JOSÉ SIMEÓN CAÑAS'

> The University, and especially the Catholic university, must be the laboratory where new models of society, more just and more Christian, are created. Its stand for the poor is formalised in the denunciation of structural sin and in the elaboration of new models, forming men, professional or not, who will be able to transform this society so that it will benefit all, and especially the poorest. (Segundo Montes, 'Las Universidades Católicas en América Latina')

The relatively small Central American University 'José Simeón Cañas' (UCA) of El Salvador has probably played a much more important role in the political scene of that country than any other Catholic university in Latin America (for example, the UCA in Managua, Nicaragua). Priests, intellectuals, insurgents and ministers (not to mention foreigners interested in the Salvadoran 'reality') sought information and advice from UCA Jesuits, arguably the most distinguished intellectuals in the country and *the* specialists of *la realidad*. The UCA achieved a rare feat: it was close to both the seat of power and its counterpower.

Studying its structure and its ideological disposition is essential to understanding not only the insurgency and the Catholic left, but also the logic of political development in El Salvador.

Throughout the 1980s, right-wing sectors of Salvadoran society portrayed the UES as a hotbed of guerrilla activity, whereas the UCA was portrayed as the insurgency's *eminence grise*. It is hard to escape the impression that the far right hated the UCA even more than the UES, this because of a number of interlocking factors. First, the UCA was led by 'foreigners' from Spain (the extreme right is very chauvinistic). Second, it was run by Jesuits. Third, it always enjoyed a good reputation, both in EI Salvador and abroad, thus making it a much more credible and daunting opponent than the UES. Fourth, the UES was consistent in and quite transparent about its support for the insurgency, whereas the UCA, by maintaining institutional and some ideological distance from the FMLN, remained a more elusive opponent. Fifth, the UCA was a vocal and articulate advocate of negotiation and peace, two blasphemous words in the extreme right's dictionary. Extremists always prefer a polarised situation, with nobody in the middle trying to 'deceive' the people.

The Magisterium

The UCA was founded in 1965 by conservative elites of strong political will in order to offer a Catholic, anticommunist university as an alternative to the increasingly radical national university. In 1964 the journal *Estudios Centroamericanos* (*ECA*), then the property of the Society of Jesus, published the following advertisement:

> Send your child to a Catholic university.
> The lay [public] university cannot raise your son into a full-grown man.
> An atheist professor, unconcerned, procommunist, may deform his personality for ever.

The founders, conservative Jesuits, were soon ousted by a younger generation of Jesuits, exponents of the nascent theology of liberation.[47] The new progressive political line was publicly proclaimed in 1970; typically, along with the announcement of an important loan granted by the Inter-American Development Bank.[48]

During the 1970s and 1980s the UCA's political orientation was dictated by a handful of Jesuit leaders, though formally the university was run by a rector and a five-member board of directors.[49] In contrast with the pattern commonly found in public universities in Latin America, the 'radicalisation' of the UCA did not result from pressure from below (that is, students); the contest typically took place at the top, among the leaders. In spite of some divisions among the faculty members[50] and the student body, the UCA liked to speak with one voice: dissenters or lukewarm supporters usually kept their opinions to themselves.[51] In contrast with the UES, the faculty members were not unionised and there is no evidence of dissatisfaction with this situation (for one thing the UCA professors were the best remunerated in the country.) All the same the students were not encouraged to form autonomous organisations, let alone political organisations.[52] In contrast with the UES, the UCA granted little power to its student body in the management of the university. This was openly acknowledged in a handbook published by the university: 'the UCA's conception of the university mission does not focus primarily on the student'.[53] Although the UCA openly sought to convert students into agents of social change, it feared student activism, considered a plague in Latin American public universities. Again the UCA handbook outlined this very clearly: 'One cannot underestimate the potential danger that [student activism] might represent for the smooth running of the university, [with] groups of students firmly resolved not to collaborate with it'.[54] If any connections were to be made with political organisations outside the campus, they had to be made by those at the top, by the university's proper authorities.

For some observers, the fact that most of the students came from the middle and upper classes explains the relative absence of student activism and extreme politicisation at the UCA. UES spokespersons have seldom resisted pointing out the social difference between this 'Catholic' and 'private' institution and their own public institution, in order to explain the latter's radical orientation.[55] As a matter of fact there is probably a correlation here, but hardly a relation of causality: most of the FMLN leaders who were mobilised at the UES were from urban, middle-class backgrounds. The UCA was still a new and relatively small university during the 1970s, and was consequently not in a position to enjoy virtual monopoly in the recruitment of middle to upper-class students. Finally, as already made clear, UCA leaders would not let their university be taken over by any outside political organisation.

In sum, in contrast with the UES, where faculty members, administrators, students and even staff were organised and/or unionised along radical political and corporatist lines, thus generating permanent political struggles within an essentially monistic (but not monolithic) power structure, the UCA was clearly led by a handful of (often charismatic) leaders who controlled both the administration and the composition and reproduction of the official politics of the university.

The UES was more democratic in the sense that power was shared by the different components of the university community: administration, faculty members, students and staff. On the other hand there is no shortage of evidence to support the view that the democratic structures within the UES were routinely manipulated by a handful of well-organised and highly partisan groups, to the exclusion of everybody else. If the UES was democratic, it was a 'popular democracy' in the historical (that is, not in the idealised) sense. So much so that in reality it would be difficult to demonstrate how the UCA was more elitist and monistic than the national university. The UES was permanently ruled like a communist country during an interregnum period; as in the USSR after the death of Lenin, when personal rivalries and competition for power were hidden behind turgid rhetoric. The UCA, on the other hand, was ruled like the Roman Catholic Church, featuring a highly centralised power wrapped in a charismatic magisterium, some mandatory social rituals, and a great deal of scope for (or organisational impotence to deal with) day-to-day, private departures from the official dogma. Conversely both institutions wished to participate in the historical mission of social change in El Salvador. Their diagnosis of the Salvadoran *realidad* was usually the same. Having in common a solid antiliberal foundation and an unmistakable sense of leadership, the UCA and the UES (the Catholic left and Marxist–Leninists) were able to go a long way along the same path, towards the university-led liberation of the Salvadoran people.

Towards Social Change

The UCA's ideology rested on one basic source of inspiration (a radical Christian inspiration) and one distinct strategy (social projection). The UCA was not a 'Catholic' university in the traditional sense, like the Evangelical University or the Don Bosco University. As Jon Sobrino, a prominent theologian at the UCA, pointed out, the Christian mission of the university 'cannot be measured in terms of religious practices'. Indeed, what mattered was the impact the university had on society, in order to shape it according to the ideals of the 'realm of God'.[56] The emphasis was not placed on meditation but on 'will' and 'action'. For all its rhetoric on the primitive Christians, theology of liberation is a *bona fide* twentieth-century ideology. The 'prophecy' celebrates the collectivist ideal against the capitalist 'reality', the *homines novi* against the *homo economicus*, 'civilisation of poverty' against 'civilisation of wealth', integral 'liberation' against narrowly defined democratisation and liberalisation. Utopia is not really a third option, but a steamy call for the eradication of liberal principles and practices in society.[57]

The strategy of 'social projection', a true *leitmotiv* of the UCA, made possible this conjugation of the Christian mission with a clear desire to foster social and political change, within the context of the specific function of the university.

Social Projection

The UCA shared with many universities throughout the world the desire to 'transform society'.[58] Although most universities do include service to the community as one of their missions, it is clear that, in the case of the UCA, university extension was primarily geared towards 'real' political change. The specific name for this kind of activity – *social projection* – was relatively new to political discourse in El Salvador, but it has since been adopted by all universities in the country.[59]

The concept of social projection was of course part of a more comprehensive discourse on the role of the Church – and in particular, of Jesuits – in society. In May 1968 Latin American Jesuits held a conference in Rio de Janeiro that produced a number of resolutions substantially more radical than the ones adopted three months later in Medellín, Colombia, by the Latin American Episcopal Conference (CELAM). The Rio declaration conveyed very clearly the Jesuits's intention to wade deeper into the different strongholds of power in Latin American society – the Jesuits, Octavio Paz (1993) argues, are the 'Bolsheviks of Catholicism'. Amongst the most salient points was the Jesuits' desire to end their 'isolation'. For all their declared intention to shed their 'image of power', the lay people targeted by the Jesuits' new strategy were clearly the shakers and movers of society: intellectuals, business persons, union leaders, professionals and politicians. Their resolve to use any available social position as a springboard for social change was reaffirmed during the Oaxtepec meeting in 1971:

> An extraordinary sphere of activity and a new style of education of unsuspected magnitude are now available to all Jesuits in Latin America. Beginning with natural associations – such as the family, or civic, religious, cultural and sports-related associations, and so on – that already exist; using all social means of communication as well as the multiple latent education-related resources that exist in each region and each community, our education can achieve

> incredible goals in a perspective of change, overcoming the rigidity of traditional institutions of education.[60]

Universities and colleges, where Jesuits had arguably left their most commendable imprint during their journey in Latin America, were especially focused upon because of their 'decisive importance in planning change in our society'.[61] As a matter of fact the UCA defined social projection as 'a function through which university activities have a direct effect on social change'.[62] This function was clearly of far greater priority than the two other traditional functions (although the three of them were defined as part of the same enterprise of social change): research for its own sake and, especially, teaching.[63] This was plainly stated by a former president of the university, Ignacio Ellacuria, who contended that 'projection and research' are 'typically progressive' whereas 'teaching' is 'typically retrograde'.[64] The opportunity to producing agents of social transformation is what reconciled the UCA with its teaching mission.

The function of 'social projection' was based on one assumption: the fundamental injustice underlying Salvadoran society, and the urgent need to turn this situation around. In a discourse commemorating the tenth anniversary of the UCA, the then president of the university, Román Mayorga Quiroz, said:

> We are of the opinion that in reality we in live in a radically unjust society. It is therefore necessary to carry out a global social process of liberation from structural oppression, whose roots are to be found in the socioeconomic class system, a system that is neither productive nor congenial to solidarity and which we have inherited from colonial times, perpetuated throughout one hundred and four years of independence.[65]

Mayorga Quiroz also contended that 'the interests of the oligarchy are the antithesis of the interests of the majority... This is one more reason why the UCA's fundamental commitment ought to be to oppose the class interests of the oligarchy, which lead to the exploitation, domination and marginalisation of the popular masses.'[66] In a study conducted by a team from the UCA, social projection was presented according to objectives dealing with the 'structural transformation of society; this means that its activities are not fundamentally oriented towards transforming individuals, but towards transforming the structures of society'.[67] Indeed the UCA 'must orient itself according to the structural elements of society, and not according to particular events... no matter how absorbing they may appear at one point or another'.[68]

The transformation of society must target three 'infrastructural' goals: 'First, a project for the nation; second, the need for leaders, formed and motivated to bring about its realisation; and third, a lucid awareness amongst the masses of the necessity for and the nature of this project.'[69] The contribution of the university to the formulation of the project was fundamental since, as Mayorga Quiroz pointed out, without a clear project, scientifically outlined by the university, 'we will be at the mercy of demagoguery, and of improvised and unscientific solutions'.[70]

What the UCA theologian Jon Sobrino has called the 'university-led liberation of the Salvadoran people' was a paradoxical enterprise, since it was both populist and self-consciously 'elitist'.[71] For Sobrino, favouring of the poor 'does not necessarily mean – and for a university this is practically impossible – that the university should have a physical and geographical presence amongst the poor'. Neither could it be limited to a change in the student body, favouring society's poorest. Rather it meant that 'the world of the poor has entered into the university, that the real problematic of the poor is taken into account as something central and that from this problematic the social reality is reckoned with, along with its legitimate interests, because they are the interests of the poor'.[72] Mayorga Quiroz justified the UCA's elitism as follows:

> We must recognise – even though it is difficult – that there is in all this [that is, in the UCA agenda] an... elitist perspective, even though it is not understood in the traditional and oppressive way. Our only justification for

> this resides in two observations: (a) we do not know, nor can we foresee for the next ten years, a magisterial perspective that would not be elitist in the socio- cultural context of Central America; (b) it would be naive to pretend that one can realise a project of liberation and social transformation in this century without leaders.[73]

Another UCA top official, Luis de Sebastián, had little doubt that social transformation must be undertaken with a clear division of labour between the university vanguard and the rearguard (the rest of the population):

> a barely literate peasant can paint the walls [that is, cover the walls with graffiti]. On the other hand a peasant can not analyse reality from a theoretical perspective. This must be done by university people, because this kind of analysis can change the social structure... [W]hen university people go on painting the walls they do not respect the division of labour and end up being not very efficient in the overall struggle for social change. Still, there is something that only university people can do: profound analysis, and the elaboration of solutions.[74]

To put it bluntly, social projection was 'popular' in the sense that the 'problematic' defined by the scientific vanguard was basically socialist. Social projection, not only at the UCA but also at the UES and other institutions, was beneficial to many communities throughout the nation. All kinds of projects involving students and faculty members alike were put in place, in a fashion that did not depart significantly from the traditional 'service to the community' sponsored by universities all around the world. But what the leaders actually had in mind was a much more dramatic structural endeavour.

The Temptation of Power

The UCA was implicated in all the political debates that convulsed the nation. As early as 1969 the UCA was invited to participate in a national conference organised by the military government of Fidel Sánchez Hernández (1967–72). The theme of the conference – agrarian reform – could hardly have been more politically sensitive. The implications were not missed by the UCA leadership, who were quick to note the meaning of this invitation for such a 'young and vigorous institution'. Only four years after its foundation, the UCA was being awarded public recogniton.[75] The war with Honduras in 1969 and then the presidential elections of 1972 (marred by fraud and military intervention) provided more opportunities for the UCA to make its presence felt in the political debate. In fact the first issue of the *ECA* as the cultural and intellectual vehicle of the UCA, rather than a vehicle of the Society of Jesus, was devoted to the infamous 'soccer war' with Honduras. In the summer of 1973, in a special issue of the *ECA* devoted to the question of agrarian reform, an editorial stated that 'our vocation as a university compels us to be present in the clarification, programming and development of any type of agrarian reform that might be implemented in our country'.[76] The UCA's expertise on agrarian reform was solicited again by the military government of Arturo Molina (1972–76). Molina was, of all the military presidents who ruled El Salvador from 1931 to 1979, the keenest to take on the landed oligarchy and to try to transform the agrarian structure.[77] He failed.

In 1973, technocrats from the Administración de Bienestar Campesino (ABC), as well as members of the armed forces, participated in seminars on agrarian reform organised by the UCA.[78] In 1972 the UCA's position on Molina's illegitimate seizure of power betrayed a cautiousness that had all but disappeared by the end of the decade: 'it is not incumbent upon us to take a position on such serious accusations. We prefer to bestow upon the qualified authorities the benefit of our trust.'[79] In 1976 the UCA supported Molina's agrarian transformation programme, and even called on the army to contribute to its realisation.[80]

This prudence should not be construed as a sign of fading resolve *vis-à-vis* its socio-political mission. In a special issue of the *ECA* entitled 'A revolutionary university or revolution in the University?', the UCA reaffirmed its intention to be proactive in the political debate. In the face of growing right-wing criticism of the UCA's 'political interference' (a criticism backed up by bombs), the UCA asserted that 'We are now more convinced than ever that this is the path we must follow as academics.'[81] In a special monograph entitled *El Salvador 1971–72, año político*, published by the UCA Research Institute, the UCA explicitly affirmed its intention to exercise 'democratic control' of the government.[82] In conformity with this, new political science courses in 1974 were purposely designed to prepare 'men and women [to be] scientifically capable and in human solidarity with the people'.[83] During the same year the UCA offered a 'seminar of political formation' to leaders of the FECCAS.[84]

In the late 1970s one of the most distinguished intellectuals at the UCA, Luis de Sebastián, wrote that 'the university is not in the business of seizing power, but it must provide what constitutes its specific contribution: appropriate knowledge to those organisations dedicated to political struggle'.[85] This did not prevent many professors from this relatively small institution from accepting government positions only a few months later.

The First Junta

Although the UCA was not formally part of the Popular Forum, an opposition coalition against the government of dictator Carlos Humberto Romero, the events at the turn of the decade clearly indicate that it was in close contact with both the civilian opposition and the coup plotters in the barracks. The UCA's fingerprints were everywhere: the Proclamation of the Armed Forces was revised and polished by an intellectual from the UCA (namely its rector). The UCA's presence was even more conspicuous in the first civilian government formed in the aftermath of the coup. Román Mayorga Quiroz himself was one of the three civilians nominated in the five-member civil–military junta.[86] General Jaime

Abdul Gutiérrez, the real representative of the army in the junta (the other one, the young officers' leader Adolfo Arnoldo Majano, proved powerless), recalls that Mayorga Quiroz was chosen by the army as a key individual because of his close links with the two most important sectors of the civilian opposition: the Church and the universities.[87] The two other civilian members were Guillermo Manuel Ungo and Mario Andino. Ungo, leader of the MNR and the UNO candidate for vice president in 1972, constituted the army's concession to the Popular Forum. Ungo taught classes at both the UCA and the UES – in fact he had taught many of the political leaders of the past twenty years. During the 1950s he was editor of *Opinión Estudiantil*, 'the fighting organ of the Salvadoran university students'.[88] In 1964 he accompanied Fabio Castillo on a trip to Moscow, when an official exchange agreement was signed between the UES and the University of Lamonosov.[89] At one point he was also director of the Research Institute at the UCA, formed in 1973. Mario Andino, however, who is usually portrayed as the representative of the private sector, was more like a ghost – he soon resigned and never had any impact one way or the other.

The UCA's presence was especially salient in the governmental bureaucracy. According to colonel Mariano Castro Morán, in a book published by the UCA, 'half of the top civil servants of the first junta were from the UCA or had had links with the UCA'.[90] When considering both the junta and the government at large, it was literally a 'government of the UCA'. Castro Morán also emphasised that most of the new leaders and top civil servants had been educated at the Externado San José.[91]

The experience of power was short-lived: most intellectuals from the UCA resigned in January 1980. In April 1980 the UCA acquired observer status in the FDR. The March–April issue of the *ECA* (1980) was entirely devoted to the programme of government presented by the Revolutionary Coordination of the Masses (CRM) and adopted by the FDR. Soon, according to Tommie Sue Montgomery, 'every one of the officials who had come out of the UCA and into the government after October 15 was working in some manner with the FDR/FMLN'.[92]

The UCA's philosophy was very different from that of the UES, but it had a similar attraction to vanguardism and, ultimately, armed struggle. Still, the the role played by the UCA was the perfect embodiment of that of the Catholic Church in the emergence of insurgency in El Salvador. Although it self- righteously proclaimed itself as the advocate of the poor, it was, and still is, a fairly elitist institution, a private college for the middle and upper classes. Although it was an advocate of radical change, it seldom refused to participate when invited by the government. In the wake of the Chapultepec accords, the UCA was instrumental in drafting the new law on education and supplied more than its fair share of members to the new Supreme Court. Theology of liberation may sound 'radical' but it was never really schismatic. This was arguably the central feature of quite a few radical movements and organisations in Latin America.

* * *

The crisis affecting the Salvadoran Catholic Church was not a unique phenomenon. It was a regional episode, generated by a combination of mutually enforcing factors: the raising of expectations in the 1960s and early 1970s in the wake of unprecedented economic growth and social mobilisation; the parallel development of bureaucratic and sometimes mobilisational authoritarian regimes; and the upsurge of repression, urban insurgency and death squad – all this in the enduring context of social inequality and exclusion of the many based on economic, cultural, gender and ethnic prejudices. The radicalisation of some sectors of the Catholic Church was also related to the countercultural trends of the late 1960s, to which Latin American cultural elites were exposed. Indeed the two most obvious factors explaining the decline of the Popular Church in Latin America were democratisation on the one hand, and the demise of the countercultural trends in Latin America and the West in general on the other hand.

Although one must be careful not to formulate definite conclusions about the Church's role in the emergence of insurgency (for lack of sufficient data), the evidence strongly suggests that its impact on the lower strata, especially in the countryside, has probably been exaggerated by most observers, whereas its influence on urban, middle-class youths, mostly through education institutions, has certainly been underestimated – if estimated at all – by the same observers. What has been missed is the fact that, as Jean Meyer points out, 'beside religious considerations, if there was a change of [political] alliance, one cannot yet find a change of problematic: it is still an alliance of the state with the Catholic Church [*du sabre et du goupillon*] ... that revolutionary Christians advocate'.[93] And the state, in Latin America, is the object of competition and yearning for the members of a fairly narrow and exclusive club where all the political resources are concentrated.

The Catholic Church has always had a concern for the poor, and one certainly cannot question the goodwill, courage and commitment of the many priests and monks who have dedicated their lives to helping the poor. But historically, this unprecedented commitment to the poor has been part of the time-honoured 'quest for societal relevance' that has characterised the Catholic Church since the Liberal reforms of the late nineteenth century.[94] The logic of the emergence of insurgency, and the Church's participation in it, is essentially the same time-honoured logic of power that has characterised political development in Latin America for centuries.

Conclusion

> Obviously, the accords of Chapultepec wouldn't have been possible without the relative de-ideologisation of both side; in this sense the signature of the accords and the compliance with the first phase of the transition – beyond international pressure – are an indication of the realism of the national political elite. (Castellanos Moya, 1993)

The contribution of this book to the understanding of insurgency in Latin America is to bring in the actors and their agendas. Central American political actors are power seekers, not solely social-class spokespersons. Their political agenda is shaped by a variety of conditioning factors, not just those derived from some compelling socioeconomic 'reality'. This 'reality', constantly invoked by politicians and scholars alike, is an intellectual construct, predicated on multiple beliefs and dispositions whose origins are both narrower (the immediate environment of ideologues) and wider (ideas shared by a generation of ideologues) than suggested by exponents of the dominant paradigm. The structural and historical grievances identified by Booth and presented as the 'most promising theories' on the roots of national revolts in Central America are supported by a significant, though not sufficient, body of evidence. An important source of dissatisfaction with the dominant paradigm stems from the discovery that residual variables related to the insurgents themselves help to explain not only the short-term causes of the emergence of Latin American insurgencies in the wake of the Cuban revolution (the so-called 'guerrillas'), but also, conceivably, the immediate causes of their development and rapid decline in the 1970s (South America) and 1980s (Central America).

In closing, four general comments can be formulated, based on the present study.

First, *bringing the actors 'back in' to Latin American studies* is warranted in order to come to terms with the political actors' fundamental liberty and responsibility. For all the awesome constraints that Latin American countries are facing – chiefly those deriving from dependency, underdevelopment and a strong authoritarian legacy – no political outcome south of the Rio Grande can be regarded as inevitable. In fact a wider variety of outcomes is imaginable in Latin America's fluid political situation than in established and prosperous democracies, where institutional rigidity, diffusion of power and rent-seeking activities breed incremental change or even gridlock. The comparatively low level of political institutionalisation in 'neo' or 'post' patrimonial states brings politics closer to the relatively undifferentiated elite. But then comes what historian Simon Schama (1989), pondering on the French revolution, has called an 'explosion of politics', when the autonomy of politics (the uncertainty of political outcomes) is enhanced, stimulated by the ascendancy of passions over interests. Violence is arguably not the opposite of power, as Hannah Arendt suggested. It is rather the paroxysm of politics. For, in the realm of violent politics, 'means become ends' and politics becomes its own environment.[1]

Second, it is possible to find in this volume *an applicability that transcends the case of El Salvador*. As indicated in Chapter 1, Latin American studies are just behind the pack when it comes to assessing the weight of political ideas in political change – see for instance the recent studies on revolutions, especially great revolutions such as the French and the Russian. More generally, my argument on the role of ideas in political change is likely to become much more mainstream in the years to come. For as Ferenc Feher (1991) suggests, Western societies are undergoing a transition towards a 'post-Machiavelian' society; that is, a society where issues related to problems of identity, justice and the good life are rapidly gaining ground at the expense of narrowly defined issues of interest representation and procedures. The early twenty-first century may well be like the late eighteenth: a period of intense production of ideas that will shape the world for decades and even centuries to come.

Third, this study has analysed not only *ideas*, but also *ideologues*. If some general and dominant passions were shared by a whole generation of countercultural actors, why did they trigger an internal war in El Salvador, insurgencies in all Latin American countries and significant instability in France, Italy and Germany, to name but a few developed nations, but nothing politically significant in, say, Canada, Costa Rica and Britain? The reason is that interconnected factors related to the insurgents' immediate environment do matter in explaining both the insurgents' political mobilisation and their impact on the polity. These factors are the ideological disposition of universities, the distribution of resources (including political resources) in universities, the relationship between university actors and the state, the size and political influence of the middle strata, plus, in this study, a crisis in two key political forces: the Catholic Church and the Communist Party, both of which conducted most of their political networking in universities. The broader structural explanation may be useful in explaining why an insurgency succeeds, and perhaps more importantly, what kind of challenges victorious insurgents are likely to face once in command of the state apparatus. Nevertheless it does not provide an obvious explanation of why, how and when specific insurgents decide to make good on their *patria o muerte* war cry.

This is not to say that ideas matter only during the emergence of an insurgency. They also matter during the second stage (the epicentre of the internal war, or what Tilly (1978) called 'multiple sovereignty'), since no insurgency in Latin America or the so-called Third World has ever conquered power without securing some support, through ideological accomodation, from the national bourgeoisie and the middle strata. And they do matter in the third and final phase of the internal war for ideological dispositions shape political agendas as well as the perception of both opportunity and threat. The case made here is that ideas matter *more* during the emergence of insurgency, because the social, economic and political constraints of the national environment are less important in shaping the nature of an incipient insurgency (organisational structure and ideological dispositions) than they are in the subsequent internal war.

My fourth and final comment is difficult to formulate but it deserves to be submitted for discussion. The Mexican writer and Nobel laureate Octavio Paz used to say that in Latin America the left have ideas, whereas the right only have interests. The implication of this riveting assertion is puzzling. It implies that the former is more inclined to embrace utopias than the latter, cutting itself off from both its own social roots and its larger environment. To be sure, ideas have played a pivotal role in restructuring the ARENA Party over the past decade. Nonetheless the shift from the extreme right to a more moderate right, and from thuggery to espousing electoral democracy, is probably easier to explain in terms of 'interests' than in terms of 'ideas'.[2] Observers are probably right to stress the importance of the realisation by some members of the Salvadoran bourgeoisie that an environment of peace and electoral democracy, as opposed to anti-Communist crusade, is more conducive to profit making in a time of economic globalisation.

On that account, a strong focus on ideas and ideologues is arguably more relevant for analysing radical insurgencies than almost any other forms of political mobilisation.

This suggests that something unusual is happening when the right starts to act in a dogmatic, fanatical way. Not that the Salvadoran right waited until the 1970s and 1980s to indulge in repressive behaviour. Systematic massacres occurred in 1932, and the assassination of political opponents has been a fixture of modern Salvadoran politics.[3] Nevertheless the kind of theology of counterrevolution developed under the charismatic leadership of Roberto D'Aubuisson was extraordinary, as was the epidemic of similar dreadful events in Argentina, Uruguay and Chile a decade earlier. Since they were in large part a response to the perceived 'communist threat', fuelled by violent actions committed by 'urban guerrillas', one can suggest that the general and dominant passions of the left had an ill-understood impact on the right, creating, in a perverse way, a common mind-set of insurgency/counterinsurgency to which both became prisoners. This is not to say that insurgents are logically and morally *responsible* for counterinsurgency. In fact the bulk of moral responsibility for the tragedy of the 1980s rests plainly on the government of El Salvador, the army, the security forces, the judicial system, the members of the economic establishment and those foreign governments who financed the death squads' activities. But it seems clear that *this* kind of counterinsurgency was to a large extent the product of *this* kind of insurgency.

Notes and References

Introduction

1. Cf. Yvon Grenier, *Guerre et pouvoir au Salvador, idéologies du changement et changements idéologiques* (Ste-Foy: Les Presses de l'Université Laval, 1994). This previous book examines primarily the period from 1977 to 1982 and, as reviewer Stephen Webre summarised, 'eschews socioeconomic causes and external intervention seeking meaning instead in the behaviour of political actors in 'the context of the historical development of the Salvadoran State'. S. Webre in *Hispanic American Historical Review,* 76:2 (May 1994), p. 367–8.
2. Tommie Sue Montgomery, *Revolution in El Salvador* (Boulder, CO: Westview Press, 1982; new edition 1994); Marta Harnecker, *Con la mirada en alto, historia de las FPL Farabundo martí a través de sus dirigentes* (San Salvador: UCA editores, 1993).
3. During the 1980s Thomas W. Walker was the quasi owner of Nicaragua in North American academia. His entire production on the Sandinistas is a monument to the uncritical, Cold-War-like approach to area studies. The parallel between Walker – as well as most American analysts of Salvadoran politics during the 1980s – and Cold War revisionists in the US, as described by John W. Holmes, is clear: 'It is the historian's obligation to try to determine the validity of the perceptions of such events, recognizing at the same time that misperceptions are historic facts. His analysis can be distorted by an anxiety to establish guilt or innocence, a weakness of much Cold War history on all sides. In the West the paranoiac simplifications of the anti-communists of the fifties provoked a new breed of Cold Warriors for whom the American conspiracy replaced the Soviet conspiracy. These revisionist historians, mostly Americans, are paradoxically guilty of megalomaniac Americanism. They see no other actor on the world scene of any consequence. The Soviet Union has only a dream-like existence, its policies all being fantasies of American conspirators. Allies of the United States, it is assumed, had neither will nor eyes of their own. Fearful of United States displeasure, expressed economically, they dumbly accepted a view of Soviet policy fabricated in Washington.' John W. Holmes, *The Shaping of Peace: Canada*

and the Search for World Order, 1943–1957, vol. 2 (Toronto: University of Toronto Press, 1982), pp. 12–13. (I thank Steve Holloway for bringing this quote to my attention.) For a more specific illustration, compare Professor Walker's rant on the 'US- manufactured Contra War' to the analysis on the 'peasant tragedy' in Nicaragua proposed by a top Sandinista official, or more recently by a former Sandinista supporter. See Alejandro Bendaña, *Una tragedía campesina, testimonios de la resistencia* (Managua: Editora de Arte, 1991) and Paul Berman, 'Untold Stories of the Revolution', *The New Yorker*, 23 September 1996, pp. 58–81. See also Yvon Grenier, 'Gringo's' Central American Revolutions', *Conflict Quarterly* vol. 14, no. 2 (Spring 1994), pp. 63–70.

4. J. Goodwin and T. Skocpol, 'Explaining Revolutions in the Contemporary Third World', *Politics & Society*, vol. 17, no. 4 (1989), p. 492.
5. See T. Wickham-Crowley, *Guerrillas & Revolution in Latin America* (Princeton, NJ: Princeton University Press, 1992), pp. 335–40 and M. Harnecker (1993) pp. 38–45.
6. Various parts of this book are adaptations of previously published material and analysis, with the editors' permission. For the first chapter: 'From Causes to Causers: the Etiology of the Salvadoran Internal War Revisited', *Journal of Conflict Studies* (Fall 1996); 'Guérilla et terrorisme en Amérique latine', *Études internationales*, vol. 19, no. 4 (Dec. 1988), pp. 613–27; 'De l'inflation révolutionnaire: guerre interne, coup d'État et changements radicaux en Amérique latine', *Études Internationales*, vol. 22, no. 1 (March 1991), pp. 47–61. For chapter 2: 'La realidad y los intelectuales: ciencias sociales, poder y transición política en centroamérica', *América Latina Hoy* (Madrid, [forthcoming] 1998); 'Chronicle of a Death Foretold: Intellectuals in the Americas', *Hemisphere*, vol. 7, no. 1 (1995), pp. 10–14. For chapter 3: 'Understanding the FMLN: A Glossary of Five Words', *Conflict Quarterly*, vol. 11, no. 2 (Spring 1991), pp. 51–75. For chapters 4 and 5: 'Vers la "libération universitaire du peuple Salvadorien": l'Université Centro-Américaine dans la transition politique au El Salvador', *Revue Canadienne d'Études du Développement* vol. 13, no. 1 (March–April 1992), pp. 7–38; *Una clase dirigente en transición: La Universidad Nacional en la crisis del poder en El Salvador* (San Salvador: FundaUngo, Serie Análisis de la Realidad Nacional, 1994), p. 31; Yvon Grenier, 'Ideology and Insurrection: Bringing the Actor Back in', *Ciencia Ergo Sum*, vol. 4, no. 3 (November 1997), pp. 265–72.

1 Challenging the Dominant Paradigm

1. Walter LaFeber, *Inevitable Revolutions, The United States in Central America*, 2nd edn (New York and London: W.W. Norton, 1993). For James Dunkerley, 'nobody in their right mind could plausibly refute the view that the Central American conflict is rooted in the economic structure of the region'. See his *Power in the Isthmus* (New York: Verso, 1988), p. 171.
2. Hence the abundance of 'fact-finding' missions organised by solidarity groups and scholarly programmes such as the LASA Nicaragua task force, occasionally followed by books offering 'new' evidence based on interviews with guerrilla leaders, talkative generals and sundry politicians, all of them repeating basically the same elementary 'reality' about the region's tragedy, the same 'alternative' policies and so on.
3. John A. Booth, *The End and the Beginning, The Nicaraguan Revolution* (Boulder, CO.: Westview Press, 1982); and 'Socio-economic and Political Roots of National Revolts in Central America', *Latin American Research Review*, vol. 26, no. 1 (1991), pp. 33–74.
4. Booth, 'Socioeconomic and Political Roots', op. cit., p. 35.
5. Ibid., pp. 34–5. For a similar perspective see Jan L. Flora and Edelberto Torres-Rivas (eds), *Central America* (New York: Monthly Review Press, 1989), pp. 32–55.
6. Equally puzzling for him is the case of Honduras; in spite of being the poorest nation in the region, it has not undergone national revolt and therefore remains impermeable to Booth's mainstream explanation (by Central American studies standards).
7. In a remarkable article, Mitchell A. Seligson contends that the Gini coefficient, indicating concentration of wealth, was one of the five highest in the world, based on Taylor and Jodice's *World Handbook of Political and Social Indicators* (SALA, 1983). The *Statistical Abstract of Latin America*, on the other hand, indicates that the Gini coefficient for economically active persons (as opposed, for instance, to household) was 0.532 for El Salvador in 1961, against 0.475 in Argentina and 0.712 for Peru in the same year. Enrique Baloyra also contends that 'while there is much concentration in the more authoritarian coffee republics (El Salvador and Guatemala), concentration is also a fact of life in democratic Costa Rica. As a matter of fact, Costa Rica and Nicaragua were the countries where the largest farms accounted for a larger proportion of the farmland than anywhere else in the isthmus.' And he concludes: 'Therefore, concentration accompanying or resulting from the

consolidation of the export model could not have been the only effective cause of authoritarian capitalism.' See Mitchell A. Seligson, 'Thirty Years of Transformation in the Agrarian Structure of El Salvador, 1961–1991', *Latin American Research Review*, vol. 30, no. 3 (1995), pp. 43–74; *Statistical Abstract of Latin America*, ed. James W. Wilkie, UCLA Latin American Center Publications, 29, Part 1, table 1419; Enrique A. Baloyra, 'Reactionary Despotism in Central America', *Journal of Latin American Studies*, vol. 15 (1983), p. 301.

8. For an overview of the literature, see Ekkart Zimmermann, *Protest, Revolt and Revolution* (Boulder, CO: Westview Press, 1990).
9. Foran points out that when Jack Goldstone reviewed the literature on revolutions in 1982, 'he placed the role of ideology on the "frontiers of research" as an underexplored area for future scholars to probe'. He also aptly contends that the 'fourth generation' is 'a return to the preoccupation of theorists as early as de Tocqueville . . . on the French Enlightenment, Brinton ("the desertion of the intellectuals"), or the structural functionalists of the second generation. (There seems to be almost nothing completely new in writings on revolution!)' See John Foran, 'Theories of Revolution Revisited: Toward a Fourth Generation?', *Sociological Theory*, vol. 11, no. 1 (March 1993), p. 9; Jack Goldstone, 'The Comparative and Historical Study of Revolutions', *Annual Review of Sociology* vol. 8 (1982), p. 204.
10. See the excellent review by Randall Collins, 'Maturation of the State-Centered Theory of Revolution and Ideology', *Sociological Theory*, vol. 11, no. 1 (March 1993), pp. 117–28.
11. François Furet, *Le passé d'une illusion, essai sur l'idée communiste au XXe siècle* (Paris: Robert Laffont/Calmann-Lévy, 1995).
12. 'Surprisingly, the vast literature on the Holocaust contains little on the people who were its executors.' Daniel Jonah Goldhagen, *Hitler's Willing Executioners, Ordinary Germans and the* Holocaust (New York: Alfred A. Knopf, 1996), pp. 5, 6.
13. Ideology and politics in the Soviet Union was not merely a reflection of the 'social base'. For Malia, 'to adapt Marx's characterization of Hegel's idealism, the Soviet system was an "inverted world", a world "standing on its head". That is to say, it was a world where (contrary to Marx's own sociology) ideology and politics formed the "base" of the system rather than its "superstructure", and where socioeconomic arrangements derived secondarily from this Party base.' Hence 'the primacy of ideology and politics over social and economic

forces in understanding the Soviet phenomenon'. Martin Malia, *The Soviet Tragedy: A History of Socialism in Russia, 1917–1991* (New York: The Free Press, 1994), pp. 8, 16.

14. Jean-François Revel, *Le regain démocratique* (Paris: Fayard, 1992).
15. For Malia, 'the idea of social science posits that, behind the obvious diversity of discrete social formations, something called "society" is the fundamental human reality, and that this "society" is basically the same everywhere, in the past no less tan in the present'. Two consequences follow from this basic assumption. First, 'politics and ideology are merely reflections of the social base', or 'subsets of the more basic global entity of society'. Second, 'the pattern of Soviet development [or any other society, for that matter] cannot be unique or sui generis, but must be essentially similar to that of other "modern" societies'. Malia, *The Soviet Tragedy*, op. cit., p. 7.
16. Perhaps the most famous and suggestive work in that line of thought is Samuel P. Huntington, *Political Order in Changing Societies* (New Haven: Yale University Press, 1968).
17. Sara Gordon, *Crisis política y guerra en El Salvador* (Mexico: Siglo XXI, 1989); Enrique Baloyra, *El Salvador in Transition* (Chapel Hill: University of North Carolina Press, 1982).
18. Two recent books represent welcome exceptions: Forrest D. Colburn, *The Vogue of Revolution in Poor Countries* (Princeton, NJ: Princeton University Press, 1994); and Eric Selbin, *Modern Latin American Revolutions* (Boulder, CO: Westview Press, 1993). See also Eric Selbin, 'Socio-cultural origins of revolutions: popular political culture and resistance, rebellion, and revolution in Latin America and the Caribbean', paper presented at the conference of the Latin American Studies Association, Washington DC, 1995.
19. For a critical appraisal of the left's contribution to Latin American social sciences from a left-wing perspective, see the excellent book by Jorge G. Castañeda, *Utopia Unarmed, The Latin American Left After the Cold War* (New York: Vintage Book, 1994).
20. It is useful to recall that many rich and democratic West European countries underwent serious problems of urban terrorism and near internal war in the 1960s and 1970s (Italy, Germany and France), not to mention ethnic-based internal strife in Spain, Britain and Yugoslavia. In May 1968, a student-led revolt came close to provoking the collapse of the constitutional order.
21. James DeNardo, *Power in Numbers* (Princeton, NJ: Princeton University Press, 1985), pp. 17–18.

22. See for instance Juan Antonio Morales and Gary McMahon (eds), *Economic Policy and the Transition to Democracy, The Latin American Experience* (New York: Macmillan/St Martin's Press, 1996).
23. The literature on the 'lost decade' is both well-known and abundant. For a general discussion on the demonstrative effect of democratisation and the corollary of 'democratic waves', see Samuel P. Huntington, *The Third Wave, Democratization in the Late Twentieth Century* (Norman and London: University of Oklahoma Press, 1991). Huntington identifies the following waves: The first (long) wave of democratisation (1828–1926), the first reverse wave (1922–42), the second (short) wave of democratisation (1943–62), The second reverse wave (1958–75) and the third wave of democratisation (1974–).
24. On the intricacies of measuring the gap between rich and poor, between and within nations, see the excellent collection of articles in Mitchell A. Seligson and John T. Passé-Smith (eds), *Development and Underdevelopment, The Political Economy of Inequality* (Boulder, CO, and London: Lynne Rienner, 1993).
25. See Juan J. Linz, 'Crisis, Breakdown and Reequilibration', in Juan J. Linz and Alfred Stepan (eds.), *The Breakdown of Democratic Regimes* (Baltimore, MD: Johns Hopkins University Press, 1978), p. 11; Guillermo de la Dehesa, 'La crisis económica Mexicana, una visión desde fuera', *Vuelta*, vol. 19, no. 223 (June 1995), p. 37. See also Pitou van Dijck and Ruud Buitelaar (eds), *Latin America's Insertion in the World Economy* (New York: Macmillan/St Martin's Press, 1995).
26. As the elected President of Brazil, sociologist and one of the founding fathers of dependency theory, Fernando Henrique Cardoso now applies neoliberal policies: other times, other paradigms'. For an overview of economic theorisation of dependency and development in Latin America, see the excellent collection in Jorge I. Domínguez (ed.), *Essays on Mexico, Central and South America, Scholarly Debates from the '50s to the '90s*, vol. 1 (New York and London: Garland Publishing, 1994); see also Seligson and Passé-Smith, *Development and Underdevelopment*, op. cit.
27. One can find a very polemical appraisal of this legacy in Robert A. Packenham, *The Dependency Movement, Scholarship and Politics in Development Studies* (Cambridge, Mass.: Harvard University Press, 1992); a more balanced overview is available in David Lehmann, *Democracy and Development in Latin America, Economics, Politics and Religion in the Postwar Period* (Philadelphia: Temple University Press, 1990).

28. Terry L. Karl, 'Dilemmas of Democratization in Latin America', *Comparative Politics*, vol. 23, no. 1 (Oct. 1990), p. 16. See also James M. Malloy and Mitchell A. Seligson (eds), *Authoritarians and Democrats, Regime Transition in Latin America* (Pittsburgh, PA: University of Pittsburgh Press, 1987).
29. Karen L. Remmer, 'The Political Impact of Economic Crisis in Latin America in the '80s', *American Political Science Review*, vol. 85, no. 3 (Sept. 1991), p. 795.
30. Karen L. Remmer, 'New Theoretical Perspectives on Democratization', *Comparative Politics*, vol. 28, no. 1 (Oct. 1995), p. 106.
31. For instance Jean Baechler argues that among the most common causes of revolution, economic deprivation and social inequality hardly matter at all. Jean Baechler, *Les phénomènes révolutionnaires* (Paris: Presses Universitaires de France, 1970).
32. As Claudio Véliz contends, diagnoses of the overarching problem of underdevelopment in Latin America are so general and self-evident as to become essentially tautological or ahistorical. In his most recent book he compares the gloomy diagnosis of the state of the Latin American economy in the late nineteenth century with a recent appraisal by ECLA: 'Only minimal modifications are required to make these two arguments, otherwise separated by a century, coalesce into a familiar diagnosis that rests on capital remaining scarce, governments continuing to be unhelpful, and bad habits stubbornly refusing to vanish.' Claudio Véliz, *The New World of the Gothic Fox, Culture and Economy in English and Spanish America* (Berkeley, CA: University of California Press, 1994), p. 182.
33. See Harry Eckstein (ed.), *Internal War, Problems and Approaches* (New York: The Free Press, 1964); Yvon Grenier, 'De l'inflation révolutionnaire: Guerre Interne, Coup d'état et Changement Radicaux en Amérique Latine', *Études Internationales*, vol 19, no. 4 (décembre 1991) pp. 57–61. Charles Tilly proposed 'multiple sovereignty' as yet another concept describing the violent competition between contenders and challengers in a polity. See Charles Tilly, *From Mobilization to Revolution* (New York: Random House, 1978).
34. See Simon Schama, *Citizens, A Chronicle of the French Revolution* (New York: Vintage Books, 1989), p. 703. See also Honoré de Balzac, *Les Chouans*, (1828) and Charles Tilly's classic work on *the Vendée* (Cambridge: Haward University Press, 1964)
35. See Walter Laqueur, *Guerrilla: A Historical and Critical Study* (London: Weidenfeld and Nicolson, 1977).

36. See Luis Mercier-Vega,*Technique du contre-État* (Paris: Belfond, 1968); Gabriel Zaïd, *De los libros al poder* (Mexico: Grijalbo, 1988); and Yvon Grenier, 'Guérilla et terrorisme en Amérique latine', *Etudes Internationals*, 19, 4 (December 1988), pp. 613–27.
37. See Jeffrey Berejikian, 'Revolutionary Collective Action and the Agent-Structure Problem', *American Political Science Review*, vol. 86, no. 3 (Sept. 1992), pp. 647–57.
38. Octavio Paz, *Obras completas*, vol. 8: *El peregrino en su patria* (Mexico: Fondo de Cultura Economica, 1993), p. 297.
39. Theda Skocpol, *States and Social Revolutions, A Comparative Analysis of France, Russia and China* (Cambridge: Cambridge University Press, 1980), p. 114.
40. Barrington Moore, *Social Origins of Dictatorship and Democracy, Lord and Peasant in the Making of the Modern World* (Boston, Mass.: Beacon Press, 1966), p. 479.
41. James C. Scott, *Weapons of the Weak, Everyday Forms of Peasant Resistance* (New Haven, CT, and London: Yale University Press, 1985).
42. Ibid., p. 247. Scott defines resistance (in fact, 'class resistance') as follows: '[it] includes *any* act(s) by member(s) of a subordinate class that is or are *intended* either to mitigate or deny claims (for example, rents, taxes, prestige) made on that class by superordinate classes (for example, landlords, large farmers, the state) or to advance its own claims (for example, work, land, charity, respect) *vis-à-vis* those superordinate classes', (ibid., p.290). See also Colburn (1994), p. 43.
43. The Peruvian writer Mario Vargas Llosa once said that the true revolution in Latin America would be to renounce to revolution. And then again, during his bid for the presidency of his country, he called for a 'revolution of liberty'. Mario Vargas Llosa, *El pez en el Agua*, (Mexico, D.F.: Seix Barral, 1993.)
44. John Walton, *Reluctant Rebels: Comparative Studies of Revolution and Underdevelopment* (New York: Columbia University Press, 1984). Forrest Colburn (1994, p. 7) similarly contends that 'There are no ready and agreed-upon indicators, though, which measure social transformation. And there is no threshold at which it can be decided whether or not sufficient transformation has taken place, or been attempted, for a political upheaval to be judged a revolution.'
45. In Latin America these ingredients have mixed with others, inherited from two matrixes: the Iberian peninsula of the Counter-Reformation and the pre-Colombian civilisations.
46. Raymond Boudon, *L'idéologie, l'origine des idées reçues* (Paris: Fayard, 1986), p. 45.

47. The Marquis de Condorcet, enthralled by the French Revolution, articulated this idea better when he envisaged 'l'espèce humaine, affranchie de toutes ses chaînes, *soustraite à l'empire du hasard*, comme à celui des ennemis de ses progrès, et marchant d'un pas ferme et sûr dans la route de la vérité, de la vertu et du bonheur'. Quoted by Keith Michael Baker in François Furet and Mona Ozouf, *Dictionnaire critique de la révolution française* (Paris: Flammarion, 1988), p. 243 (emphasis added). Closer to this case study, Carlos Fuentes once cited an indigenous poet who offered the following intelligence: 'Los que tienen el poder de contar los dias, tienen el poder de hablarle a los dioses.' Carlos Fuentes, *El Espejo enterrado* (Mexico: Fondo de Cultura Económica, 1992), p. 106.
48. Octavio Paz, *Itinerario* (México: Fondo de Cultura Económica, 1993), p. 37
49. For a classical exposition of this argument, see Clifford Geertz, 'Ideology as a Cultural System', in David Apter (ed.), *Ideology and Discontent* (Glencoe, Ill.: The Free Press, 1964), pp. 47–76.
50. 'All language, even the language of liberty, ends up converting itself in a prison.' Octavio Paz, 'El Caracol y la sirena: Rubén Dario', reproduced in *Obras completas;* vol. 3 *Fundación y disidencia, Dominio hispánico* (Mexico: Fondo de Cultura Económica, 1994), p. 138.
51. Quoted in Jean-François Revel, *La connaissance inutile* (Paris: Grasset, 1988), p. 347. In a remarkable essay on reactionary historian Joseph de Maistre, E. M. Cioran captures in an elegantly crafted paragraph (so much so that I dare not translate it) the extravagance not only of the ideological discourse, but of *any* discourse on the human experience: 'Le tête-à-tête avec l'idée incite à déraisonner, oblitère le jugement, et produit l'illusion de la toute-puissance. En vérité, être aux prises avec une idée rend insensé, enlève à l'esprit son équilibre et à l'orgueil son calme. Nos dérèglements et nos aberrations émanent du combat que nous menons contre des irréalités, contre des abstractions, de notre volonté de l'emporter sur ce qui n'est pas; de là le côté impur, tyrannique, divagant, des ouvrages philosophiques, comme d'ailleurs de tout ouvrage. Le penseur en train de noircir une page sans destinatire se croit, se sent l'arbitre du monde... Chaque doctrine contient en germe des possibilités infinies de désastre: l'esprit n'étant constructif que par inadvertance, la rencontre de l'homme et de l'idée comporte presque toujours une suite funeste... Pour émettre la moindre opinion sur quoi que ce soit, un acte de bravoure et une certaine capacité d'irréflexion sont nécessaires, ainsi

qu'une propension à se laisser emporter par des raisons extra-rationnelles.' E.M. Cioran, *Exercices d'admiration, Essais et portraits* (Paris: Gallimard, 1986), pp. 15, 51, 65.

52. Ibid., p. 179.
53. For abundant illustrations of this, see Régis Debray, *Loués soient nos seigneurs, Une éducation politique* (Paris: Gallimard, 1996). See also Yvon Grenier, 'Chronicle of a Death Foretold: Intellectuals in the Americas,' *Hemisphere*, 7, 1 (1995), pp. 16–17.
54. Thomas Jefferson similarly concluded: 'State a moral case to a ploughman and a professor. The former will decide it as well and often better than the latter because he has not been led astray by artificial rules.' Quoted in Robert A. Dahl, *Democracy and Its Critics* (Hew Haven, CT: Yale University Press, 1989), pp. 59–60.
55. Karl-Werner Brand talks about the *zeitgeist*, a 'social mood' or 'cultural climate' corresponding to different periods of history, and about the cyclical reappearance of movements embracing various critiques of modernisation. With regard to the vertical connection, the following are some of the factors conditioning the intellectuals' orientation, according to Karl Mannheim: 'the social background of the individual; the particular phase of his career curve – whether he is on the upgrade, at a plateau, or on the downgrade; whether he moves up individually or as a member of a group; whether he is blocked in his advancement or thrown back on his initial situation; the phase of a social movement in which he participates – the initial, middle, or the terminal shape; the position of his generation in reaction to the other generations; his social habitat; and, finally, the type of aggregation in which he performs.' Karl Mannheim, 'The Problem of the Intelligentsia: an Inquiry into its Past and Present Role', *Essays on the Sociology of Culture* (London: Routledge & Kegan Paul, 1956), p. 158. See also Karl-Werner Brand, 'Cyclical Aspects of New Social Movements: Waves of Cultural Criticism and Mobilization Cycles of new Middle-Class Radicalism', in Russell J. Dalton and Manfred Kuechler (eds), *Challenging the Political Order* (New York: Oxford University Press, 1990), pp. 23–42.
56. Cf. Philippe Sollers, *Improvisations* (Paris: Folio, collection Essais, 1991), p. 22.
57. In Marx's England proper, revolt was animated by reactionary longing for a return to the past and came primarily from dying traditional handicrafts, not the factories. See Craig Calhoun, *The Question of Class Struggle* (Chicago, Ill.: University of Chicago Press, 1982).

58. On the subtle interdependency of this import/export process, see Bertrand Badie, *L'État importé* (Paris: Fayard, 1992); and Richard M. Morse, 'The Multiverse of Latin American Identity, 1920–1970', in Leslie Bethell (ed.), *Ideas and Ideologies in Twentieth Century Latin America* (Cambridge and New York: Cambridge University Press, 1996), pp. 3–132. For an analysis of the impact of foreign ideas on the intellectual development of Central America, see Andrés Pérez, 'Social Sciences and Social Reality in Central America', *CEPAL Review*, vol. 50 (Aug. 1993), pp. 147–62; Castañeda (1994), p. 180.
59. Some economists are attempting to cram the fascinating phenomenon of fad – so central in our mass consumption societies – into scientific economics. For instance 'fads are due to informational cascades', reckon Sushil Bikhchandani, David Hirshleifer and Ivo Welch, three economists from the University of California at Los Angeles. They recognise that people often have only limited knowledge; some things are unknown, or cost too much to find out. But everyone knows something. So, by watching what others do, each consumer can tap their information and so improve his own decision-making. See 'Yes, Ten Million People Can Be Wrong', *The Economist*, 19 February (1994), p. 81.
60. Jean-François Revel, *Le regain démocratique* (Paris: Fayard, 1992), p. 170.
61. Lewis A. Coser, *Men of Ideas: A Sociologist View* (New York: The Free Press, 1965), p. 137.
62. For comparative perspective on the role of intellectuals in the emergence of ethnic tensions in Yugoslavia, see Svetlana Slapsak, 'Bestial Words, Bestial War', *The New York Times*, 25 May 1993.
63. See for instance Jack Goldstone, *Revolution and Rebellion in the Early Modern World* (Berkeley, CA: University of California Press, 1991).
64. Skocpol (1980), p. 17.
65. Theda Skocpol, 'Cultural Idioms and Political Ideologies in the Revolutionary Reconstruction of State Power: A Rejoinder to Sewell', *Journal of Modern History*, vol. 57 (1985), p. 95. Skocpol uttered those unstructuralist words in response to insightful criticisms formulated by William H. Sewell, who reproached her for some of her comments on ideology in *States and Social Revolution* (1980); for instance when she contended that 'It cannot be argued that the cognitive content of ideologies *in any sense* provides a predictive key to... the outcomes of the Revolution.' See W.H. Sewell, 'Ideologies and Social Revolutions: Reflections on the French Case',

Journal of Modern History, vol. 57 (1985), pp. 57–85 (quotation on p. 59). See also Skocpol's 'revisionist' approach in her 'Rentier State and Shi'a Islam in the Iranian Revolution', *Theory and Society*, vol. 11, no. 3 (1982), pp. 265–303.

66. On El Salvador, see for instance John Foran, 'A Theory of Third World Social Revolutions: Iran, Nicaragua and El Salvador Compared', paper presented at the meeting of the International Sociological Association, Madrid, 1990, quoted in J. Foran, 'Theories of Revolution Revisited: Toward a Fourth Generation', *Sociological Theory*, vol. 11, no. 1 (March 1993), p. 14; Jean Daudelin and Yvon Grenier, 'Violence politique et transition à la démocratie en Amérique centrale: une grille d'analyse', in Jacques Zylberberg and François Demers (eds.), *L'Amérique et les Amériques* (Ste-Foy: Les Presses de l'Université Laval, 1992), pp. 713–34, and 'Political Pacts and Democracy: Lessons from El Salvador and Nicaragua', *Latin American Essays*, vol. VII (Kean College, PA: Middle Atlantic Council of Latin American Studies, 1994), pp. 79–100
67. Colburn (1994).
68. Ibid., p. 15.
69. For a critical view on the intellectual ambiance in the US-based Latin American Studies Association, see Alfred G. Cuzán, 'The Latin American Studies Association vs. the United States: the Verdict of History', *Academic Questions*, vol. 7, no. 3 (Summer 1994), pp. 40–55.
70. John Walton suggests the opposite in his *Reluctant Rebels* (1984).
71. As Forrest D. Colburn points out, 'The many contemporary revolutions show . . . that there is little necessary linkage between structural origins and outcomes' (Colburn, 1994, p. 15).
72. See interesting the comments by Ignacio Ellacuria in 'Universidad y política', *ECA*, vol. 383 (Sept. 1980), pp. 807–24.
73. See Matt D. Childs, 'An Historical Critique of the Emergence and Evolution of Ernesto Che Guevara's *Foco* Theory', *Journal of Latin American Studies*, vol. 27 (1995), p. 604. In his memoirs, Régis Debray recalls a discussion with Fidel Castro when the *líder máximo* made the case that three men can start a war of liberation in Latin America (Debray, 1996, p. 85).

2 From Causes to 'Causers'

1. Michael Radu (ed.), *Violence and the Latin American Revolutionaries* (New Brunswick and Oxford: Transaction Books, 1988), p. 1.

2. When Jorge G. Castañeda wrote that 'the idea of revolution itself, central to Latin American radical thought for decades, has lost its meaning', he showed tremendous courage (Castañeda, 1994, p. 241).
3. For insightful comments on the act of speaking on behalf of someone else, see Pierre Bourdieu, *Ce que parler veut dire* (Paris: Fayard, 1982).
4. The concept of the 'unattached intellectual' was borrowed and disseminated in the *République des lettres* by Karl Mannheim. After some disgruntling feedback on his use of the concept, he attempted to clarify his argument as follows: 'Let us re-emphasize at this point that intellectuals do not form an exalted stratum above the classes and are in no way better endowed with a capacity to overcome their own class attachments than other groups. In my earlier analysis of this stratum I used the term 'relatively uncommitted intelligentsia' (relativ freischwebende intelligenz)... The epithet 'relative' was no empty word. The expression simply alluded to the well-established fact that intellectuals do not react to given issues as cohesively as for example employees and workers do.' Karl Mannheim, 'The Problem of the Intelligentsia: an Inquiry into its Past and Present Role', *Essays on the Sociology of Culture* (London: Routledge & Kegan Paul, 1956), pp. 105–6.
5. Castañeda (1994), p. 177.
6. François Bourricaud, 'The Adventures of Ariel', *Daedalus*, Summer 1972, p. 113; see also Yvon Grenier, 'Chronicle of a Death Foretold' op. cit.
7. During the 1960s Cuba provided military assistance for the insurgencies in all Latin American nations except Mexico. Even the Black Panthers operated a guerrilla training centre in Cuba! See Castañeda (1994), p. 68, note 20; Childs, 'An Historical Critique of the Emergence and Evolution of Ernesto Che Guevara's Foco Theory', *Journal of Latin American Studies*, 27 (1995) p. 598.
8. As Timothy Wickham-Crowley sums up: 'In their initial stage, guerrilla movements begin among the highly educated offspring of rural elites and the urban middle and upper classes.... In the subsequent stage of the movement, peasants come to dominate in numbers, while power remains in the hands of those with higher status and education' (Wickham-Crowley, 1992), p. 29. As regards age, according to an FPL leader 'Ninety percent of the activists were youths from seventeen to twenty years old.' Quoted in Harnecker (1993), p. 157. The social profile of the revolutionary messiah does not seem to have changed a great deal since the Middle Ages, for as

Norman Cohn asserts in his classic study of millenarian movements: 'Unlike the leaders of the great popular risings, who were usually peasants or artisans, *prophetae* were seldom manual workers or even former manual workers. Sometimes they were petty nobles; sometimes they were simply impostors; but more usually they were intellectuals or half-intellectuals – the former priest turned freelance preacher was the commonest type of all.' Norman Cohn, *The Pursuit of the Millennium, Revolutionary Millenarians and Mystical Anarchis of the Middle Age* (New York: Yale University Press, 1970), p. 285.

9. See Shirley Christian, *Revolution in the Family* (New York: Random House, 1985); Samuel Stone, *The Heritage of the Conquistadors, Ruling Classes in Central America from Conquest to the Sandinistas* (Lincoln and London: University of Nebraska Press, 1990).
10. For a courageous denunciation of this retreat from the barricades by a tenured American professor, see James Petras, 'The Metamorphosis of Latin America's Intellectuals', *Latin American Perspectives*, vol. 17, no. 2 (Spring 1990), pp. 102–12. For a critical analysis of non-governmental organisations as promoters of democratic forms of government, see Laura Macdonald, *Supporting Civil Society* (New York: Macmillan/St.Martin's Press, 1996); Michael W. Foley, 'Laying the Groundwork: The Struggle for Civil Society in El Salvador', *Journal of Interamerican Studies and World Affairs*, vol. 38, no. 1 (Spring 1996), pp. 67–104.
11. A good illustration of how the existence of this type of 'club' transcends functional roles and the very porous dividing line between political and non-political roles is provided by the Salvadoran Dental Society, which, during the national crisis of the fall of 1979, issued a political statement on the ground that 'the violent events of the past days cannot be overlooked by whoever considers oneself as a *good Salvadoran* ... This is time to be serious, for the country is in danger and *only the assistance of good Salvadorans* can save it.' See 'Pronunciamiento de la sociedad dental de El Salvador ante la realidad nacional', *ECA*, nos 372–3 (Oct.–Nov. 1979), p. 1015.
12. See the excellent collection in Kay Lawson and Peter H. Merkl (eds.), *When Parties Fail, Emerging Alternative Organizations* (Princeton, NJ: Princeton University Press, 1988).
13. Contemporary agrarian reforms, incidentally, provide an excellent illustration of this idiosyncrasy: still a pressing need for most Latin American countries, they are also the modernisers' Trojan horse, permitting the penetration of

urban, would-be national political structures (ergo, struggles) into the countryside. See the excellent Merilee S. Grindle, *State and Countryside, Development Policy and Agrarian Politics in Latin America* (Baltimore, MD, and London: Johns Hopkins University Press, 1986).

14. Debray (1996), p. 124.
15. Rafael Guidos Vejar, 'La crisis política en El Salvador', *ECA*, nos 369–70 (July–Aug. 1979), p. 523.
16. Horacio Castellanos Moya, *Recuento de incertidumbres, cultura y transición en El Salvador* (San Salvador: Editorial Tendencias, 1993), pp. 50–1.
17. He was deemed responsible for the assassination of the Archbishop Oscar Romero by the UN-sponsored Commission of Truth (1993). He died of cancer on 20 February, 1992 at the age of 48.
18. ARENA, 'Principios ideológicos y objetivos', *ECA*, nos 396–7 (Oct.–Nov. 1981), p. 1064.
19. See ARENA, *Principios, Objetivos y Lineamientos del Programa de Gobierno* (San Salvador, 1989), and *Principios, Objetivos y Estatutos* (San Salvador, n/d).
20. ARENA, 'Pronunciamiento y exigencias', *ECA* nos 396–7 (Oct.–Nov. 1981), p. 1066.
21. In 1981 ARENA positioned the PDC to 'the right of the communist movement', whereas the PDC stamped ARENA as a 'right wing atheist' party. See ARENA, 'El Partido ARENA saluda al soldado salvadoreño en su día', *ECA*, nos 390–1 (April–May 1981), p. 450, and 'Análisis de la situación actual: mensaje del Lic. Julio Alfredo Samayoa, Secretario General del Partido [PDC]', *ECA* nos 390–1 (April–May 1981), p. 455.
22. Gordon (1989), p. 310.
23. Tilly (1978), p. 78.
24. Castañeda (1994, p. 39) is right when he declares that 'if the left in Latin America has a democratic ancestry today, it lies above all in the Communist parties' penchant for elections, nonviolence, and alliances: the right strategy, perhaps, though quite likely for the wrong reasons.'
25. The history of the Masonic lodge and its political influence in El Salvador is still to be written. The military-led PCN (Partido de Conciliación Nacional) did not shy away from using the well-known triangle as its logo.
26. This explain why, in El Salvador as in many Latin American countries, the radical activism of the 1960s and 1970s was to be found as much, if not more, in these normally 'conservative' (in North America and Europe) disciplines. New ideology, traditional pattern of political mobilisation!

27. See the interview by Carlos Ernesto Mendoza in *Análisis* (San Salvador), vols 9–10 (Sept.–Oct. 1988), pp. 47–59.
28. Pondering on the difficulty of enlisting people from the popular sectors during the 1970s, an FPL leader asserted the following: 'I think this was caused by our understanding that we ought not to work with just any sectors, but only with the most sensible. We did not try to work with workers in general, or with peasants in general; instead we started by openly seeking the collaboration of ANDES ... which was the most ready to fight during the early 1970s. It turned out that we were right to think that we could expand our movement through this strategy. ANDES played an extremely important role in organising the peasantry and high school students, the latter being very receptive [to our message] as a result of the living situation of the youths. Students were ready to organise politically and to go to the streets' quoted in Harnecker, 1993, p. 125.
29. The argument that revolution is brought about not by the rigidity of the old regime, but by its careless attempt to reform itself, has been made repeatedly since de Tocqueville.
30. See especially Victor Bulmer-Thomas, *The Political Economy of Central America since 1920* (Cambridge: Cambridge University Press, 1988); and Gordon (1989).
31. See for example Charles W. Anderson, 'El Salvador: The Army as Reformer', in Martin Needler (ed.), *Political Systems of Latin America* (New York: Van Nostrand Reinhold, 1970), pp. 70–92; James Dunkerley, *Power in the Isthmus, A Political History of Modern Central America*, (London, New York: Verso, 1988). 352; John D. Martz, *Central America, The Crisis and the Challenge* (Chapel Hill, NC: University of North Carolina Press, 1959), 80–111.
32. Gordon (1989).
33. Goldstone (1991), p. xxiv.
34. CEPAL, *Indicadores socioeconómicos para el desarrollo*, Comisión Economica para America Latina (CEPAL), 1980. For a discussion on the connections between urbanisation and modernisation, see Huntington, *Political Order in Changing Societies* (New Haven: Yale University Press, 1968), pp. 72–78.
35. El Salvador, Ministerio de Planificación, *Indicadores Económicos y Sociales* (San Salvador, Jan.–June 1980), p. 185.
36. José Napoléon Duarte (1964–70), José Antonio Morales Ehrlich (1974–78) and Carlos Rebollo Herrera (1970–74).
37. The US' influence was not confined to building up the 'centre' and fostering democratisation, as was generally the case during the Cold War; Washington also supported the cat that could immediately catch the mouse (that is, the 'communist

guerrilla'); the cat in this case being the reactionary army and the infamous security forces. For a good analysis of the contradictory US policy in El Salvador, see A.J. Bacevich, James Hallums, R.H. White and T.F. Young, *American Military Policy in Small Wars: The Case of El Salvador* (special report, Institute for Foreign Policy Analysis, Tufts University, 1988).

38. At this point it is useful to remember, with, ortega y Gasset, that behind, or underneath, ideological constructs, there are deeply rooted mind-sets shaped by time-honoured beliefs, long preexisting the importation of any foreign ideological discourse. Glen C. Dealy contends that 'It is from Aquinas, Rousseau and Auguste Compte, rather than from Marx and Lenin, that Central Americans ultimately derive their common political orientation. Nationalistic movements everywhere in the area attest more to a hoary agrarian desire for unity and justice provided by strong central government than to any new affinity for an alien ideology of middle-class property owners or exploited industrial workers.' On democracy he argues that 'Latin Americans have a democratic tradition but not a pluralistic one. They embrace a pre-Lockeian view of popular sovereignty: the people may collectively overthrow an unjust prince, but for them to put effective checks upon his daily behavior or term in power is practically unheard of.' On human rights: 'While human rights in general are defended throughout the area, individual rights are not.' Hence, 'if rights were common instead of individual, it seemed logical to name them and characterize them as collective goals to be sought rather than as freedoms to be protected – thus the list of 'social rights' guaranteed by contemporary Central American constitutions and the popular tendency to associate freedom with bread, schools and hospitals.' David Lehmann also points out that 'Common to all the radical projects of the time [the 1970s] was the vision of a final stasis, in which the contradictions of society and economy would be overcome and a state of harmony achieved – again reflecting the influence of Catholic thought.' See Glen C. Dealy, 'Pipe Dreams: The Pluralistic Latins', *Foreign Policy*, vol. 57 (Winter 1984/85), pp. 115–16, 117; David Lehmann, *Democracy and Development, in Latin America, Economics, Politics and Religion in Postwar Period (Philadalphia, P.A: Temple University Press, 1990)*, p. 50 Jacques Zylberberg, 'Des acteurs étatiques: Léviathan en Amérique', *Études Internationales*, vol. 17, no. 2 (June 1986), pp. 249–78.

39. Pierre Bourdieu called that the *effet de science*. See his excellent *Homo Academicus* (Stanford, CA.: Stanford University Press, 1988).

40. Debray (1996), pp. 153, 240–1.
41. For a thoughtful portrait, see Lehmann, *Democracy and Development*, op. cit.
42. See Gordon (1989).
43. See Rudolph P. Atcon, *La Universidad Latinoamericana/the Latin American University* (Bogotá: ECO Revista de la Cultura de Occidente, 1966).
44. Ministry of Education, El Salvador, *Documentos de la reforma educativa*, vol. 3 (San Salvador, 1970).
45. Manuel Luis Escamilla, *La reforma educativa salvadoreña* (San Salvador: Ministerio de Educación, 1975); UES, Secretaria de Planificación, *Diagnóstico global de la UES*, Tome 1 (San Salvador, 1972), pp. 75–80; Proyecto UCA/PREDE-UCA, *La investigación y la docencia en la educación universitaria de El Salvador* (San Salvador, 1990), p. 73.
46. UCA, *Universidad y sociedad, lecturas para el curso de admisión a la UCA* (San Salvador: UCA, 1989), p. 66; see also Román Mayorga Quiroz, *La universidad para el cambio social* (San Salvador: UCA editores, 1978), p. 25.
47. Edelberto Torres-Rivas, 'Ciencia y conciencia sociales en Centroamérica', *Polémica* vol. 8 (1989), p. 5; CSUCA, *Confederación Universitaria Centroamericana, 1948–1973* (San José: CSUCA circa 1973); Fernando Flores Pinel, 'La Universidad de El Salvador, una encrucijada política difícil', *ECA*, nos 361–2 (Nov.–Dec. 1978), p. 892 (see in Flores Pinel the list of donors – international and wealthy Salvadorans – to the National University during that period).
48. Cf. John Beverley and Marc Zimmerman, *Literature and Politics in the Central American Revolutions* (Austin: University of Texas Press, 1990), p. 47; Richard M. Morse, *Resonancias del Nuevo Mundo* (Mexico: Editorial Vuelta, 1995), p. 233.
49. Torres-Rivas, 'Ciencia y conciencia sociales', op. cit.
50. For Gilbert W. Merkx, 'the expansion of area studies following [the] passage of Title VI led to the dissemination of new and more objective information about foreign areas, criticism of U.S. foreign policy, and exposés of the mistakes made by national security agencies... The relationship of the area studies community to U.S. cold-war policy was therefore not marked by dependence and support but rather by autonomy and even confrontation.' Gilbert W. Merkx, 'Foreign Area Studies, Back to the Future?', *Lasa Forum*, vol. 26, no. 2 (Summer 1995), pp. 5, 6.
51. The Peace Corps programme also had an unintended repercussion in the Third World. As Forrest Colburn (1994, p. 17) points out: 'Peace Corps volunteers, too, while often

dismissed as agents of imperialism, contributed to the radicalization of Ethiopian students.'

52. This end of this countercultural trend in the West, and especially in the United States, coincided with the stagnation of living standards in the mid-1970s. Conservative trends re-emerged with what economist Paul Krugman labelled the 'age of diminished expectation'.

53. Although the countercultural trend in the 1960s (The new left) was substantially different from the one that existed in Europe during the 1920s and 1930s (Romanticism), both shared a common antiliberal creed. Furthermore, in both instances cultural protest preceded political protest. See Zev Sternhell (ed.), *L'éternel retour, contre la démocratie, l'idéologie de la décadence* (Paris: Presses de la Fondation nationale des sciences politiques, 1994).

54. The following is an interesting extract from Colburn (1994, p. 35) about Nicaragua: 'Pictures of ranking Sandinistas on display at the Museum of the Revolution in Managua are illuminating. Taken in the '60s, the pictures reveal students with long hair, sideburns, mustaches, and beards. All the hair, and the style in which it is brandished, attest to the awareness among Nicaraguan youth in the '60s and '70s of what their peers were up to in places as distant as Berkeley and Paris. In 1986, a New York journalist, Paul Berman, interviewed Omar Cabezas, a Sandinista leader and the author of a celebrated memoir of guerrilla life. Their discussion and Berman's conclusion are generalizable: "Cabezas was happy to reminisce . . . He brought up names like Danny Cohn-Bendit, the Paris student leader of 1968. Berkeley and Kent State came to his lips. When the Kent students were massacred in 1970, Cabezas organized a memorial meeting at León . . . I think he wanted it understood that he and his comrades weren't as isolated as might be imagined. They were part of the big world . . . Fantasy in prosperous Western Europe and North America became realism in many poor countries of the world".' The article quoted by Colburn is Paul Berman, 'Nicaragua 1986', *Mother Jones*, December 1986. See also Miguel Huezo Mixco, 'Literatura sin revolución', *Tendencias* (San Salvador), vol. 24 (Oct. 1993), p. 25.

55. V.S. Naipaul, 'Argentina', *New York Review of Books*, vol. 39 (30 Jan. 1992), p. 14, quoted by Colburn, ibid., p. 48.

56. Castañeda (1994), pp. 78, 128.

57. Marxism became a dominant passion in Western universities only after the Second World War. According to Furet (1995, p. 325) 'between the two wars [Marxism] was more common among writers than professors'.

58. See Steven Palmer, 'Carlos Fonseca and the Construction of Sandinismo in Nicaragua', *Latin American Research Review*, vol. 23, no. 1 (1988), pp. 91–109.
59. See interviews with Jorge Schafik Handal in Miguel Bonasso and Ciro Gómez Leyva, *El Salvador, cuatro minutos para las doce, conversaciones con el comandante Schafik Handal* (Mexico: Periodistas Asociados Latinoamericanos, 1992), p. 24.
60. DRU, May 1980, reproduced in *ECA* no. 379. See also Cienfuegos (1993), p. 13; Harnecker (1993), p. 41. In neighbouring Nicaragua the Sandinistas were quite ready to admit their debt to the comrades of the Sierra Maestra. Matt Childs reminds us that 'Tomás Borge described Fidel Castro as "the resurrection of Sandino, the answer to our reservations, the justification of the dreams of heresy of a few hours before". The influence of the Cuban Revolution is further reflected in the opening lines of the Sandinista oath: "Before the images of Augusto César Sandino and Ernesto Che Guevara, before the memory and the heroes and martyrs of Nicaragua, Latin America and all of humanity, before history: I place my hand on the red-and-black banner that signifies *Patria Libre o Morir!*"' Childs, 'An Historical Critique of the Emergence and Evolution of Ernesto Che Guerara's *Foco* Theory', *Journal of Latin American Studies*, 27 (1997), p. 597. Tomas Borge himself talks about Nicaragua's 'impermeability' to advanced ideology (that is, Marxism–Leninism) until 1960: 'the apparent impermeability of Nicaragua was broken by the Cuban Revolution. The struggle in the Sierra Maestra influenced Nicaraguan political life. From then on, the Nicaraguan rebellion nurtured itself with Lenin, Che Guevara, Ho Chi-Minh and other revolutionaries.' Tomas Borge, *La paciente impaciencia* (Managua: Editorial Vanguardia, 1989), pp. 90–1.
61. Castañeda (1994), p. 97.
62. Castro's record on the unification of the left in Latin America is nevertheless contradictory. As Childs points out 'while it is undoubtedly true that the left's overall following increased as a result of Castro's victory, at the same time it became increasingly sectarian and divided'. Childs, 'An Historical Critique', op. cit., p. 596.
63. Castañeda (1994), p. 74 (emphasis added).
64. Ibid., p. 16.
65. Ibid., p. 184.
66. See Simon Leys, *Les habits neufs du président Mao* (Paris: Champ Libre, 1971).
67. For an epic presentation of the advent of Marxism–Leninism among the Central American intelligentsia, see Claudio

Bogantes and Ursula Kuhlmann, 'El surgimiento del realismo social en Centroamérica, 1930–1970', *Revista de Crítica Literaria Latinoamericana*, vol. 17 (1983), pp. 39–64.

68. According to Robert Packenham (1992, p. 234), 'Marxism as a compelling intellectual orientation declined even in France – *especially* in France – where it had once been dominant. This example was particularly significant for Latin American Marxist intellectuals, so sensitive to French influences.' Forrest Colburn (1994, p. 16) similarly contends that 'the beginning of the end [of Marxist influence in the West] was probably the wave of revisionist interpretations of the Soviet Union by Parisian intellectuals in the '70s.' See also the excellent book by Jeannine Verdès-Leroux, *Le réveil des somnanbules, Le parti communiste, les intellectuels et la culture (1956–1985)* (Paris: Fayard/Minuit, 1987).

69. Edelberto Torres-Rivas, *Centroamérica: la democracia posible* (San José, CR: EDUCA/FLACSO, 1987), p. 131.

70. On the use of paradox and contradictions in ideological constructions, see Raymond Boudon, *L'art de se persuader des idées douteuses, fragiles ou fausses* (Paris: Fayard, 1990).

71. Packenham, (1992), p. 209; see also Jacques Zylberberg, 'Modèles d'État, modèles de croissance: Le cas latinoaméricain', *Civilisation*, vols 1–2 (1980), pp. 60–72.

72. One of the best analysis of this disposition among Latin American social scientist can be found in Charles Bergquist, 'In the Name of History: A Disciplinary Critique of Orlando Fals Borda's *Historia doble de la costa*', *Latin American Research Review*, vol. 25, no. 3 (1990), pp. 156–76.

73. There are countless illustrations of this mind-set in Transito Rivas and Hilda Elizabeth Miranda Luna, *Crisis de la educación superior universitaria y las posibilidades de solución para la Universidad de El Salvador* (San Salvador: Editorial Universitaria, 1990).

74. See for instance LP-28, 'Programa de Gobierno Democrático Popular de las Ligas Populares 28 de Febrero' and MIPTES, 'Plataforma ideológica del Movimiento Independiente de Profesionales y técnicos de El Salvador', both in *ECA*, nos 377–8 (March–April 1980), pp. 52, 358. Since scientific materialism and historical materialism are synonymous, one can find other statements, such as that in an FMLN communiqué, where its enemies are condemned to representing 'the antihistory, the lie and the obscurantism of the nation'. In FMLN, 'Proclama del FMLN a la nacion, la revolución democrática', mimeo, 24 September 1990, p.11.

75. Torres-Rivas, 'Ciencia y conciencia sociales', op. cit., p. 8.

76. Ibid., p. 5.
77. Cf. *Revista de Ciencias Sociales*, vol. 33 (Sept. 1986).
78. Miguel De Castilla Urbina, 'Aproximación de una historia de las Ciencias Sociales en Nicaragua', *Revista de Ciencias Sociales*, vol. 33 (Sept. 1986), p. 57 (emphasis added).
79. Carlos Figueroa Ibarra, 'Ciencias sociales y sociedad en Guatemala', *Revista de Ciencias Sociales*, vol. 33 (Sept. 1986), p. 30 (emphasis added).
80. Mario Lungo, 'El desarrollo de las Ciencias Sociales en El Salvador y su aporte al conocimiento de la realidad del país', *Revista de Ciencias Sociales*, vol. 33 (Sept. 1986), p. 53.
81. For Daniel Levy, 'Costa Rica's universities... rarely exhibit the degree of either leftism or disruption found in Colombia, Ecuador, Mexico, or Venezuela. Student protests, demonstrations, and propaganda are generally rather mild at the University of Costa Rica (the nation's only university until the '70s).' Daniel C. Levy, 'Latin American Student Politics: Beyond the '60s', in Philip B. Altbach (ed.), *Student Political Activism: An International Reference Handbook* (New York: Greenwood Press, 1989), p. 322. See also Gonzalo Ramirez Guier, 'Una interpretación de la evolución de las ciencias sociales en Costa Rica', *Revista de Ciencias Sociales*, vol. 33 (Sept. 1986), pp. 93–105.
82. Torres-Rivas, 'Ciencia y conciencia sociales', op. cit., p. 9.
83. Sergio Ramirez, '6 falsos golpes mortales contra la literatura centroamericana', *ABRA*, vol. 2, no. 19 (San Salvador, January–February 1977), p. 10. For very similar testimonies on the intellectual atmosphere of the 1960s and 1970s by Chilean intellectuals, see Jeffrey M. Puryear, *Thinking Politics, Intellectuals and Democracy in Chile, 1973–1988* (Baltimore, MD: Johns Hopkins University Press, 1994), p. 18 ff.
84. Torres-Rivas, 'Ciencia y conciencia sociales', op. cit., p. 12. Richard Morse formulates the same comment about 'developmentalist' intellectuals in the 1950s and early 1960s, who had precious little time to 'recycle and transform the ideologies that they were importing'. Richard Morse, *Resonancias del nuevo mundo* (México: Vuelta, 1995), p. 233.
85. Zaïd (1988), p. 30. Mario Vargas Llosa also recalls that: 'Until the First World War, more or less, the Latin American intellectual elite was almost always of the right, Francophile or "hispanist" and violently and condescendingly anti-American... Since the Mexican revolution [1910], intellectuals in Latin American became 'progressive'... They took up anti- Americanism, coloring it with economic and political hues.' Quoted in Castañeda (1994), p. 291.

86. *The Globe and Mail*, Toronto, 4 April 1996, p. A16.
87. In a way, the ideological construct *la realidad* is structurally similar to the new catchword of (mostly Western) 'armchair decolonisers': postcolonialism. As Jasper Goss points out, 'the problem of whether postcolonialism is a material condition... or a strategy to arrive at a broader postcolonial condition or both, is unclear.' What is more, 'postcolonial critics... have guaranteed themselves the position of armchair decolonisers, with the primacy of a textual role being the most prominent in anti-colonial struggle.' One again, intellectual ambiguity supplies the fig leaf for an unambiguous enterprise of self-promotion. Jasper Goss, 'Postcolonialism: Subverting Whose Empire?' *Third World Quarterly*, vol. 17, no. 2 (1996), pp. 239–50.
88. Daniel Pécaut, *Entre le peuple et la nation: Les intellectuels et la politique au Brésil* (Paris: Éditions de la maison des sciences de l'homme, 1989), p. ix.
89. Mario Benedetti, 'Situación del intelectual en la América Latina', *Literatura y arte nuevo en Cuba*, quoted in Douglas Salamanca, 'Literatura, Sandinismo y Compromiso', *Revista Iberoamericana*, vol. 157 (Oct.–Dec. 1991), p. 854.
90. Arturo Arias, 'Literary Production and Political Crisis in Central America', *International Political Science Review*, vol. 12, no. 1 (1991), p. 19.
91. Quoted in H. H. Gerth and C. Wright Mills (eds), *From Max Weber: Essays in Sociology* (New York: Oxford University Press, 1958), p. 143.
92. Castilla Urbina, 'Aproximación', op. cit., p. 62. This theoretical undertaking was made possible, according to the author, by Fonseca's mastery of 'dialectic materialism and the political economy of Marx and Engels', in addition to a 'profound knowledge of the history of Nicaragua and of the wars of liberation of other peoples'.
93. UCA, *Universidad y sociedad, lecturas para el curso de admisión a la UCA* (San Salvador: UCA editores, 1989), p. 199.
94. Jon Sobrino, 'Inspiración cristiana de la Universidad', *ECA*, no. 468 (Oct. 1987), p. 701 (emphasis added).
95. Editorial, '1982, año decisivo para El Salvador', *ECA* nos 399–400 (Jan.–Feb. 1982), p. 8.
96. *La realidad* is practically an icon for the Mexican writer Rosario Castellanos, who advocates *l'art engagé*. 'Now, committed with what? With *la realidad*. The political commitment [of the artist] consists in transcribing with the best and richest esthetic means... this reality that we have managed to

contemplate, to discover and that we want to transmit to others.' Quoted in Salamanca, 'Literatura, Sandinismo y Compromiso', op. cit., p. 851.

97. Cf. 'Crisis Social, Papel de la Universidad', *Cuadernos universitarios*, vol. 6 (San Salvador, 1986), pp. 13, 14.
98. Ignacio Ellacuria, 'La UCA ante el doctorado concedido a Monseñor Romero', *ECA*, no. 437 (March 1985), p. 171.
99. UCA, *Universidad y sociedad*, op. cit., p. 203
100. Ignacio Ellacuria, 'Utopía y profetismo desde América latina: un ensayo concreto de soteriología histórica', *Revista latinoamericana de teología*, vol. 17 (May–Aug. 1989), p. 150.
101. Editorial, 'La ofensiva de noviembre ¿fin de la guerra?' *ECA*, nos 495–6 (Jan.–Feb. 1990), p. 10.
102. In fact one could perhaps make the following case: the more the elite, and the intellectual elite in particular, is cut off from the aspirations of the masses, the more likely it is to manufacture 'realist inflation'; that is, a self-serving ideological assumption where the twin contradictions of scientific morality and the popular elites are conjugated.

3 Revolution within the Revolution

1. One year before, the Communist Party, via its electoral facade the UDN, joined two other parties (the PDC and the social-democratic MNR) to create the UNO. The UNO coalition fielded candidates at the 1972 presidential elections: José Napoléon Duarte (PDC) for president and Guillermo Ungo (MNR) for vice-president.
2. Born in 1935 to an upper-class family from San Salvador, he was arrested in 1960 during the Lemus dictatorship. He escaped from jail in the aftermath of an earthquake and went into exile (Mexico, Western Europe, Cuba and Czechoslovakia). He returned to El Salvador only in 1973, where he was accused of being a CIA spy and executed in 1975 on the order of the top command of the ERP. See 'Dalton, fusilado por Espia de la CIA: FPL', *Excelsior* (Mexico), 10 March 1980; for mournful comments from a bewildered friend, see Régis Debray, 'Gracias Roque...', *ECA*, no. 330 (April 1976), pp. 248–50
3. Resistancia Nacional, 'Mensaje a la nación con audacia hacia el futuro', *Análisis* (San Salvador), May–June 1992, p. 330.
4. Marco Antonio Grande, 'Dialéctica del desarrollo del FMLN', (2 articles), *Análisis*, vol. 5 (San Salvador, May 1988), p. 25.

5. The limited unity achieved with the formation of the FMLN in 1980 was in itself a considerable feat (as in Nicaragua, Fidel Castro was apparently instrumental in convincing the rebels to coalesce into a military front instead of killing each other). The competing vanguards could barely talk to each other during the 1970s, and sometimes resorted to violence to express their hatred. In their various manifestoes and proclamations published during that period, one finds recurrent rhetoric just where the usual Leninist anthems were used *in extenso*: counter-revolutionary, imperialist's ally, revisionist, bureaucratism and so on. See for instance the inflammatory exchange between the FAPU and the BPR over the issue of the agrarian 'transformation', sponsored by the military government (upon which, incidentally, both had essentially the same position: that it was an imperialist plot). Cienfuegos (1993), p. 20. See *ECA*, nos 335–6 (Sept.–Oct. 1976), pp. 629–30; see also in Cabarrus (1983).
6. Cienfuegos (1993), p. 10.
7. Details of the origins of the various groups often differ among observers and participants (even their foundation dates – the PRTC's for instance – are sometimes the object of controversy). This suggests that behind the soup of acronyms, of which insurgents appear to be particularly fond, lies a muddle of anxious activists vying for peer-recognition and a place in history. For an overview, in addition to the books of Marta Harnecker and Fermán Cienfuegos already quoted, see Jorge Schafik Handal, 'We Have No Alternative to Armed Struggle', *World Marxist Review* (Oct. 1980); interviews with Schafik Handal in Miguel Gonasso and Ciro Gómez Leyva, *Cuatro minutos para las doce, conversaciones con el comandante Schafik Handal* (Mexico: Periodistas Asociados Latinoamericanos, 1992); Salvador Samayoa and Guillermo Galvan, 'El movimiento obrero en El Salvador ¿Resurgimiento o Agitación?' *ECA*, nos 369–70 (July–Aug. 1979), pp. 591–600; Italo López Vallecillos, 'Rasgos sociales y tendencias políticas en El Salvador (1969–1979)', *ECA*, nos 372–73 (Oct.–Nov. 1979), pp. 863–84. For a critical perspective by two former 'renegades', see Javier Rojas, *Conversaciones con el comandante Miguel Castellanos* (Santiago, Chili: Editorial Andante, 1986); and Marco Antonio Grande, 'Dialéctica del desarrollo del FMLN', op. cit.
8. For most of the internal war, the top leaders of the five organisations of the FMLN were Eduardo Sancho (RN, *nom de guerre* Fermán Cienfuegos), Francisco Jovel (PRTC, Roberto Roca), Jorge Shafik Handal (PC), Salvador Sánchez Cerén (FPL, Leonel Gonzalez) and Joaquín Villalobos (ERP, René Cruz). See 'Comunicado de la Dirección Revolucionaria

Unificada (DRU-PM) anunciando la formación del Frente "Farabundo Marti" para la Liberación Nacional (FMLN)', *ECA*, nos 384–5 (Oct.–Nov. 1980), pp. 1092–3.

9. During the emergence of the insurgency, as Fermán Cienfuegos (Eduardo Sancho) concedes, the main focus was on 'creating the military apparatus... during the first years we did not put much emphasis on the issue of the masses'. Cienfuegos (1993), p. 21. Some documents lead one to believe that PM (Pontico-military) organisations were tied to distinct 'military' wings: that is, the Popular Armed Forces of Liberation (FAPL/FPL), the Armed Forces of National Resistance (FARN/RN), the Popular Armed Forces of Liberation (FARPL/PRTC) and the Armed Forces of Liberation (FAL/PCS). All these military wings, sometimes called the Popular Army of Liberation (EPL), were first coordinated by the Unified Revolutionary Direction (DRU-1980). However, since the DRU was sometimes called the Unified Revolutionary 'Political-Military' Direction (DRU-PM) it is hard to know which groups – the military or the political-military – the DRU coordinated. Moreover it remains unclear whether, or when, the DRU (PM) was supplanted by the FMLN.
10. Cienfuegos (1993), p. 32.
11. This militaristic orientation at the expense of the mobilisation of the masses was sometimes criticised among the Salvadoran left. See for example the special issue of *ECA*, no. 465 (July 1987). It was also far from being the excluse preserve of the Salvadoran left. As Castañeda (1994, pp. 270–1) points out, 'an entire wing of the left has been nothing but militaristic for at least thirty years'.
12. See the candid remarks of pro-insurgents Samayoa and Galvan, 'El movimiento obrero en El Salvador', op. cit.
13. Cienfuegos (1993), pp. 20–1.
14. Quoted in Harnecker (1993), p. 124 (emphasis added).
15. Ibid., p. 136.
16. Ibid., p. 137.
17. Cienfuegos (1993), p. 41.
18. Apparently the FDR also included the Social Democratic Party, a ghost organisation whose unassuming leader, Reni Roldan, was Ungo's running mate (on the Convergencia Democratica ticket) during the presidential elections of March 1989). The CD, created in 1987, served as the electoral vehicle of the FDR during the late 1980s. Ungo once explained the difference between the PSD and the MNR by pointing out that whereas the PSD was 'social-democrat', the

MNR was 'socialist-democrat'. See his interview in *Análisis*, vols 9–10 (San Salvador, Sept–Oct. 1988), pp. 60–71.

19. FDR-FMLN, 'Pacto político', *ECA,* no. 461 (March 1987), pp. 281–2.
20. Quoted in Harnecker (1993), p. 359.
21. Régis Debray, *Lutte armée et lutte politique en Amérique latine* (Paris: Maspéro, 1967), p. 94.
22. Max Weber, *Economy and Society*, vol. 2 (New York: Bedminster Press, 1968), p. 906.
23. The Grupos de Acción Revolucionaria (GAR), the Frente Unido de Acción Revolucionaria (FUAR), the Movimiento Revolucionario Abril y Mayo (mimicking the Movement of the 26 of July in Cuba), the Acción Revolucionaria Salvadoreña (ARS), the Movimiento de Izquierda Radical (MIR), the Comisiûn Nacional de Masas (CONAMAS), the Frente Revolucionario de Unidad Popular (FRUP), and many others.
24. The Rafael Antonio Arce Zablah Brigade (ERP), the Urban Commando Mardoqueo Cruz (PRTC), the Pablo Castillo Metropolitan Front (FPL), the Clara Elisabeth Ramírez Metropolitan Front, and so on.
25. Y. Grenier, 'Understanding the FMLN, A Glossary of Five Words', *Conflict Quarterly*, 2 (Spring 1991), pp. 51–75.
26. On forced recruitment – which apparently lasted only for few years in the mid 1980s – see the comments by FPL leaders in Harnecker (1993), pp. 245, 246; see also Americas Watch, *El Salvador's Decade of Terror, Human Rights since the Assassination of Archbishop Romero* (New Haven and London: Yale University Press, 1989).
27. According to Fermán Cienfuegos (1993, p. 43), in 1981 the FMLN's finance commission (COFIN) was already in possession of some 10 million dollars, received from international solidarity movements Cienfuegos, *Veredas de audacia*, 43.
28. Cienfuegos (1993), p. 12
29. Ibid., p. 9.
30. Communiqué no. 1 of the FPL, *ECA*, nos 342–3 (April–May 1977), p. 321
31. Harnecker (1993), p. 94.
32. Timothy P. Wickham-Crowley contends that 'by both act and ideology...the Salvadoran guerrillas have set themselves apart from almost all other regional revolutionaries', and that 'the closest parallel to their acts seems to be *Sendero Luminoso*'. See his 'Understanding Failed Revolution in El Salvador: A Comparative Analysis of Regime Types and Social Structures', *Politics and Society*, vol. 17, no. 4 (1989), p. 519.

33. The best critical review of this generation's commitment to Leninism is to be found in Castañeda (1994).
34. For Colburn, 'The key to successful insurrections has not been, as is so often romanticized, an alliance between guerrillas and peasants. Instead, what has been indispensable is the ability of revolutionaries to weld together a broad coalition of groups – large segments of the middle class, the peasantry, and foreign interests' (Colburn, 1994, p. 46). Colburn should have mentioned, first and foremost, the national bourgeoisie.
35. In the January 1981 agreement between the FMLN and the so-called young officers of the Salvadoran army (*Juventud Militar*) it is stated that 'the new army will accept the FMLN-FDR as the vanguard of the people and the revolution, and obey the Democratic Revolutionary Government (GDR)'. See FMLN and Juventud Militar, 'Pacto político de la Juventud Militar y las Fuerzas del FMLN', *ECA*, nos 387–8 (Jan.–Feb. 1981), p. 92.
36. 'FMLN General Command Issues Year-End Message', broadcasted on Radio Venceremos (2 Jan. 1990), translated in *FBIS-LAT*, Vol. 90, no. 5 (8 Jan. 1990), p. 25.
37. As Cienfuegos (1993, p. 15) recalls, in the early 1970s 'practically all organisations were pretending to be the vanguard ... trying to seize this role from the PC'.
38. Harnecker (1993), p. 132.
39. Ibid., p. 137.
40. Ibid., p. 344.
41. Ibid., p. 345.
42. Ibid., pp. 200–1.
43. Ibid., p. 221.
44. Ibid., p. 199.
45. Ibid., pp. 199–200.
46. Ibid., p. 96.
47. Ibid., p. 346.
48. Ibid., p. 202.
49. Ibid., p. 147.
50. Ibid., pp. 344–5.
51. Ibid., p. 221.
52. See for example T. Wickham-Crowley, 'Understanding Failed Revolution in El Salvador: A Comparative Analysis of Regime Types and Social Structures', *Politics and Society*, vol. 17, no. 4 (1989), pp. 511–37; Manus I. Midlarsky and Kenneth Roberts, 'Class, State, and Revolution in Central America: Nicaragua and El Salvador Compared', *Journal of Conflict Resolution*, vol. 29, no. 2 (June 1985), pp. 163–94; Matthew Soberg Shugart,

'States, Revolutionary Conflict and Democracy: El Salvador and Nicaragua in Comparative Perspective', *Government and Opposition*, vol. 22, no. 1 (Winter 1987), pp. 13–32.

53. Wickham-Crowley, 'Understanding Failed Revolution', op. cit., p. 521.
54. As an FPL leader admitted: 'For us it was a real challenge to maintain a certain simplicity when we were talking to the people.' Quoted in Harnecker (1993), p. 346.
55. Ibid., p. 201.
56. Ibid., p. 199.
57. To be sure, Reagan's support of the counterinsurgency cause in El Salvador was virtually unqualified.
58. Peter Berger, *Pyramids of Sacrifice, Political Ethics and Social Change* (New York: Anchor Books, 1976), p. 81. Timothy Wickham-Crowley's attempt to explain why guerrillas are successful (or not), based on various 'sources of peasant support' (state and agrarian structures, rebellious cultures and social ties) is predicated on the assumption that, ultimately, insurgents must behave in a way that is consonant with peasants' needs and aspirations. This approach carries its own inevitable conclusion: a successful revolution, at all stages of its evolution, is one that brings historical demands to the fore. This approach yields some valuable, though quasi-tautological, results when comparing relatively successful insurgencies with total failures – such as Guevara's *foco* in Bolivia. But that's about it. Was the FSLN in Nicaragua more successful than the FMLN in bartering sundry benefits for political support from the peasants or 'the masses'? Because Wickham-Crowley's approach plays down the mobilisational, top-down dimension of *all* insurgencies of the Castro generation, it limits the capacity to explain: (1) why peasant 'support' seems to exist only where insurgents already enjoy a quasi monopoly of the legitimate use of force in a given territory; (2) why most peasants do not actively support any armies from the city and usually vote with their feet when military conflict spills into their region; and (3) how 'peasants' demands evolve from an agenda that is always substantially different from the insurgents' agenda – (as Che Guevara deplored many times, peasants are very petit-bourgeois) to one that is in similar or at least compatible with it. Wickham-Crowley (1992), chapters 6 and 7.
59. See the comments by John McAward, senior consultant for Freedom House, in Joseph S. Tulchin (ed.), *Is There a Transition to Democracy in El Salvador?* (Boulder, CO, and London: Lynne Rienner, 1992), p. 59 et seq.

60. Quoted in Castañeda (1994), pp. 241–2. Likewise Fermán Cienfuegos (Eduardo Sancho) contends that 'the experience has demonstrated that one cannot impose a line to the masses, nor can you impose a revolutionary mode of thinking'. He continues: 'For instance one cannot impose a Marxist-Leninist ideology on our people, who are Christian. The problem is not to convert all the masses into Marxists, but to win them to the political project proposed by the FMLN' (Cienfuegos, 1993, p. 46). For an interesting comparative perspective, see David Stoll, *Between Two Armies in the Ixil Towns of Guatemala* (New York: Columbia University Press, 1993).
61. Cienfuegos (1993), p. 51.
62. Seligson's comments on this question deserve to be quoted at length: 'When we find that an identical condition (such as the predominance of landless laborers in western El Salvador) is associated in one instance with a major uprising (in the 1932 rebellion) and in another with quiescence (in the 1980s), we must be led to conclude that the alleged causal factor is entirely spurious.' In correction with the economic conditions of rebellion in the most conflictive zones of El Salvador, Seligson concludes that 'the particular conditions of the regions themselves are not responsible for the violence and that government repression of real or imagined guerrilla bands caused major escalation of the violence and forced otherwise neutral bystanders to chose between "two armies".' M. A. Seligson, 'Agrarian Inequality and the Theory of Peasant Rebellion', *Latin American Research Review*, vol. 31, no. 2 (1996), pp. 152, 155.
63. Douglas Kincaid, 'Peasants into Rebels: Community and Class in Rural El Salvador', *Comparative Study of Society and History*, vol. 29 (1987), p. 477. This author points out, for instance, that the Communist Party's 'ideological exhortations' were 'ineffective'.
64. See Jeffrey Paige, *Agrarian Revolution: Social Movements and Export Agriculture in the Underdeveloped World* (New York: Free Press, 1975); Carlos Samaniego, 'Movimiento campesino o lucha del proletariado rural en El Salvador', *Estudios sociales centroamericanos*, vol. 25 (1980), pp. 125–44.
65. Even an author such as Jenny Pearce, who comes as close as academic publishing (and common sense) allows to suggesting that the FMLM was a sort of popular Messiah, cannot pinpoint many 'guerrilla controlled' areas in the autumn of 1984. See Jenny Pearce, *Promised Land, Peasant Rebellion in Chalatenango, El Salvador* (London: Latin American Bureau, 1986), p. viii.

66. As a matter of fact the overwhelming majority of FMLN leaders, including quite a few leaders of peasant organisations, elected San Salvador as their domicile after the Chapultepec accords.
67. Furet (1995), p. 250, note 2 (emphasis added).
68. Grande, 'Dialéctica del desarrollo del FMLN', op. cit., p. 23.
69. This thesis is masterfully articulated in Gabriel Zaid, 'Enemy Colleagues, A Reading of the Salvadoran Tragedy', *Dissent*, Winter 1982, pp. 13–39.
70. Cienfuegos (1993), p. 18.
71. See the BPR and other groups' and parties' positions on the 'agrarian transformation' in *ECA*, vols 335–6 (Sept.–Oct. 1976).
72. The junta nationalised the banks and external trade, and launched an agrarian reform that, according to Merilee S. Grindle (1986, pp. 134–6), was the most extensive non-socialist land reform in Latin America. See also M. A. Seligson, 'Thirty Years of Transformation in the Agrarian Structure of El Salvador, 1961–1991', *Latin American Research Review* 30, 3 (1995), pp. 73–74. See also his reply to comments by Martin Diskin and Jeffrey Paige Seligson, 'Agrarian Inequality', op. cit.
73. Quoted in Harnecker (1993), pp. 348–9.
74. 'Pacto político de la juventud militar y las fuerzas del FMLN', *ECA*, nos 387–8 (Jan.–Feb. 1981), pp. 91–2.
75. 'Proclama de la Fuerza Armada de El Salvador', *ECA*, nos 372–3 (Oct.–Nov. 1979), pp. 1017–18.
76. Quoted in *Excélsior* (Mexico City), 6 March 1980, and in Zaid, 'Enemy Colleagues', op. cit., p. 16. See also ERP, 'El ERP ante la situación nacional', *ECA*, nos 372–3 (Oct.–Nov. 1979), p. 1023.
77. Cienfuegos (1993), p. 25.
78. Quoted in Harnecker (1993), p. 212 (emphasis added).
79. 'Programa de gobierno de la Unión Nacional Opositora', *ECA*, no. 341 (March 1977), p. 220 (emphasis added).
80. Castañeda (1994), p. 180.
81. Quoted in Harnecker (1993), pp. 344, 348.
82. R. Cardenal (1987), pp. 452–6 (emphasis added).
83. Torres-Rivas (1987), p. 142. James Malloy noticed a similar pattern in a radical faction of the Bolivian MNR: 'One of the most consistent characteristics of this primary group, especially Los Grupos de Honor after 1946, was an orientation to action and an involvement in what one MNR leader calls *la mística de la revolución violenta*. They were more interested in the seizure than the use of power'. James Malloy, *Bolivia: the*

Uncompleted Revolution (Pittsburgh, PA: University of Pittsburgh Press, 1970), p. 160.

84. Rafael Guido Béjar, 'El centro político y la reproducción del consenso', *Tendencias*, vol. 23 (Sept. 1993), p. 21. See also Yvon Grenier, 'Una clase política en transición', *Tendencias*, vol. 14 (San Salvador, Oct. 1992).
85. The UCA's University Institute for the study of Public Opinion (IUDOP) published numerous polls throughout the 1980s showing popular dissatisfaction with the war in general and the FMLN's economic sabotage in particular. Of course this resulted in part from successful government propaganda and the control of the media by right-wing and extreme-right-wing factions.
86. Sara Miles and Bob Ostertag, 'FMLN New Thinking', *NACLA, Report on the Americas*, vol. 23, no. 3 (Sept. 1989), pp. 15–38.
87. Joaquin Villalobos, 'A Democratic Revolution for El Salvador', *Foreign Policy*, vol. 74 (Spring 1989), pp. 103–22, *Una revolución en la izquierda para una revolución democrática* (San Salvador: Ediciones Arcoiris, 1992). The FMLN's national convention of December 1994 still called for unity, but also for internal elections for the nomination of candidates (instead of nomination from above) and for internal democracy.
88. 'Pacto de San Andrés, Desarrollo: el nuevo nombre de la paz', (I and II), *Proceso*, (San Salvador) 6 and 14 June 1995; Partido Demócrata (en organización), *Apuesta total a la paz*, (San Salvador), March 1995.
89. In an interview with the author (San Salvador, 29 June 1995), Sonia Aguiñada Carranza, an ERP-FMLN turned PD member of the legislative assembly (ERP-PD) denied that the ERP was ever Marxist–Leninist beyond some strategic alliance with other factions of the FMLN.
90. FMLN, 'Plan económico', *ECA*, no. 557 (March 1995), p. 291. See also FMLN, 'Propuestas ante el paquete de medidas económicas impulsado por el gobierno', *ECA*, nos 555–6 (Jan.–Feb. 1995), p. 147–9.
91. Castellanos Moya (1993), p. 21.
92. Terry L. Karl, 'Imposing Consent? Electoralism vs. Democratization in El Salvador', in Paul Drake and Eduardo Silva (eds), *Elections and Democratization in Latin America, 1980–85* (San Diego: CILAS/Center for U.S.-Mexican Studies/IOA, 1986). See also E.S. Herman and F. Broadhead, *Demonstration Elections: U.S.-Staged Elections in the Dominican Republic, Vietnam, and El Salvador* (Boston: South End Press, 1984).

93. Adam Przeworski, *Democracy and the Market* (Cambridge, MA: Cambridge University Press, 1992), pp. 18–19.
94. See Guillermo O'Donnell and P. Schmitter, *Transitions from Authoritarian Rule, Tentative Conclusions about Uncertain Democracies* (Baltimore, MD: John Hopkins University Press, 1986), p. 71; Diane Ethier (ed.), *Democratic Transition and Consolidation in Southern Europe, Latin America and Southeast Asia* (New York: Macmillan/St Martin's Press, 1990).
95. See ARENA, *Manual del dirigente* (San Salvador: ARENA, 1990). For an original interpretation of the extreme right's crusades in Latin America, see Frank Graziano, *Divine Violence* (Boulder, CO.: Westview Press, 1992).
96. As the former guerrilla Marco Antonio Grande pointed out, 'the Salvadoran problem was seen by the left as a problem of class struggle and seizure of power, not as a problem defined in terms of democratising the system'. Grande, 'Dialéctica del desarrollo del FMLN', op. cit., p. 23.
97. Przeworski falls into this trap when he contends that 'one should not forget that the success of the Pacto de Punto Fijo cost Venezuela the largest guerrilla movement in Latin America. Exclusion requires coercion and destabilizes democratic institutions'. Przeworski, *Democracy*, op. cit., pp. 90–1.
98. Linz, 'Crisis, Breakdown, and Reequilibration', in Juan L. Linz and Alfred Stepan eds, *The Breakdown of Democratic Regimes* (Baltimore: John Hopkins University Press, 1978), p. 6.
99. Among them, the absence of an independent and effective judicial system, the high level of political violence, the constant fear felt by the population, the impunity of military and security forces, the death squads' activities, and so on.
100. Linz, 'Crisis, Breakdown, and Reequilibration', op. cit., pp. 14–15.
101. See Daniel Wolf, 'ARENA in the Arena: Factors in the Accommodation of the Salvadoran right to Pluralism and the Broadening of the Political System', *LASA Forum*, vol. 23, no. 1 (Spring 1992), pp. 10–18.
102. Przeworski, *Democracy*, op. cit., p. 74.
103. Goodwin and Skocpol, 'Explaining Revolutions in the contemporary Third World,' *Politics and Society*, vol. 17, no. 4 (1989), p. 495.
104. See for example 'Las elecciones de 1985 ¿Un paso adelante en el proceso de democratización?' *ECA*, no. 438 (April 1985), pp. 205–14.
105. Editorial, 'Elecciones aleccionadoras', *ECA*, nos 473–4 (March–April 1988), p. 156.

106. Ibid., p. 165.

4 The University Vanguard

1. On the political role of universities in Latin America, see Germán Arciniegas, 'Intellectuals and Politics of Latin America', in Cole Blasier (ed.), *Constructive Change in Latin America* (Pittsburgh, PA: University of Pittsburgh Press, 1968); Syed Hussein Alatas, *Intellectuals in Developing Societies* (London: Frank Cass, 1977); Rudolph F. Atcon, *The Latin American University* (Bogotá: ECO Revista de la Cultura de Occidente, 1966); Marta Harnecker, *Estudiantes, cristianos e indígenas en la revolución* (México: Siglo Veintiuno Editores, 1987); John P. Harrison, 'The Role of the Intellectual in Fomenting Change: the University', in John J. TePaske and Sidney Nettleton Fisher (eds), *Explosive Forces in Latin America* (Columbus, Ohio: Ohio State University Press, 1964), pp. 30–1; Daniel C. Levy, 'Latin American Student Politics: Beyond the 1960s', in Philip B. Altbach (ed.), *Student Political Activism: An International Reference Handbook* (New York: Greenwood Press, 1989), pp. 315–37; Joseph Maier and Richard W. Weatherhead (eds), *The Latin American University* (Albuquerque, NM: University of New Mexico Press, 1979); Kalman Silvert, 'The University Student', in Peter G. Snow (ed.), *Government and Politics in Latin America* (New York: Holt, Rinehart and Winston, 1967), pp. 367–84.
2. Political activism often arises with the surfacing of purely academic grievances, which complicates the identification and analysis of 'political' mobilisations in universities. For instance in San Miguel in the early 1970s, political activism arose in the Instituto Nacional as a result of students' refusal to pay for their exams. Interview with FMLN leader Mauricio Gonzalez (FPL), San Salvador, 29 June, 1995. See also See Paulino Gonzalez, 'Las luchas estudiantiles en Centroamerica, 1970–1983', in Daniel Camacho and Rafael Menjivar (eds), *Movimientos populares en Centroamerica* (San José, CR: EDUCA, 1985), p. 259.
3. For an hemispherical application of this typology, see Yvon Grenier, 'Chronicle of a Death Foretold, Intellectuals in the Americas,' *Hemisphere*, 7, 1 (1995), pp. 10–17.
4. For Lipset, this is a common feature of developing countries, where 'the university alone must modernize the society', and

where universities 'are also almost solely responsible for the conduct of intellectual life in general in their own countries.' Seymour Martin Lipset, 'University Students and Politics in Underdeveloped Countries', *Comparative Education Review* vol. 19, no. 1 (Feb. 1966), p. 132.

5. See Ronald Newton, 'On "Functional Group", "Fragmentalism", and "Pluralism", in Howard J. Wiarda (ed.), *Politics and Social Change in Latin America, The Distinct Tradition* (Amherst, Mass.: University of Massachusetts Press, 1982), pp. 133–60.
6. Ivan Vallier, 'Religious Elites: Differentiations and Developments in Roman Catholicism', in S. M. Lipset and Aldo Solari (eds), *Elites in Latin America* (New York: Oxford University Press, 1967), p. 193.
7. Glen C. Dealy, *The Public Man, An Interpretation of Latin American and Other Catholic Countries* (Amherst, Mass.: University of Massachusetts Press, 1977), and *The Latin Americans, Spirit and Ethos* (Boulder, CO.: Westview Press, 1992). For François Bourricaud, the typical Latin American intellectual is 'generally uninterested in pure learning or theoretical knowledge'. As a group, 'their interest focused almost exclusively on problems such as dependence and national identity, leading them to question the social mission of the intelligence, rather than the critical function of intelligence'. François Bourricaud, 'The Adventures of Ariel', *Daedalus*, Summer 1972, p. 113.
8. Fernando Uricoechea, 'Los intelectuales latinoamericanos y el desarrollo de sus sociedades', *Revista Mexicana de Sociología*, vol. 29, no. 4 (Oct.–Dec. 1967), pp. 789–90.
9. Ignacio Ellacuría, 'Universidad y política', *ECA*, no. 383 (Sept. 1980), 809.
10. Lipset, 'University Students', op. cit., p. 134. For a parallel with Eastern Europe, see G. Konrad and I. Szelenyi, *The Intellectuals on the Road to Class Power* (New York: Harcourt Brace Jovanovich, 1979).
11. Hussein Alatas, *Intellectuals in Developing Societies*, op. cit., p. 56.
12. Lipset, 'University Students', op. cit., p. 142. Octavio Paz similarly contends that the student's exasperation 'does not originate from particularly harsh living conditions, but from the very paradox coextensive to the student's condition: during all those years spent in the isolation of universities and graduate schools, the kids experience an artificial situation, being half privileged and secluded, and half dangerous and irresponsible. Add the extraordinary agglomeration in

learning establishments and other well-known factors of segregation: real human beings in an unreal world.' Octavio Paz, *Obras completas, El peregrino en su pátria* (Mexico: Fondo de Cultura Económica, 1993), p. 273. Samuel P. Huntington (1991, p. 144) cut through the nuances with the following statement: 'Students are the universal opposition; they oppose whatever regime exists in their society'.

13. Dealy, *The Public Man*, op. cit., p. 23.
14. Ibid., p. 24. Lipset also points out that 'countries in which governments may be toppled by the political action of the military, are often the same nations in which student activity is of major significance.' Lipset, 'University Students', op. cit., p. 143.
15. See C. Véliz, *The Centralist Tradition in Latin America* (Princeton, NJ: Princeton University Press, 1980), p. 148.
16. The well-known essay by Salvador De Madariaga comes to mind: 'Man and Universe in Spain', in Hugh M. Hamill, *Dictatorship in Spanish America* (New York: Alfred A. Knopf, 1966), pp. 29–35.
17. Mario Monteforte Toledo, 'Los intelectuales y la integración centroamericana', *Revista Mexicana de Sociología*, vol. 29, no. 4 (Oct.–Dec. 1967), pp. 835–6.
18. Most publications deal with the educational aspects and only indirectly with the political dimension. For an overview see Miguel Angel Durán, *Historia de la Universidad* (San Salvador: Editorial Universitaria, Colección Tlatoli, 1975 [1941]); Mario Flores Macal, 'Historia de la UES', *Anuario de Estudios Centroamericanos* (1976); Yvon Grenier, *Universities, Intellectuals and Political Transition: the Salvadoran Case* (Montréal: McGill University, Centre for Developing-Area Studies, Discussion Paper No. 71), p. 48; Gustavo Mallat, *Realidad de la educación universitaria en El Salvador* (San Salvador: FUSADES, documento de trabajo no. 22, 1991); Fernando Reimers (coordinator), *La educación en El Salvador de cara el siglo XXI, Desafíos y oportunidades* (San Salvador: UCA Editores; Instituto para el Desarrollo Internacional [Harvard University] and Fundación Empresarial para el Desarrollo Educativo, Universidad Centroamericana José Simeón Cañas, 1995); UCA/PREDE-OEA, *Datos e información para las hipótesis del estudio sobre la educación superior en El Salvador*, Coord. Mario Cerna Torres (San Salvador, 1989); UCA/PREDE-OEA, *La investigación y la docencia en la educación universitaria de El Salvador* (San Salvador, June 1990).
19. J. Dunkerley, *Power in the Isthmus, A Political History of Modern Central America*, (London NY: Verso, 1988), p. 421, note 86.

20. Norma G. De Herrera, 'Crónica de una Universidad intervenida, 1980–1982', *El Universitario*, May–June 1982, p. 2.
21. Mario Salazar Valiente, *El Salvador: autonomía universitaria y despotismo oligárquico-castrense* (San Salvador: Editorial Universitaria, 1980), pp. 11–12.
22. 'Decreto de erección de la Universidad de El Salvador', San Salvador, 16 February 1841, reproduced in Jose Antonio Cevallos, *Recuerdos Salvadoreños* (San Salvador: Ministerio de Educación, 1965), pp. 341–3.
23. This reflected a regional pattern, as Carlos Tünnermann points out: 'In Latin America the university was created before the rest of education, and for a very long time it was the only institution that provided post-secondary teaching.' See Carlos Tünnermann, *Estudios sobre la teoría de la Universidad* (San José: Editorial Universitaria Centroamericana, 1983), p. 253. One may recall that Latin America already had some thirteen universities when Harvard University was founded in 1636.
24. Joseph Maier and Richard W. Weatherhead (eds), *The Latin American University* (Albuquerque, NM: University of New Mexico Press, 1979), p. 7.
25. Duran, *Historia de la Universidad*, op. cit., pp. 87–8.
26. Bradford E. Burns, 'The Intellectual Infrastructure of Modernization in El Salvador, 1870–1900', *The Americas*, vol. 41, no. 3 (Jan. 1985), p. 62.
27. FEUR-FSD, *Plan general de gobierno de las autoridades universitarias para el período 1967–1971* (San Salvador, n/d), p. 11, quoted in UCA/PREDE-OEA, *La investigación y la docencia*, op. cit., p. 135. On the influence of the Córdoba movement in the UES, see Luis Argueta Antillón (former rector), 'La reedición de la reforma universitaria de Córdoba, una necesidad histórica', *Estudios Sociales Centroamericanos*, vol. 48 (Sept.–Dec. 1988), pp. 17–27.
28. *Resoluciones y Recomendaciones votadas por el Primer Congreso Centroamericano de Universidades* (Guatemala, CA, Nov. 1948), p. 50.
29. The Confederación Universitaria Centroamericana regroups together the national (public) universities of the Central American region, including the UES.
30. For an assessment of the intellectual's role at the end of the nineteenth century, see Burns, 'The Intellectual Infrastructure', op.cit., pp. 57–82; Paul W. Borgeson, 'El Salvador', in David W. Foster (ed.), *Handbook of Latin American Literature* (New York and London: Garland Publishing, 1987), pp. 517–27.
31. CSUCA, *Confederación Universitaria Centroamericana, 1948–1973* (San José: CSUCA, n/d [circa 1973]), Appendix 1.

32. Ibid., Appendix 2.
33. See Patricia Parkman, *Nonviolent Insurrection in El Salvador, The Fall of Maximiliano Hernández Martínez* (Tucson, AZ: University of Arizona Press, 1988).
34. For instance Medardo González Trejo, former student of philosophy and president of AGEUS, was a top leader of the FPL (*nom de guerre*: comandante 'Milton'). Besides AGEUS there was the Federation of Salvadoran University Student (FEUS), which according to Tom Barry was 'operating on a more political level' than AGEUS; and the Federation of Revolutionary Salvadoran Student (FERS), linked to an insignificant and fading FMLN organisation: the Movement for Bread, Land, Work and Liberty (MPTL). See Tom Barry, *El Salvador, A Country Study* (Albuquerque, NM: The Inter-Hemispheric Education Resource Center, 1990), p. 105.
35. See Beverley and Zimmerman, (1990), p. 123; Monteforte Toledo, 'Los intelectuales', op.cit., pp. 835–6; Hector F. Oqueli Colindres, 'El movimiento estudiantil', *ABRA* (San Salvador), vol. 1, no. 8 (1975), pp. 13–30; Gonzalez, 'Las luchas estudiantiles', op.cit., pp. 238–92.
36. Gonzalez, 'Las luchas estudiantiles', op.cit., p. 250. For the first congress of university students, see *El Universitario*, 24 Feb. 1969, p. 1, quoted in Fernando Flores Pinel, 'La Universidad de El Salvador, una encrucijada política dificil', *ECA* nos 361–2 (Nov.–Dec. 1978), p. 892.
37. In a book recently published by the UES press, the authors assert that 'the struggle for the control and hegemony of the UES have been the most conspicuous features of the recent years of its history'. Tránsito Rivas and H. Miranda Luna, *Crisis de la educación superior universitaria y las posibilidades de solución para la Universidad de El Salvador* (San Salvador; Editorial Universitaria, 1990) p. 37.
38. See Roque Dalton, *El Salvador* (La Havana: Encyclopedia Popular, 1965), pp. 115, 133.
39. See Stephen Webre, *José Napoleón Duarte and the Christian Democratic Party in Salvadoran Politics* (Baton Rouge and London: Louisiana State University Press, 1979), pp. 28–9, 31–6; Dalton, *El Salvador*, op.cit., pp. 115,137; Flores Macal, 'Historia de la UES', Anuario dé Estudios Centroamericanos (1976) op.cit., pp. 197–135.
40. 'According to the arielist conception, political action consists essentially of preaching. And it so happens that the supreme preacher is the university professor.' Bourricaud, 'The Adventures of Ariel', op.cit., p. 123.

41. See UES, Secretaria de Planificación, *Diagnóstico global de la UES*, tome 1 (San Salvador, 1972) pp. 120, 123.
42. The CSU was opposed to the *puertas abiertas* in 1968, before the student revolt made it change its position. For its position in 1968, see Secretaria de Planificación, *Diagnóstico global de la UES* op.cit., p. 83.
43. See UCA/OEA-PREDE, *La investigación y la docencia*, op.cit., p. 142. In the preamble of the decree repealing the Organic Law of 1951, it is stated 'That the UES electoral mechanisms invaliedated the democratic longing for a secret vote and for the administrative responsibilities to be performed by capable people; and that on the other hand [teachers] lived under the constant threat of destitution for sectarian or partisan motives.' See El Salvador, Asamblea Legislativa, Decreto no. 41, in *Diario Oficial* (San Salvador), 19 July 1972, p. 6631.
44. See details in Flores Macal, 'Historia de la UES', op.cit., p. 134.
45. El Salvador, Asamblea Legislativa, Decreto no.138, in *Diario Oficial* (San Salvador), 18 October 1972, pp. 9670–9. The new law was inspired by recent political development at the UES. Hence Article 5 stipulated that university education will be essentially democratic, [and] respectful of the distinct philosophical and scientific tendencies that inform human thinking.... University education must not manifest itself as participation in partisan political activities'. Article 6 stated that academic liberty would be recognised as long as it was used 'with the exclusive purpose of teaching and research'. Article 47 specified that 'its faculty members [*sus órganos ni sus funcionarios*] must not intervene in activities related to partisan politics, or divert into such activities any facilities of the university'. Finally, the new law gave professional corporations – political conservatives – a say in the General Assembly as well as in the University Superior Council. The law was reformed in December 1978 (Decree 108) to increase the number of professors in the General Assembly by reducing the number of student (from 2 to 1 per faculty) and professional (from 3 to 1 per faculty) representatives. The measure did not produce the expected results, since the professors were very much allied with the students' organisations at the time. See *ECA*, nos 363–4 (Jan.–Feb. 1979), pp. 92–9. See also Ignacio Ellacuria, 'La ley orgánica de la UES', *ECA*, no. 290 (Dec. 1972), pp. 749–61.
46. Salazar Valiente, *El Salvador*, op.cit., pp. 62–3.
47. For the formation of the CAPUES, see Decree no. 247 in *Diario Oficial* (San Salvador), 1 April 1977, pp. 24–5.

48. In 1977 the army granted the presidential seat to Molina's minister of defence, General Carlos Humberto Romero, after another fraudulent election in which the UNO even sought to field a military candidate (Colonel Ernesto Claramount). In November 1977 Romero imposed his 'Public Order Law', removing the final legal obstacle to full-fledged repression of the opposition. Romero was overthrown in October 1979 by a military coup, supported by a broad coalition of political parties, unions and even an ultra-leftist organisation (the LP-28).
49. Decree no. 363, in *Diario Oficial* (San Salvador), 7 October 1977, pp. 4–5.
50. Flores Pinel, 'La Universidad de El Salvador', p. 899. Another author describes the climate in this period as follows: 'At this very moment the UES could be defined as a physical space where a group of persons lock themselves in to study ways of attacking each other.' Erick Cabrera, 'El caos académico- administrativo de la UES', *ECA*, no. 345 (July 1977), p. 502. See also UCA/PREDE-OEA, *Datos e informaciones*, op.cit., pp. 297–9.
51. UCA/PREDE-OEA, *La investigación y la docencia*, op.cit., p. 203.
52. The candidates for rector were Félix Antonio Ulloa and Héctor Dada Hirezi, both well-known intellectuals and political activists. See UCA/PREDE-OEA, *La investigación y la docencia*, op.cit., pp. 167–175.
53. See 'Universidad de El Salvador en el Frente Democrático Revolucionario' (interview with rector Felix Antinio Ulloa), *El Universitario* (San Salvador), 15 May 1980, p. 3.
54. Loc cit.
55. UCA/PREDE-OEA, *Datos e informaciones*, op.cit., pp. 307–8. The earthquake of 10 October, 1986 also caused huge damage to the university's infrastructure. The extent of the damage ranged from 40 per cent for certain edifices to complete destruction for others. See Coordinación Universitaria de Investigaciones Científicas (CUIC), 'La UES ante la crisis generada por el terremoto de octubre', *Estudios Sociales Centroamericanos*, vol. 42 (Sept.–Dec. 1986), pp. 7–12.
56. UCA/PREDE-OEA, *La educación y la docencia*, op.cit., pp. 182–4.
57. Beside sheer repression, other means were used by the state to suppress the UES: (1) economic strangulation during the 1980s, which forced the UES to 'transnationalise' itself (that is, to seek support outside the country); (2) an ongoing campaign aimed at denigrating UES officials, carried out by government officials and the right-wing media; (3) the systematic privatisation of higher education, on order to 'reduce

the scope of the UES's influence on the profession and the ideological shaping of students'. See UCA-PREDE/OEA, *La educación y la docencia*, p. 268.

58. Rene Mauricio Mejía Mendez, 'La universidad en el exilio', paper presented at the second Conference in support of the UES, Hotel Alameda, 19 April 1990.
59. During various informal discussions with UES officials by this author during the summer of 1995, it appeared that many did not have a vivid recollection of this plan, as though it was simply a political statement made at the time, like many others made before or after 1988.
60. The Council comprises the rector, the deans of each faculty, the directors of the two University Regional Centres in San Miguel and Santa Ana (created in 1969) and representatives of the professors
61. This author was assured that the plan was widely discussed within the university community. See UES, *Plan de desarrollo, 1988–1992* (San Salvador: UES, 1988).
62. According to Tránsito Rivas and Miranda Luna, who try to apply the spirit of the political project to curricular reform, the 'UES's reform and new curriculum must be valued as political projects with implications in the area of education'. Rivas and Luna, *Crisis de la educación superior*, op.cit., p. 52. For a theoretical treatment, see Francisco Gutiérrez, *Educación como praxis política* (Mexico: Siglo XXI, 1984).
63. UES, *Plan de desarrollo*, op.cit., p. 12.
64. Ibid., pp. 12–13.
65. See Gabriel Zaïd, *De los libros al poder* (Mexico: Grijalbo, 1988).
66. UES, *Plan de desarrollo*, op.cit., p. 56.
67. UES, 'Análisis sobre la democracia salvadoreña y el actual proceso electoral de diputados y alcades', *ECA*, nos 473–4 (March–April 1988), p. 274 (emphasis added).
68. UES, *Plan de desarrollo*, op.cit., p. 16.
69. Ibid., pp. 16, 17.
70. Ibid., p. 17 (emphasis added). In another declaration the UES defines democracy by saying that its 'culmination' is 'the satisfaction of basic needs, through the access of all to material and cultural goods and services'. See UES, 'Posición de la UES ante los acuerdos tomados en la reunión cumbre de presidentes de Centroamérica: Esquipulas II', *ECA*, nos 466–7 (Aug.–Sept. 1987), p. 649.
71. UES, *Plan de desarrollo*, op.cit., pp. 17–18 (emphasis added).
72. Ibid., p. 18 (emphasis added).
73. Ibid., p. 18.

74. Ibid., p. 19.
75. Ibid., p. 27.
76. Ibid., p. 56.
77. Ibid., p. 55.
78. Ibid., p. 20.
79. See for example, UES Coordinación Universitaria de Investigación Científica (CUIC), ¿Que es y como realizar actualmente la proyección social en la Universidad de El Salvador?' *Estudios Sociales Centroamericanos*, vol. 46 (Jan.–April 1988), p. 12.
80. Interview by the author in San Salvador, 23 July 1990. Over recent years the debate on the nature of the university's political engagement has namely concerned the university's position during elections, an issue somewhat complicated by the participation of Democratic Convergence (CD) in the 1989 presidential contest. The CD was an offshout of the FDR, which may be broadly considered as the FMLN's political wing.
81. UES, *Plan de desarrollo*, op.cit., p. 21.
82. UES, 'La situación política y el proceso electoral', *ECA*, nos 426–7 (April–May 1984), p. 367 (emphasis added).
83. UES, 'La UES ante el anuncio del diálogo, 13 de octubre de 1984', *ECA*, nos 432–3 (Oct.–Nov. 1984), p. 855. (emphasis added).
84. UES, 'Análisis sobre la democracia salvadoreña y el actual proceso electoral de diputados y alcades', *ECA*, nos 473–4 (March–April 1988), p. 273 (emphasis added).
85. UES, 'La paz es constitucional', *ECA*, nos 483–4 (Jan.–Feb. 1989), p. 151.
86. Fabio Castillo, *Cuarta memoria anual del período rectoral 1991–1995* (San Salvador: Ciudad Universitaria, June 1995).
87. At one point Castillo contends that 'broad sectors of the university community' are 'mobilised by hatred'. Ibid., p. 45.
88. Ibid., p. 3.
89. Ibid., p. 17.
90. Ibid., p. 30.
91. Ibid., p. 49.
92. Ibid., p. 54.
93. Movimiento para la Concertación Universitaria (MCU), *Propuesta de plataforma para la construcción de la Universidad de El Salvador hacia el próximo siglo [Universidad de El Salvador, Proceso Electoral 1995–1999]* (San Salvador: Ciudad Universitaria, 17 April 1995).
94. Ibid., p. 4.

5 The Catholic Church, Social Change and Insurrection

1. To mention but a few publications on the subject: Edwin Eloy Aguilar, José Miguel Sandoval, Timothy J. Steigenga and Kenneth M. Coleman, 'Protestantism in El Salvador: Conventional Wisdom versus Survey Evidence', *Latin American Research Review*, vol. 28, no. 2 (1993), pp. 119–40; Americas Watch, *El Salvador's Decade of Terror, Human Rights since the Assassination of Archbishop Romero* (New Haven and London: Yale University Press, 1989) Philip Berryman, *The Religious Roots of Rebellion: Christians in Central American Revolutions* (New York: Maryknoll, Orbis Books, 1984); Carlos Rafael Cabarrús, *Génesis de una revolución: análisis del surgimiento y desarrollo de la organización campesina en El Salvador* (México: Ed. de la Casa Chata, 1983); Jorge Caceres Prendes, 'Radicalización política y pastoral popular en El Salvador, 1969–79', *ECA*, nos 407–8 (Sept.–Oct. 1982), pp. 93–153; Rodolfo Cardenal, *El poder eclesiástico en El Salvador* (San Salvador: UCA editores, 1980), and *Historia de una esperanza, vida de Rutilio Grande* (San Salvador: UCA editores, 1987); Salvador Carranza, 'Una experiencia de evangelización rural parroquial, Aguilares, septiembre de 1972–agosto de 1974', *ECA*, nos 348–9 (Oct.–Nov. 1977), pp. 838–54; Jorge Carredes Prendes, 'Radicalización política y pastoral popular en El Salvador, 1969–1979', *Estudios Sociales Centroamericanos*, vol. 11, no. 33 (December 1982), pp. 93–153; CEB (Comunidades Eclesiales de Base), 'Pronunciamiento de las Comunidades Cristianas de Base ante la situación de la Iglesia en el momento actual', *ECA*, nos 396–7 (Oct.–Nov. 1981), pp. 1075–6; Ana Cristina Cepeda *et al.*, ' "Orientación" y "Justicia y Paz", reformismo y radicalismo en la Iglesia salvadoreña' (2 parts), *ECA*, no. 230 (Oct. 1973), pp. 705–728, and *ECA*, nos 303–4 (Jan.–Feb. 1974), pp. 51–80; 'Los Jesuitas ante el pueblo salvadoreño,' *ECA*, no. 344 (June 1977), pp. 434–50; Penny Lernoux, *Cry of the People* (Harmondsworth: Penguin, 1982); Tommie Sue Montgomery, 'The Church in the Salvadoran Revolution', *Latin American Perspectives*, vol. 10, no. 1 (Winter 1983), pp. 62–87; Ivan D. Paredes, 'La situación de la iglésia católica en El Salvador y su influjo social', *ECA*, nos 369–0 (July–August 1979), pp. 601–14. On the relation between the church and radical politics in Latin America, see Jean Meyer, *Historia de los cristianos en América Latina, siglos XIX y XX* (Mexico: Vuelta, 1991).

2. See for instance Jenny Pearce, *Promised Land: Peasant Rebellion in Chalatenango, El Salvador* (London: Latin American Bureau, 1986). According to two scholars: 'With the end of the war and the move toward open electoral politics, one of the major challenges facing both San Francisco and San Antonio [two locations where the authors studied Christian communities] is the loss of lay pastoral agents to political movements, especially the FMLN.' Philip J. Williams and Anna L. Peterson, 'Evangelicals and Catholics in El Salvador: Evolving Religious Responses to Social Change', paper presented at the international congress of the Latin American Studies Association, Washington, DC, 28–30 September 1995, p.11.
3. Malia (1994) p. 44.
4. Meyer, *Historia de los cristianos*, op.ct., p. 340.
5. Quoted in Harnecker (1993), p. 151.
6. Gino Germani, *Politica y sociedad en una época de transición, de la sociedad tradicional a la sociedad de masas* (Buenos Aires: Editorial Paidos, 1966).
7. It is worth noting that for all the sympathy that some priests expressed for the insurgency, to this author's knowledge only one priest actively participated in the armed struggle: Ernesto Barrera, killed in 1978. One can find no exception to this rule anywhere in Latin America.
8. The 'ideal-typical liberal', according to Stephen Holmes, is 'more distressed by poverty and personal dependency... than by inequality of income or wealth.' Marxism, along with most socialist theories of the nineteeth century, is not entirely dissimilar to liberal theory since it celebrates the universal goodness of material progress. Theology of liberation, on the other hand, is 'ideal-typical anti-liberal', for it condemns inequality while promoting the redeeming virtues of poverty. See Stephen Holmes, *Passions and Constraint, On the Theory of Liberal Democracy* (Chicago and London: University of Chicago Press, 1995), p.15.
9. This was confirmed by many FMLN militants in informal discussions, and by Eduardo Sancho (nom de guerre: Fermán Cienfuegos, leader of the RN faction) during an interview in San Salvador in July 1994.
10. He also contends that 'too much has been asked of the idea of a 'popular Church' in Latin America, and the weight of the Vatican's history, tradition, and hierarchical structures have often been underestimated'. Castañeda (1994), p. 217. The excellent report by Mark Hammer on the massacre at El Mozote, as well as an article produced by a team of

researchers from the University of North Carolina, reveal a fundamental new religious development in El Salvador: a tremendous growth of Protestantism in the lower strata of Salvadoran society (and as far away from urban centers as El Mozote, situated in one of the hotbeds of insurgency – the department of Chalatenango) over the past two decades. Aguilar *et al.* estimate that Protestants made up about 12 per cent of the population by the late 1980s. A more recent survey conducted by a team from the UCA, presents the following statistics: Catholics, 56.7 percent; Evangelical, 17.8 per cent; no religion, 23.2 per cent; others, 2.3 per cent. The case can certainly be made that this phenomenon, in contrast with the success of the Popular Church, has been underestimated or simply ignored until recently because it did not fit easily with the dominant discourse on the causes of revolution in El Salvador. See Aguilar *et al.*, 'Protestantism in El Salvador', op. cit.; Mark Danner, 'The Massacre at El Mozote', *The New Yorker*, 6 December 1993; Instituto Universitario de Opinión Pública, 'La religión de los Salvadoreños', *ECA* no. 563 (Sept, 1995), pp. 849–62.

11. In an editorial in the weekly *Orientación* (21 May 1973) Romero thundered against 'these schools that teach demagogy and Marxism', and against professors 'who should not even call themselves Christians.' Quoted in Charles J., Beirne, 'Jesuit Education for Justice: The Colegio in El Salvador, 1968–1984', *Harvard Educational Review*, vol. 55 (Feb. 1985), p. 10.
12. CONIP, 'Comunicado de la Coordinadora Nacional de la Iglesia Popular, Monseñor Oscar Arnulfo Romero a nuestros hermanos cristianos y al pueblo en general', *ECA*, no. 383 (Sept. 1980), pp. 906–8.
13. The slogan 'Be a patriot, kill a priest', uttered by the death squad Unión Guerra Blanca (UGB) in 1977, is a chilling reminder of the far right's attitude towards the Popular Church. On the other hand, repression was not without its backlash, since it produced martyrs for both the Church and the opposition. As the priest Ivan D. Paredes points out, 'if the Church is persecuted, then the people will intuitively understand that this is happenning because it is defending the people, and because the Church is part of the people'. Cabarrús also asserts that the CEBs 'contain an element that is perhaps not primarily religious; this revolutionary experiment is a passion: a political passion! What gives all its thrill to politics is the risk with which one lives it, and the heroic connotations that stems from it.' See Paredes, 'La situación de la iglésia católica en El Salvador', op.cit., p. 611; Cabarrús, (1983), p. 157.

14. Cabarrús (1983).
15. At the end of the 1970s, 13.7 percent (30 out of 219) of diocesan priests and 84 percent (183 out of 218) of members of religious orders were foreign-born. Among the latter, 85 came from Spain, 46 from Italy, 24 from the US, 11 from Guatemala, 10 from Costa Rica and 8 from Mexico; most of them, therefore, from outside Latin America. See Paredes, 'La situación de la iglésia católica en El Salvador', op.cit., p. 605.
16. 'In the cotton belt', continues Kincaid, 'the dispersed and fragmented hamlets of landless laborers presented much more difficult terrain for creating local organizations'. Kincaid, 'Peasants into Rebels: Community and Class in Rural El Salvador, *Comparative Study of Society and History*, 29 (1987), p. 489.
17. Webre (1979).
18. PDC/Tendencia Popular, 'Mensaje de la Tendencia Popular Demócrata Cristiana a la convención nacional del partido y al pueblo salvadoreño', *ECA*, nos 377–8 (March–April 1980), pp. 374–6.
19. For an openly hostile view of theology of liberation from inside the Salvadoran Church, see Freddy Delgado, *La Iglesia Popular nació en El Salvador, Memorias de 1972 a 1982* (Mexico City, n/d).
20. Montgomery, 'The Church', op.cit., p. 86. See also Castellanos Moya, (1993), p. 29.
21. All the FPL leaders interviewed by Marta Harnecker (1993) as well as the leaders of other organisations (Joaquin Villalobos and Eduardo Sancho in particular) readily admitted that problem.
22. This seems to have been a constant problem for liberation theologians throughout Latin America. Daudelin and Hewitt, for instance, indicate that 'in a recent interview, the well-known progressive archbishop of São Paulo, Cardinal Paulo Arns, admits that the progressives' rhetoric turned people away'. Jean Daudelin and W. E. Hewitt, 'Churches and Politics in Latin America: Catholicism at the Crossroads', *Third World Quarterly*, vol. 16, no. 2 (1995), p. 229.
23. Quoted in Harnecker (1993), p. 126.
24. Ibid., p. 201.
25. Quoted in Pearce, *Promised Land*, op.cit., p. 128.
26. Quoted in Harnecker (1993), p. 155.
27. Montgomery, 'The Church', op.cit. As one of the pioneers of this experiment (Father Salvador Carranza from Spain) testified: 'Given the concentration of clergy in narrow urban

sectors of society, it seemed urgent to reach out to the marginalised majorities, which meant reaching out to the world of the countryside, which is the great human and religious reserve of this country.' Carranza, 'Una experiencia de evangelización', op.cit., p. 838.

28. According to T. S. Montgomery, 'With a growing frequency that disturbs traditional members of the Church, CEB members have moved beyond purely religious concerns to political issues. Nowhere in Latin America has this been more true or had more profound consequences than in El Salvador.' She also contends that 'while [Archbishop Oscar] Romero reflected the pastoral strain of liberation theology, about one-third of the younger priests had adopted a more Marxist-influenced variation which emphasized the need for the people to transform reality.' Montgomery, 'The Church', op.cit., pp. 67, 69.
29. Ernesto Cardenal, in an interview for the French newspaper *Le Monde* (15 March 1979), claimed that 'an atheist revolutionary knows God, but a bishop who supports a dictatorship does not'.
30. Carranza, 'Una experiencia de evangelización', op.cit.
31. Castañeda (1994), p. 217.
32. Cabarrus (1983), p. 156.
33. Anna L. Peterson claims that a group of priests and nuns from Belgium were amongst the first organisers of these groups, in a poor urban community (Zacamil) located behind the UES campus. According to her, the model emulated was that of San Miguelito in Panama city, initiated by Leo Mahon, a priest from Chicago. Anna L. Peterson, 'Religion and Collective Identity in El Salvador', paper presented at the international congress of the Latin American Studies Association, Los Angeles, 24–26 September 1992.
34. Paredes, 'La situación de la iglésia católica en El Salvador', op.cit., p. 607 (emphasis added).
35. Cabarrus (1983), p. 262.
36. Matt D. Childs underlines the same pattern in the Castroist insurgency in Cuba: 'Another interesting aspect of the Second Declaration of Havana is its *childlike portrayal of the peasantry*. The earlier statement of Guevara in *Guerrilla Warfare* of "a genuine interaction" whereby "leaders teach the people" and "people teach the leaders" is replaced by the stronger vanguard position that the peasantry need appropriate "revolutionary" and "political leadership" owing to their "uncultivated state".' Matt D. Childs, 'An Historical Critique of the Emergence and Evolution of Ernesto Che Guevara's

Foco Theory, *Journal of Latin American Studies*, 27 (1995) p. 612 (added emphasis).

37. Carranza, 'Una experiencia de evangelización', op.cit., p. 839.
38. Ibid., p. 844 et seq.
39. Ibid., p. 840. The natural leaders chosen by the missionaries needed to have their nomination ratified by the CEB. But we are aware of no case where the latter vetoed such an important decision made by the missionaries.
40. Ibid., pp. 841, 849. It was ensured that the delegates and CEBs were integrated into a wider network: 'one never let them alone, for they were under the supervision of other older delegations, or of a foreign collaborator or of another community'. (ibid., p. 841).
41. Ibid., pp. 838–9. See also Rivera y Damas' communique at the seventh regional conference of 'Justice and Peace' (Centro Metodista de Costa Rica, 16–21 October 1977), in *ECA*, nos 348–9 (Oct.–Nov. 1977), pp. 805–14.
42. Carranza, 'Una experiencia de evangelización', op.cit., p. 842.
43. Ibid., p. 851.
44. According to Brenan, it was the anti-clerical reforms of the 1830s that left the Spanish Church insecure, causing it to seek protection from the rich and powerful. Gerald Brenan, *The Spanish Labyrinth: An Account of the Social and Political Background of the Civil War* (New York and Cambridge: Cambridge University Press, 1969), pp. 37–57. See also Norman Cohn, *The Pursuit of the Millennium: Revolutionary Millenarians and Mystical Anarchists of the Middle Ages* (New York: Oxford University Press, 1970); Raj Desai and Harry Eckstein, 'Insurgency, the Transformation of Peasant Revolution', *World Politics*, vol. 4 (July 1990), p. 449.
45. Daudelin and Hewitt, 'Churches and Politics in Latin America', p. 227.
46. Castañeda (1994), p. 217.
47. For instance Francisco Peccorini Letona, a far-right Jesuit who was director of the *ECA* from 1952 to 1954 (when it was the official organ of the Society of Jesus). Peccorini was assassinated on 15 March 1989, by an FMLN urban commando.
48. The same pattern occurred at the Jesuit-led Externado San Jose, a college that apparently preceded the UCA in the realm of radical politics (although both institutions were very close). See 'El Externado piensa asi', *ECA*, no. 296 (June 1973), pp. 399–422.
49. The following description is still move or less valid today, but it relates specifically to the 1970s and 1980s.

50. According to then Secretary General Mario Cerna Torres, about a third of faculty members displayed a political commitment along the lines indicated by the university authority (interview with the author, San Salvador, July 1990).
51. See Luis de Sebastián, 'La proyección social debe cambiar la injusticia estructural: De Sebastian', *El Universitario* (San Salvador, UES), vol. 6 (15 May 1979), p. 11.
52. In the mid 1970s the UCA authorities were challenged by a short-lived student organisation linked to the insurgency (the FUR-30), which organised demonstrations and occupied university buildings. This experience strengthened the UCA's resolve to tighten its control over student organisations.
53. Universidad Centroamericana (UCA), *Universidad y sociedad, lecturas para el civiso de admisión a la UCA* (San Salvador UCA editores, 1989), p. 208.
54. Ibid. In order to prevent student activism, the UCA avoided 'massification': in 1980 it UCA still had no more than 2500 students. S. M. Lipset contends that 'the larger the university, the greater the absolute number of those with dispositions to political activity and the stronger their mutual support, organization and resources. Larger student bodies will also heighten the tendency towards the formation of an autonomous student culture resistant to the efforts of the university administration to control it.' S. M. Lipset, 'University Students and Politics in Underdeveloped Countries,' *Comparative Education Review*, 19, 1 (February 1966), p. 145.
55. For instance Transits Rivas and Hilda Elizabeth Miranda Lumna, *Crisis de la educación superior universitaria y las posibilidades de solución para la Universidad de El Salvador* (San Salvador: Editorial Universitaria, 1990).
56. Jon Sobrino, 'Inspiración cristiana de la Universidad', *ECA*, no 468 (October 1987), p. 698.
57. On the notions of 'prophecy' and 'utopía', see Ignacio Ellacuria, 'Utopía, profetismo desde América Latina: un ensayo concreto de soteriología histórica', *Revista Latinoamericana de Teología* vol. 17 (May–Aug. 1989), pp. 141–84.
58. For an overview of the public universities' self-defined missions in Central America, see appendix 1 and 2 in *Confederación Universitaria Centroaméricana, 1948–1973* (San José: CSUCA, Secretaría General, 1974), pp. 74, 90. For the objectives of private institutions in the same region, see Jorge Mario Garcia Laguardia, *Legislación universitaria de América Latina* (Mexico: UNAM, 1973), p. 210.

59. See for instance *Situación de la educación universitaria en El Salvador* (San Salvador: Centro de Investigaciones Tecnológicas y Científicas [CENITEC], Dirección de Seminarios, 1989).
60. Document of Oaxtepec, Mexico, 1971, quoted in 'El Externado piensa asi', *ECA*, no. 296 (June 1973), p. 414. See also Beirne, 'Jesuit Education for Justice', op. cit.
61. See 'Declaración de los jesuitas sobre la reorganización de la actividad apostólica', *ECA*, no. 260 (August 1968). See also Beirne, 'Jesuit Education for Justice', op. cit., pp. 1–19.
62. UCA, *Universidad y Sociedad*, op. cit., p. 192.
63. For a classic definition of the university's mission, see José Ortega y Gasset, *Mission of the University* (Princeton, NJ: Princeton University Press, 1944), p. 62.
64. Ignacio Ellacuria, 'Universidad y política, *Estudius Controamericanos (ECA)*, 383 (september 1980), p. 21. This position is reaffirmed in an official UCA publication; 'the three functions are interrelated and have a unique goal, which is ... really and effectively to inflict social change'. UCA, *Universidad y sociedad*, op. cit., p. 191. See also Román Mayorga Quiroz, *La Universidad para el cambio social*, p. 16.
65. Román Mayorga Quiroz, 'La UCA hacia el futuro', *ECA*, nos 324–5 (Oct.–Nov. 1975), p. 601.
66. Mayorga Quiroz, *La Universidad para el cambio social* (San Salvador: UCA Editores, 1978) op. cit., p. 176.
67. Proyecto UCA/PREDE-OEA, *La investigación y la docencia en la educación universitaria de El Salvador* (San Salvador, June 1990), p. 51.
68. UCA, *Universidad y Sociedad*, op. cit., p. 188.
69. Mayorga Quiroz, 'La UCA hacia el futuro', op. cit., p. 601.
70. Ibid.
71. Jon Sobrino, 'Compañeros de Jesús–El asesinato-martirio de los jesuitas salvadoreñas', *ECA*, nos 493–4 (Nov.–Dec. 1989), p. 1064.
72. Jon Sobrino, 'Inspiración cristiana de la Universidad', *ECA*, no 468 (Oct. 1987), p 701.
73. Mayorga Quiroz, *La Universidad para el cambio social*, op. cit., p. 124.
74. De Sebastián, 'La proyección social', op. cit., p. 11.
75. *ECA* nos 324–5 (Oct.–Nov. 1975), p. 708. See also Baloyra (1982), p. 45.
76. *ECA* nos 297–8 (July–Aug. 1973), p. 427.
77. 'Agrarian transformation' was preferred to 'agrarian reform', a concept tantamount to communism for the landed oligarchy.
78. Mayorga Quiroz, *La universidad para el cambio social*, op. cit., p. 53.

79. See the editorial '¿Votaciones populares?' *ECA*, nos 282–2 (March–April 1972), p. 126. The editorial following the fraudulent election of Carlos Humberto Romero (1977–79) is not bereft of gentleness with regard to Romero and his predecessor. Cf. 'Cambio de gobierno en El Salvador', *ECA*, no. 345 (July 1977).
80. See *ECA*, nos 335–6 (Sept.–Oct. 1976). This issue is entirely devoted to the project of agrarian transformation. The UCA soon withdrew its support when it became clear that the government would cave in to pressures from the economic elites. See the editorial '¡A sus órdenes mi capital!' *ECA*, no. 337 (Nov. 1976), pp. 637–43.
81. *ECA*, nos 281–2 (March–April 1972), p. 123.
82. *ECA*, no. 296 (June 1973), p. 322.
83. Cf. 'La política en Centroamérica', *ECA* no. 312 (Oct. 1974), p. 661.
84. Cabarrús (1983), pp. 159–60; Cardenal (1987), p. 436.
85. De Sebastián, 'La proyección social', op. cit., p. 11.
86. See 'Pronunciamiento de la UCA ante la nueva situación del país,' *ECA*, nos 375–6 (Jan.–Feb. 1980), pp. 5–20. The first junta lasted only 75 days; on 1 January, 1980 the junta and most members of the cabinet resigned. To replace Mayorga Quiroz, Ungo and Andino, an unknown surgeon (José Ramón Avalos Navarrette) and two prominent Christian Democrats (José Antonio Morales Ehrlich and Héctor Dada Hirezi) were recruited. The latter was in fact an intellectual: a former director of the economics department at the UCA and former candidate for rector of the UES. Dada soon offered his resignation, to be replaced by another Christian Democrat: José Napoléon Duarte.
87. Cf. Carlos Ernesto Mendoza in *Análisis*, vols 9–10 (Sept.–Oct. 1988), pp. 47–59. See also the interview by Mendoza with Guillermo Manuel Ungo in the same issue.
88. Victor Manuel Valle, 'La educación universitaria en El Salvador: un espejo roto en los 1980's', paper presented at the meeting of the Latin American Studies Association, Washington DC, 6 April 1991.
89. Proyecto UCA/PREDE-OEA, *La investigación y la docencia,* op. cit., p. 112.
90. Mariano Castro Morán, *Función política del Ejercito salvadoreño en el presente siglo* (San Salvador: UCA editores, 1987), p. 278.
91. Ibid., pp. 278–9.
92. Montgomery, 'The Church', op. cit., p. 75.
93. Meyer (1991), p. 75.

94. Daudelin and Hewitt, 'Churches and Politics in Latin America', op. cit., p. 227.

Conclusion

1. The idea that politics can become its own environment was first formulated by Professor Jacques Zylberberg in a conversation with the author.
2. Castellanos Moya (1993, p. 21) contends that 'the de-ideologisation of the right has been a less perceptible and uniform process' than the de-ideologisation of the left.
3. For Castellanos Moya (ibid., p. 18), 'right now, the fact that people question and raise doubts about the viability of political assassination [in El Salvador] to solve political controversy, would indicate a new attitude, a mutation'.

Select Bibliography

AMERICAS WATCH (1991) *El Salvador's Decade of Terror, Human rights since the Assassination of Archibishop Romero* (New Haven and London: Yale University Press).

ARENDT, H. (1984) *On Revolution* (New York: Penguin Books).

ATCON, Rudolph F. (1966) *The Latin American University* (Bogotá: ECO, Revista de la Cultura de Occidente).

BALOYRA, Enrique (1982) *El Salvador in Transition* (Chapel Hill, NC: The University of North Carolina Press).

BARON CASTRO, Rodolfo (1978) *La población de El Salvador* (San Salvador: UCA Editores).

BETHELL, Leslie (ed.) (1996) *Ideas and Ideologies in Twentieth Century Latin America* (New York and Cambridge: Cambridge University Press).

BEVERLEY, John and ZIMMERMAN, Marc (1990) *Literature and Politics in the Central American Revolutions* (Austin: University of Texas Press).

BOOTH, John (1982) *The End and the Beginning, The Nicaraguan Revolution* (Boulder, CO., and London: Westview Press).

BOUDON, Raymond (1986) *L'idéologie* (Paris: Fayard).

BOUDON, Raymond (1990) *L'art de se perduader des idées douteuses, fragiles ou fausses* (Paris: Fayard).

BOURDIEU, Pierre, *Homo Academicus* (Stanford, CA: Stanford University Press, 1988).

BOURDIEU, Pierre (1982) *Ce que parler veut dire* (Paris: Fayard).

BRACAMONTE, José A. and SPENCER, David E. (1995) *Strategy and Tactics of the Salvadoran FMLN Guerrillas: Last Battle of the Cold War, Blueprint for Future Conflicts* (New York: Greenwood Publishing).

BROWNING, David (1971) *El Salvador, Landscape and Society* (Oxford: Clarendon Press).

BULMER-THOMAS, Victor (1987) *The Political Economy of Central America since 1920* (Cambridge, Mass.: Cambridge University Press).

CABARRUS, Carlos Rafael (1983) *Génesis de una revolución: análisis del surgimiento y desarrollo de la organización campesina en El Salvador* (Mexico: Edición de la Casa Chata).

CARDENAL, Rodolfo (1987) *Historia de una esperanza, vida de Rutilio Grande* (San Salvador: UCA editores).

CASTAÑEDA, Jorge G. (1994) *Utopia Unarmed, The Latin American Left After the Cold War* (New York: Vintage Books).
CASTELLANOS MOYA, Horacio (1993) *Recuento de incertidumbres, Cultura y transición en El Salvador* (San Salvador: Editorial Tendencias).
CASTRO MORAN, Mariano (1987) *Función política del Ejercito salvadoreño en el presente siglo* (San Salvador: UCA editores).
CIENFUEGOS, Ferman (1993) *Veredas de audacia, Historia del FMLN* (San Salvador: Arcoiris).
COLBURN, Forrest D. (1994) *The Vogue of Revolution in Poor Countries* (Princeton, NJ: Princeton University Press).
COLINDRES, Eduardo (1977) *Fundamentos económicos de la burguesía salvadoreña* (San Salvador: UCA editores).
DANNER, Mark (1994) *The Massacre of El Mozote, A Parable of the Cold War* (New York: Random House).
DEALY, Glen C. 1992) *The Latin Americans, Spirit and Ethos* (Boulder, CO.: Westview Press).
DEBRAY, Régis (1996) *Loués soient nos seigneurs, Une éducation politique* (Paris: Gallimard).
DEBRAY, Régis (1967), *Révolution dans la Révolution? Lutte armée et lutte politique en Amérique Latine* (Paris: Maspéro).
DeNARDO, James (1985) *Power in Numbers* (Princeton, NJ: Princeton University Press).
DOLJANIN, Nicolas (1982) *Chalatenango: La guerra descalza* (Mexico: Editorial El Dia).
FEHER. Ferenc (1991) 'La Experencia de la Libertad', in *La Palabra Liberada*, coord. gen. Octario Paz and Enrique Krauze, Mexico D.F.: Fundacíon Cultural televisa editorial Vuelta, p. 24.
FLORES MACAL, Mario (1978) *Orígenes de las formas de dominación en El Salvador* (San José: Avances de Investigación, no. 29).
FURET, François (1995) *Le passé d'une illusion, essai sur l'idée communiste au XXe siècle* (Paris: Robert Laffont/Calmann-Lévy).
GOLDSTONE, Jack (1991) *Revolution and Rebellion in the Early Modern World* (Berkeley, CA: University of California Press).
GONASSO, Miguel and GOMEZ LEYVA, Ciro (1992) *Cuatro minutos para las doce, conversaciones con el comandante Schafik Handal* (Mexico: Periodistas Asociados Latinoamericanos).
GORDON, Sara (1989) *Crisis política y guerra en El Salvador* (Mexico: Siglo XXI).
GRENIER, Yvon (1994) *Guerre et pouvoir au Salvador: idéologies du changement et changements idéologiques* (Sainte-Foy: Les Presses de l'Université Laval, coll. Société et Mutations).
GRINDLE, Merilee S. (1986) *State and Countryside, Development Policy and Agrarian Politics in Latin America* (Baltimore, MD, and London: The Johns Hopkins University Press).

HARNECKER, Marta (1993) *Con la mirada en alto, historia de las FPL Farabundo martí a través de sus dirigentes* (San Salvador: UCA editores).

HUNTINGTON, Samuel P. (1968) *Political Order and Changing Societies* (New Haven: Yale University Press, 1968), p. 269.

HUNTINGTON, Samuel P. (1991) *The Third Wave, Democratization in the Late Twentieth Century* (Norman and London: University of Oklahoma Press).

JUHN, Tricia (1996) *Negotiating Peace in El Salvadon, Civil-Military Relations and the Conspiracy to End the War*, (London: Macmillan, IPE Series, 1998)

LAWSON, Kay and MERKL, Peter H. (eds). (1988) *When Parties Fail, Emerging Alternative Organizations* (Princeton, NJ: Princeton University Press).

LEVY, Daniel (1986) *Higher Education and the State in Latin America, Private Challenges to Public Dominance* (Chicago, Ill., and London: University of Chicago Press).

LINDO-FUENTES, Héctor (1990) *Weak Foundations: The Economy of El Salvador in the Nineteenth Century, 1821–1898* (Berkeley and Los Angeles, CA: University of California Press).

MAFFESOLI, Michel (1984) *Essais sur la violence, banale et fondatrice* (Paris: Librairie des Méridiens, coll. "sociologies au quotidien").

MALIA, Martin (1994) *The Soviet Tragedy, A History of Socialism in Russia, 1917–1991* (New York: The Free Press).

MALLOY, James M. and SELIGSON, Mitchell A. (eds.) (1987) *Authoritarians and Democrats, Regime Transition in Latin America* (Pittsburgh, PA: University of Pittsburgh Press).

MAYER, Joseph and WEATHERHEAD, Richard W. (eds.) (1979) *The Latin American University* (Albuquerque, NM: University of New Mexico Press).

MENA SANDOVAL, Emilio (n/d) *Del ejercito nacional al ejercito guerrillero* (San Salvador Ediciones Arcoiris).

MENJIVAR, Rafael (1979) *Formación y lucha del proletariado industrial salvadoreño* (San Salvador: UCA editores).

MEYER, Jean (1991) *Historia de los Cristianos en América Latina, siglos XIX y XX* (Mexico: Editorial Vuelta).

MIGDAL, Joel S. (1974) *Peasants, Politics, and Revolution* (Princeton, NJ: Princeton University Press).

MONTGOMERY, Tommie S. (1982) *Revolution in El Salvador, Origins and Evolution* (Boulder CO.: Westview Press).

PACKENHAM, Robert A. (1992) *The Dependency Movement, Scholarship and Politics in Development Studies* (Cambridge, Mass.: Harvard University Press).

PAZ, Octavio (1993) *Obras completas, El peregrino en su pátria* (Mexico: Fondo de Cultura Económica).

PECAUT, Daniel (1989) *Entre le peuple et la nation, les intellectuels et la politique au Brésil* (Paris: Maison des sciences de l'homme).

REVEL, Jean-François (1992) *Le regain démocratique* (Paris: Fayard).

SCHAMA, Simon (1989) *Citizens, A Chronicle of the French Revolution* (New York: Vintage Books).

SCOTT, James C. (1985) *Weapons of the Weak: Everyday Forms of Peasant Resistance* (New York and London: Yale University Press).

SKOCPOL, Theda (1980) *States and Social Revolutions, A Comparative Analysis of France, Russia and China* (Cambridge: Cambridge University Press).

STOLL, David (1993) *Between Two Armies in the Ixil Towns of Guatemala* (New York: Columbia University Press).

TILLY, Charles (1978) *From Mobilization to Revolution* (New York: Random House).

TORRES-RIVAS, Edelberto (1987) *Centroamérica: la democracia posible* (San José: EDUCA/FLACSO).

TULCHIN, Joseph S. (ed.) (1992) *Is There a Transition to Democracy in El Salvador?* (Boulder, CO and London: Lynne Rienner).

UCA/PREDE-OEA (1990) *La investigación y la docencia en la educación universitaria de El Salvador* (San Salvador).

VÉLIZ, Claudio (1994) *The New World of the Gothic Fox, Culture and Economy in English and Spanish America* (Berkeley, CA: University of California Press).

VERDES-LEROUX, Jeannine (1987) *Le réveil des somnanbules, Le parti communiste, les intellectuels et la culture (1956–1985)* (Paris: Fayard/Minuit).

WALTON, John (1984) *Reluctant Rebels: Comparative Studies of Revolution and Underdevelopment* (New York: Columbia University Press).

WEBRE, Stephen (1979) *José Napoleon Duarte and the Christian Democratic Party in Salvadorean Politics, 1960–72* (Baton Rouge and London: Louisiana State University Press).

WHITE, Alistair (1973) *El Salvador* (Boulder, CO: Westview Press).

WICKHAM-CROWLEY, Timothy P. (1992) *Guerrillas and Revolution in Latin America* (Princeton, NJ: Princeton University Press).

ZAID, Gabriel (1988) *De los libros al poder* (Mexico: Grijalbo).

Index

DATE DUE